THE NATIONAL TRUST
GUIDE TO

Dark Age and Medieval Britain

400-1350

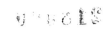

THE NATIONAL TRUST
GUIDE TO

Dark Age and Medieval Britain

400-1350

Richard Muir

with photographs by Richard Muir

George Philip/The National Trust
The National Trust for Scotland

British Library Cataloguing in Publication Data

Muir, Richard, 1943—
    The National Trust guide to Dark Age and Medieval Britain, 400–1350.
    I. Great Britain—History—Anglo-Saxon period, 449–1066
    2. Great Britain—History—Medieval period, 1066–1485
    I. Title
    941   DA152

ISBN 0-540-01090-1

© Richard Muir 1985

Published by George Philip, 12–14 Long Acre, London WC2E 9LP, in association with The National Trust and The National Trust for Scotland.

TITLE PAGE ILLUSTRATION Rievaulx Abbey, North Yorkshire.
END-PAPERS Caernarfon Castle, Gwynedd.

Illustration Acknowledgements
All photographs, with the exception of the following, were provided by Dr Richard Muir. *Aerofilms* pp. 96–7; *Cambridge University Collection of Air Photographs* pp. 54–5, p. 70, p. 77, p. 80 (above), pp. 120–1, p. 184, p. 234. The photograph on p. 23 is reproduced by permission of Bury St Edmunds Museum. Diagrams and drawings are reproduced by kind permission of the following: *The Archaeological Journal* p. 63 (drawn by S. T. James); *Michael Joseph* p. 201 (based on a plan from *Medieval Monasteries of Great Britain* by Lionel Butler and Chris Given-Wilson); *Cedric de la Nougerede* p. 61; *Phillimore & Co* p. 235, p. 237 (based on plans from *The Towns of Medieval Wales* by Ian Soulsby); *The Royal Commission on Historical Monuments (England)* p. 88; *Dr Warwick Rodwell* p. 164. The plan of Kidwelly Castle, p. 113, is based on a Crown Copyright plan. It is reproduced by permission of the Controller of Her Britannic Majesty's Stationery Office and the Royal Commission on Ancient and Historical Monuments in Wales. The map 'Aspects of Dark Age Britain' is based on the Ordnance Survey's *Britain in the Dark Ages* and reproduced with the permission of the Ordnance Survey.

Contents

Introduction: Two Steps Back

It seemed that no sooner had the Romans arrived than the troops began building the Great Highway. It had carried the legions far from the quiet heartland to their battles and strongholds in the west. But that was long ago. People could not remember the details of the conquest which had turned them into Romans, and in the modern world of the late fourth century they mattered very little. There were not so many troops on the road now. Many of those that passed spoke coarse foreign tongues which the people did not understand. They were a rather bizarre crowd, soldiers of fortune and probably best avoided. But the road was still busy, its slabs and cobbles worn down by the creaking carts and the clattering hooves of the pack horses, oxen and sheep: the life-blood of the economy pulsing along the metalled arteries and dusty capillaries of the transport network, moving from field and workshop to market and port. Travellers gathered in the roadhouse, the tired old men sitting by the roadside, avoiding the raucous hubbub of the young bloods, to watch the traffic and tell their tales.

When old men gather one can be fairly sure that soon the sages will assert that 'things are not what they were' and, moreover, that 'the country is going to the dogs'. Sometimes, they are right. It was not so long ago that the barbarians had burst through the Great Wall, and in no time at all the rich, placid and unguarded countrysides of the south were ravaged by them – outlandish Scots from Ireland, the tattooed Picts and despised North Sea pirates. Farmsteads and mansions had perished in flames, gentlefolk were slaughtered – the whole affair was both incredible and intolerable. Frontier skirmishes were one thing, but this was an outrage, still likely to form the centrepiece of any conversation.

The talk of looting and disorder prompted Placidus to go and check his baggage train. He was a dealer in pots and general merchandise, who plied the roads of southern England. When he returned he described how he had seen the troops – if you could call them troops – working on the new barrier – if you could call it a barrier – which was supposed to close the road to any future invaders. It was no wall, just a bank and ditch of an archaic design. But at least it showed that something was being done, even if it provoked uncomfortable memories of the great barbarian conspiracy and raid.

Of course, the politicians were to blame – them and the army commanders. And Rome itself was a den of iniquity. Taxes were so high that the entrepreneurs found it hard to prosper. So how was all the money being spent? Having damned the politicians and government and exhausted most other age-old pre-occupations of the propertied classes, the greybeards turned to the reliable stand-bys of farming and the weather.

Cassavus was a dealer in grain and hides and was just returning from a business trip to the northern garrisons. Coming south from York he had seen the chalk hills to the east standing white against the slate sky, with the gorged rivers clouded grey with mud and silt. The countryside was wearing out. A land which had been famed throughout the ages for its horn and corn was beginning to stagger under the burden of its swollen population. Here in the low-lands there was not an acre of waste ground to be seen. Woods had been hacked back to their cores, leaving just enough standing to meet the demand for timber. The sod had been turned wherever there was half a hope of an adequate harvest, and every remaining field held its full quota of cattle or sheep.

Yet Solinus was more optimistic. No amount of grumbling and prophecy could extinguish the pleasure of anticipation. He had sold his properties in the town and was on his way to a new home and the lifestyle of the gentleman farmer. All the wealth that had eluded the tax collectors had been invested in a villa, bought at a fearful price, but now enlarged, modernized and fitted with new mosaic floors, central heating and baths, which would surely be the envy of the neighbourhood. His only regret was that he had not followed the affluent herd and made the move years ago. In the meantime the value of urban property had plummeted, the prestige of town life had evaporated and the neighbourhood had become seedy and decrepit. It was even beginning to smell.

Having reached the comfortable consensus that, though times were bad, they could scarcely get much worse, the old men pattered away towards their beds.

Time proved them wrong, for things would get much worse than they could possibly have imagined. Their sons would live to witness the complete collapse of Roman power in Britain, and Rome would be so beset by enemies that its leaders could do no more than advise the people of far-off Britain to look out for themselves as best they could. For lack of better inspiration their grandchildren would join in the difficult pretence of being Romans still. Eventually their dynasties would sink in a sea of turmoil and decay, the farmlands would surrender to thorn and forest, and plague would assail the survivors. Four centuries would pass before the signs of recovery were clear, four more before the recovery approached completion.

But even catastrophes such as these could not extinguish the Great Highway. In the early decades of the fourteenth century an inn stood close to the site of the Roman roadhouse. One quiet corner was the preserve of the old men, and there they could reminisce and grumble, peering through the shutters at the travellers passing by. Things, they agreed, were not what they were. The great king had died at the ripe old age of sixty-eight, and the new king, Edward II (1307–27), was held in low esteem. One could scarcely imagine a less likely successor to the magnificent father. Common gossip could not be expected to excuse Edward's previous unmanly dependence on the foreign courtier Piers Gaveston by remembering his lonely childhood and his haughty and terrifying father. It was even said that Edward II enjoyed the rustic crafts of thatching and hedging. Imagine this! The son of Edward I, knee-deep in mud, laying a hedge! And now the news was filtering back that the king's enormous English army had been defeated by the Scots at Bannockburn. It was not the consequences but the humiliation which rankled – this and the thought of the taxes which would be raised to put the Scots back in their place. People in the south had little to fear; doubtless the Scots would be crushed again – let the wretched northerners worry about that.

It was not easy to blame the king for the weather, but let the facts speak for themselves. It was true that a sequence of years preceding his coronation had been afflicted by summer droughts, but since then only one year out of eight had produced even a half-respectable harvest. There had been a year of autumn flooding, followed by one with a bitter winter and a parched summer; another similar; summer drought; a mediocre year; a return to the autumn floods, and then a year in which the rain never seemed to abate.

To confirm their complaints the sages peered through the shutters, where the streams from the thatch dimpled the mud beneath. Out in the murk a band of sodden and ragged travellers followed a hand-cart. Robert, a merchant from Bath, thought that he recognized them as peasant refugees from the black Devonshire moors, on their way to look for work in London or some other city. Henry, a local yeoman, knew better. He recognized the faces of the tenants from a neighbouring estate. They had been evicted the day before to make way for sheep. Compassion had little place in the conversation of these men of substance, and soon the talking explored the idle, evasive and pig-headed characters of modern working folk. It was soon agreed that they bred like rabbits, never thinking ahead, and were much more trouble than they were worth. Sheep – now they were different; one could almost hear the mental cogwheels turning as the farmers present did their calculations.

And then the conversation turned to generalities – the uneasy relations between the king and the 'Lords Ordainers', the committee of Church and baronial interests; taxation; the disgraceful state of some monasteries; the deterioration of the farmland; and back to the iniquities of the weather and the latest royal scandals. Yes, things were bad. So bad they could scarcely get much worse and would probably

soon get better. On this more hopeful note the companions went their separate ways.

But before too long things would get far worse than the pessimists could have imagined. Between them our grumblers had twenty grandchildren. When the Great Pestilence arrived in 1348 it killed eight of them and three more would die when the plague returned a few years later. Those who survived would see peasants revolt or openly defy their masters, while costs rocketed as the workers who survived the epidemics bargained for the sale of their now precious labour. The towns and countrysides seemed half empty and whole parishes lay silent. Oxen stood bloated in the cornfields and dogs snarled over the corpses of their masters.

Today the Great Highway is a sleek trunk road, and a sign entices travellers to the fourteenth-century inn. In truth, it has burned down twice since the last of the fourteenth-century timbers were removed. It used to be the *Bull*, and then it was the *King's Head* and the *George*. For the last couple of years it has been *Ye Olde Butt and Trencher*. A man at the brewery thought of that. He also thought of the 'oaken' beams of blackened pine, the 'Elizabethan-effect' strips stuck across the sash windows to create diamond panes, the chickens in baskets and the open-plan bar. But he left a little snug where the locals could lurk: the old codgers seemed so out of place in the olde worlde setting. So there they sit and watch as the traffic roars by, streaked by the silt which blows from the fields while the Phantoms and Tornadoes rend the sky. And there they sit and grumble. They say that things are not what they were, so bad in fact that they could scarcely get much worse.

*   *   *

This book covers the time between the shock of the Roman collapse and the catastrophe of the Great Pestilence. In many ways it is the story of a long recovery and the ways in which the works of man transformed the scene as civilization advanced. It picks up the story where the preceding volume, *The National Trust Guide to Prehistoric and Roman Britain*, closed, and so forms a part of a continuing story. This is a guide to Dark Age and medieval Britain, and is, just like its predecessor, a particular sort of guide. Had I attempted to provide a viable description of every medieval castle, then the book would run into several volumes. Had I done the same for every medieval church, then it would overflow the bookshelves and spill across most of the carpet. This is an attempt to introduce the monuments of the ages in their context and explain their meaning. Hopefully then, this book will give the information that will enable a visitor to a medieval castle, church or fragment of countryside not mentioned here to appreciate the factors and formative processes involved in the creation of what they see. As a pure gazetteer a book of this size would be a pretence of little worth, but as a guide I hope that it will escort the reader through the wonderful heritage of relics and prove a reliable companion.

Professor W. G. Hoskins is an outstanding landscape historian. One of his less publicized skills has been the ability to know his audience and appreciate exactly how to communicate with each level of enthusiasm, from that of the academic expert to that of the tourist who might become a convert to the enjoyment of the past. Anyone who deliberately writes for one audience always runs the risk of attack by members of another. When I wrote a 'popular' book about lost villages I was roasted in an academic journal, deliciously obscure even among the local historians of the East Midlands where it circulates. Firstly, it was said that I had written for middle-class people who eat muesli; secondly I had enthused and advised people to explore sites in god-forsaken windswept places, and thirdly I had called medieval peasants, 'peasants'. After much careful thought I am still unable to form an opinion about muesli, or even spell it with certainty. I cannot resist the thought that were more desk-bound historians to visit our god-forsaken historical sites then, one way or another, their subject would benefit. But the question of the peasants raises more interesting issues. In a book such as this I might seek to win favour with the more pedantic academic reviewers by using obscure terminology. I could explain at length how early work on English peasant society was done by people with names like Seebohm and Vinogradoff, with the introduction of assumptions about society which were more appropriate in the recent worlds of east central Europe than that of medieval England. For further protection I could pack the text with imposing references, like: see Beckett, J. V., 'The Peasant in England: A Case of Terminological Confusion?', *The Agricultural History Review* 32 (1984), part II, pp. 113–23. I could also cram the pages with academically respectable jargon and lull the reviewer by being as boring and impenetrable as possible.

Of course, most readers would quite sensibly throw the book away and, far worse, decide that the history of our legacy of monuments and landscape was very boring and not for them. And so there is no apology for seeking to write in language that will entice the uncommitted rather than repel. Great pains have been taken to safeguard the factual accuracy of the themes introduced, even if the sites or excavations which have yielded the evidence have not always been cited. In some important respects this is a controversial or radical text – or at least it would have been had it appeared just a few years ago. But I think that most leading archaeologists will now agree with the demotion of the Saxons and the emphasis on the depths of the collapse from the heights of Roman Britain, and the slowness of the recovery. Since the apparent certainties of earlier years are being overturned a measure of imagination or intuition has been needed to link the story together, but there has been no attempt to gloss over the fact that there are many things which are still mysterious.

Mention of the 'Saxons' brings us to a more than semantic problem. I hate the word and doubt that any but the earliest Saxon settlers would have recognized themselves as such. Wherever possible I have substituted a word such as 'English', but this also creates ambiguities. Because the term 'Saxon' is so deeply entrenched in descriptions of this period I have retained it in phrases like 'Saxon churches', and can only wait for some brighter spark to invent a better name for the people of many different backgrounds and identities living in England in the centuries before the Norman Conquest.

Assisting my efforts to say the right things, two former co-authors and fine archaeologists, Christopher Taylor and Humphrey Welfare, have very kindly commented on my drafts, while Catherine Hills gave me valuable comments on the final manuscript. But all credit to the author for any factual mistakes included. Thanks are also due to Nina Muir, particularly for the many hours devoted to compiling the accompanying maps. In preparing this book I have been under no pressure from The National Trust, and all the sites included are there purely on their merits. I would like to thank Robin Wright for having enabled me to write without any restraint, and any opinions and value judgements which may seem to emerge from the text are entirely my own.

1
Into an Age of Darkness

In this year John the Baptist showed his head to two monks who came from the east to worship in Jerusalem, at a place which once was Herod's residence. At that same time Marcian and Valentinian reigned; and at that time came the Angles to this land, invited by king Vortigern, to help him overcome his enemies. They came to this land with three warships, and their leaders were Hengist and Horsa. First of all they slew the enemies of the king and drove them away, and afterwards they turned against the king and against the Britons, and destroyed them by fire and by the edge of the sword.

The Anglo Saxon Chronicle, 448.

At Reculver in Kent a ruined Norman and an older Saxon church were built inside the old Roman fort of the Saxon Shore. Most of the old Shore forts attracted missionaries and churches in the early centuries of the Christian era.

In 1914, on the eve of World War I, Edward Grey, Viscount Fallodon, said: 'The lamps are going out all over Europe; we shall not see them lit again in our lifetime.' So it must have seemed some fifteen centuries earlier, as the Roman Empire, the greatest empire that the world had ever known, shrank and crumbled. European civilization slithered and then plummeted into the abyss of the Dark Ages. Historians and others who seek portholes through the heavy mists of time see the Roman stage only dimly lit, but often some fascinating details can be discerned. At the end of the Roman act it might seem that a safety curtain had come adrift, slowly rumbling down to obscure the stage. Centuries pass before the curtain is raised again and we glimpse the later phases of Saxon and Celtic civilization. What dramas were enacted while the stage was dark?

To comprehend the disasters and disruptions of the Dark Ages it is necessary to know something of the triumphs which preceded the chaos. In Britain,

Roads proved to be the most durable part of the Roman legacy. Here, beside Roman Dere Street and near Heighington in Co. Durham, Legs Cross, probably a Saxon construction, stands by a crossroads. Dere Street, its course marked by hedgerows, is still an important north-south routeway.

the pacification of the landscape and its exploitation for farming had been quite thoroughly accomplished by the close of the Bronze Age. Iron Age Britain was a well-peopled and heavily-exploited land, but also a place that was fraught with tribal rivalries and fragmented between a series of provincial political and economic spheres. Perhaps it was the remarkable British grain harvest (as well as the quest for prestigious victories and for an end to British attempts to destabilize the continental Celts) which drew the legions of Claudius to the Channel shores in AD 43.

All Britain except the north of Scotland fell under Roman control or influence, and although the Roman way was not always a just or gentle way, the country prospered. For the first time there was a central authority which could plan and integrate the development of the different provinces, binding them together with a superb system of roads, punctuating the countryside with towns and markets, securing it with camps and forts, and directing commerce along far-reaching imperial trade routes.

While the British peasants responded to the new conditions by adopting a more commercial form of farming or by developing crafts and trades, the aristocracy frequently adopted Roman culture – and many of them found much in the foreign lifestyle that was to their liking. With the economic successes greatly exceeding the failures, this prosperous outpost of the Empire flourished. Britain now supported a population which some experts believe numbered around six million. Although there were more than sixty towns of different sizes and standings, the great bulk of the population lived in rural settings, so that many countrysides were more densely peopled than today.

This expansion and prosperity could not continue for ever. Economic ills which afflicted the Empire affected Britain too; political rivalries sapped the unity of the system – and Britain produced more than its share of pretenders to the imperial throne. Meanwhile increasing population pressure and tribal wars amongst the 'barbarian' peoples who jostled around the fringes of the Empire caused imperial armies to be ever on the move, seeking to vanquish invaders and seal the gaps in the frontiers. Increasingly the Romans and their supporters were obliged to rely upon mercenary troops, often recruited from the ranks of the barbarian raiders themselves. Increasingly, too, imposing and almost impregnable fortifications were superseded by ramshackle defence works, manned by ramshackle troops.

These ancient contests and tribulations still find their expression in the landscape of Britain. During the third century a number of troublesome raids were launched against the southern and eastern coasts of England by Saxon pirates. At Richborough in Kent the monument which commemorated the Roman landing was – most symbolically – converted into a watch tower. Carausius, who commanded the Channel fleet, succeeded in stemming the raids, and a great system of Saxon Shore forts was built, with those at Reculver in Kent and Brancaster in Norfolk being joined by new links in the chain at Bradwell-on-Sea (Essex), Portchester (Hampshire), Lympne and Richborough (Kent), Burgh Castle (Norfolk) and Walton Castle (Suffolk). (Carausius made a bid for independence from Rome in 286, and in the latter part of the century the forts helped to buttress his position as well as to deter the barbarians.) Around 330 a new fort was added to the system at Pevensey in East Sussex, while other coastal forts were built to guard the western coasts, at Cardiff and Lancaster. It is clear from the often majestic ruins visible today that the power to construct massive fortifications still flourished in Roman Britain, even though the towns were beginning to decline.

But the threats to the country came from many directions. In addition to the Saxon problem in the south and east, the Scots of Ireland threatened the western seaboard and the Picts posed a challenge to the northern frontier. In fortifying the south, the north had been drained of manpower and the defences around Hadrian's Wall were decaying. In the great barbarian raid of 367 a conspiracy of Scots, Picts, Saxons and Franks wrought widespread havoc; the Great Wall was overrun and war bands surged into parts of England which had enjoyed security and complacency for centuries. Although forces under Count Theodosius succeeded in repulsing the invaders and some northern defences were restored, the end of Roman rule in Britain was coming into view. Another military coup in Britain by the army commander Magnus Maximus in 383 added to the disruption and resulted in a weakening of the garrison as the troops which accompanied him to campaign on the continent never returned. The problems confronting the Empire were not confined to its island appendage, and with barbarians threatening the imperial heartland, Rome chose to defend itself rather than its distant possessions.

The declining powers and all-pervading insecurity of late-Roman Britain may best be represented by the Bokerley Ditch on the Hampshire-Dorset boundary: not a great stone wall in the remoter fringes of the Empire, but a defensive earthen bank and ditch construction built in the fourth century to control movement in an area which had once been as safe and placid as anywhere in the Empire. It contrasts

During the last century of Roman rule some linear earthworks of an ancient design were built to close roads to invaders and guard estates. Bokerley Ditch on the Dorset/Hampshire boundary was built to meet an unidentified threat about 320, refurbished around the time of the disastrous barbarian conspiracy and raid of 367, and again refurbished about a year before the Roman collapse.

strikingly with the confident and imposing fortifications built in the earlier phases of Roman rule.

The gaps in Britain's defences had become too many to be plugged. Troops were siphoned off to shore up the continental Empire, led by Constantine III, another pretender from Britain. 'Dad's army' units and unreliable mercenaries could not sustain the calm and security essential to settled commerce and urban life, while the British leaders lacked the confidence, unity and discipline needed to weld their forces together to ensure a stable and attractive future. But at least they squeezed some dignity from the torpor and confusion of their situation, for with Rome no longer able to sustain the embattled province – able only to advise that the British should care for themselves as best they could – in 410 the native leaders seized their independence from the failing Empire. In the same year the imperial capital, Rome, was taken by the barbarians.

The end of this phase of civilization in Britain did not come suddenly. For many years to come the upper classes sought to act and live like Romans: probably they regarded themselves as more Romans than Britons. It was a creeping, frustrating and debilitating decay rather than a sudden and outright conquest which characterized the last chapter in the story of Roman Britain. The Empire had been an intricate system of interlocking parts, but now things just would not work any more. As uncertainty prowled the countryside, the peasants and tradesmen took refuge in self-sufficiency, while the wealthy landowners left their farms in the care of agents and retreated to the walled towns. Robbed of their economic and administrative leadership over the countryside, the towns, meanwhile, had become like generals without armies. Market places became overgrown, sewage and water systems broke down, and civic regulations and practices were neglected.

There was no longer anyone to mend the highways, bring the wares from kiln or forge to market, repair the roof or fix the drains. The Roman Britons were left with administrative systems and service infrastructures which were now too complex to be operated – and the barbarians and insurgents ensured that they would not have time to learn but had to concentrate on readjusting. The once great and unified province disintegrated into a series of jealous, insecure and introspective little Englands. The rule of law surrendered to the rule of petty tyrants, despite the efforts to retain a unified kingdom under 'kings' Vortigern and his rival Ambrosius.

In the countryside, some of the villas, the farms and country seats of the larger landowners, continued to function for a while, like the recently excavated Bancroft villa near Milton Keynes in Buckinghamshire. Here there was an optimistic and lavish refurbishment in the 340s; impressive mosaics were laid down and a new bath house and plunge bath were provided. The villa continued to be occupied until well into the fifth century, as did several other excavated examples. In the towns the pattern of survival was very uneven. In a few places a reduced and debased occupation may have continued right through to the urban revival of the later Saxon kings. Some places, though no longer functioning as towns, retained their leadership over the surrounding lands and emerged as administrative centres. Others gradually collapsed into squalor and then disintegrated, as strangers built their shanties in the once-elegant streets and courtyards, or cultivated vegetables where suburbs had stood. Several towns must have shared the fate of Cambridge, peacefully occupied by Romanized Britons and Saxons in the closing days of the Empire, but described by Bede as a 'decayed little city' in the seventh century. It does not seem that the great cities died suddenly when the legions left, wreathed in flames and pillaged by barbarians, and even in the decades that saw the eviction of Rome the then dilapidated and decaying town of

Wroxeter (Shropshire) enjoyed a redevelopment of the area around the *basilica* or law-court, with a neat complex of timber-framed buildings being purposefully set out. Meanwhile, at St Albans in Hertfordshire, civic standards were preserved until the fifth century was well advanced, and a Roman fountain at Carlisle in Cumbria was still winning admirers in the seventh century. At London, Canterbury and York and, perhaps, at Gloucester urban life seems to have survived, though in a less splendid manner than before. But in most places the towns had begun to decay in the fourth century, long before the collapse of Roman rule.

Ideas about the end of Roman Britain are in a state of flux. In the nineteenth century and the earlier part of this century, archaeology was not regarded as a particularly dignified and prestigious field of academic study. Most accounts of this period were constructed by historians. Historians deal with documents, and when there are no documents available they are forced to deal in legends and to improvise

Although the decay of Roman town life was evident a century before the collapse of Roman power in Britain, fragments of the Roman townscape and road pattern survive to this day – like this gate at Lincoln.

St Albans Cathedral incorporates masses of Roman brick, gathered from the ruins of Verulamium *nearby.*

the tricky bits. Documents for this period, the blackest of the Dark Age nights, scarcely exist, and so a heavy reliance was placed on the feverish writings of the monk, Gildas, who may have been based in Chester. To hope that Gildas might have provided an objective description of the decline of Roman Britain is rather like expecting a detached account of Muslim fundamentalism from the late Shah of Persia.

Around 540, when he would have been forty-three years old, Gildas, a Celtic monk possibly from the Clyde region and perhaps educated in Wales, wrote his book *The Ruin and Conquest of Britain*. This was a tirade against the rulers and ecclesiastics of his times, which was prefaced by an account of fairly recent historical events. He wrote several generations after the eviction of the Romans, and so he apparently did not consider himself to be a Roman. His narrative reflects the changed outlook, while legends, half-

truths and mistakes or outright inventions were filtered through the indignation and malevolence of the embittered author. His general historical thesis was that debauched, inept and avaricious rulers had allowed Roman civilization and Christianity to wither in the face of assaults by vile barbarians. Legend told that Vortigern (or 'Overlord') invited the Saxon war leaders, Hengist and Horsa, to Britain around 428, when they arrived with three boat-loads of mercenaries who were hired to defend Britain against their kinsmen. These hirelings were followed by more and more Saxons, until the tables turned on their paymasters. Gildas writes: 'Then a pack of cubs burst forth from the lair of the barbarian lioness, coming in three *keels*, as they call warships in their language.' He continues: 'In just punishment for the crimes that had gone before, a fire heaped up and nurtured by the hand of the impious easterners spread from sea to sea. It devastated town and country round about, and, once it was alight, it did not die down until it had burned almost the whole surface of the island and was licking the western ocean with its fierce red tongue.... All the major towns were laid low by the repeated battering of enemy rams; laid low, too, all the inhabitants – Church leaders, priests and people alike, as the swords glinted all around and the flames crackled.'

And so we inherited a blood and thunder version of the fall of Roman Britain. The Saxons, it was said, slew the British and drove the survivors into the northern and western fastnesses. Then these bloodthirsty barbarians set about carving an agricultural landscape out of the virgin wildwood. What nonsense! How could a few boat-loads of mercenaries wreak genocide and eviction on a civilization numbering several million members? And if there had been a primeval wildwood blanket which had defied Roman cultivation, it would certainly have been more than a match for the Saxon peasants. When we strip the story of myth, legend and polemic then almost all that we know for certain is that, within a few centuries of the Roman eviction, most, but not all, of the provincial dynasties had Saxon names, and most, but not all, of the people in England were apparently adopting an evolved Saxon dialect.

It is time now to meet the Saxons. The Saxon settlement was not an organized occupation and the Saxons were not a homogeneous people. Bede described three distinct groups of Germanic settlers in his history of the English Church and people; 'These newcomers were from the three most formidable races of Germany, the Saxons, Angles, and Jutes. From the Jutes are descended the people of Kent and the Isle of Wight and those in the province of the West Saxons opposite the Isle of Wight who are called Jutes to this day. From the Saxons – that is, the country known as the land of the Old Saxons – came the East, South and West Saxons. And from the Angles – that is, the country know as Angulus, which lies between the provinces of the Jutes and Saxons and is said to remain unpopulated to this day – are descended the East and Middle Angles, the Mercians, all the Northumberland stock (that is, those peoples living north of the river Humber), and the other English peoples.'

It is most unlikely that things were this simple. There was no single concerted Saxon invasion – no Eisenhower or Montgomery figure, no 'D-Day', and no Saxon beach-masters shouting 'Angles to the left and Jutes to the right'. The people who were bracketed together as 'Saxons' (Sassenachs) by the British probably included folk from the tribes of Old Saxony and adjacent areas, Frisians, Suebians and Franks – mainly people from the North Sea margins of Germany and from Holland and Denmark, with the provinces of Schleswig and Holstein being the principal areas of emigration. The reasons for their departure are not clear. The climate was worsening and perhaps population had outstripped the resources of the flat, flood-prone continental margins – recent archaeological work seems to have revealed serious crop failures in the Saxon homelands during the migration period. But this was also the great age of continental migrations, as tribes and embryonic nations shifted, collided and merged, swirling in the vacuum caused by the collapsing Roman Empire. The newcomers must have shared some loose sense of identity as Anglo-Saxons or Anglians, but it seems unlikely that their sense of loyalty extended far beyond the local group and its leader. Amongst the continental tribal groupings of Europe they were neither particularly advanced nor particularly powerful. But for many years they had lived almost cheek by jowl with the Roman Empire, had bought its trade goods, envied its manufactures and achievements and, in many cases, had served in its armies.

The Saxons had established firm footholds in Britain well before the Roman collapse. Some may have enlisted as mercenaries, warriors recruited to buttress the province against the recurrent barbarian raids. Others probably came as craftsmen, and others still as peasant settlers, folk who did not grab the best land but occupied poorer ground on the fringes of the established estates. For many years these immigrants lived peacefully alongside their Romanized neighbours, and evidence of this co-existence has been excavated at places such as Cambridge, Winchester (Hampshire), Caister-on-Sea and Caistor-by-Norwich (Norfolk), West Stow (Suffolk) and York. After the break with Rome there probably was a demand for Saxon mercenaries to shore up the defences of Britain. As the political situation deteriorated, boat-loads of settlers must have arrived uninvited, probing the coast for weak spots, combing the countryside for poorly-defended or neglected niches where they could resume their peasant lifestyles. Sometimes the mercenaries must have rebelled against their employers, seized lands in lieu of unpaid wages, used their weapons to take over an estate, or capitalized on British quarrels to settle on lands ravaged by war. Whatever the details of the take-over, very gradually the reins of local power tended to be grasped by Saxon hands.

Yet the newcomers could never have been more than a small minority and their rise to power could not have been swift or absolute. On many estates the change of landowner may have been of little consequence to the peasant tenants, who simply continued to till the lands, gather the harvest, milk and shear. In most places the cultural transition was slow in coming. In Dorset the people around Wareham still regarded themselves as Roman Britons, writing in Latin and choosing British names until as late as about 800: five inscribed Christian tombstones of this period were found during the rebuilding of Wareham church. At the other end of the country, Cumbria remained a British-speaking land until much later. In the far west, British independence was only really broken in 838, following a defeat of the Cornish by Egbert, King of Wessex (802–39), at Hingston Down. In Yorkshire, York was in British hands until about 600; the Celtic kingdom of Elmet, with Leeds

West Stow in Suffolk, a remarkable attempt to recreate the buildings of a pagan Saxon settlement upon the sites of the dwellings and workshops of an excavated settlement of this period.

as one of its centres, survived until 617, and the impression created by the archaeological remains in many parts of Yorkshire and elsewhere is that of a small minority Saxon population living peacefully alongside the British until a phase of Saxon expansion late in the sixth century. Even in the presumed Saxon heartland of eastern and southeastern England, the area lying within a triangle with its apices at Canterbury, Cirencester (Gloucestershire) and Colchester (Essex) seems to have remained much more Roman and British than Saxon in character until about 600.

So it seems that the Roman eviction from Britain was followed by a prolonged period during which Roman/British culture remained dominant throughout most parts of the country. The Saxons were always a small minority, with the immigrants probably numbering only a few tens of thousands, and their political domination of British life was only achieved slowly and on a piecemeal basis.

This interpretation is supported by a more detailed picture of Saxon settlement in Sussex which has been gradually elucidated by Martin Welch. Here it seems that the main influx of settlers from northwest Germany took place around the middle of the fifth century. The Saxon settlements of this period are concentrated in an area between the rivers Ouse and Cuckmere – a locality notably lacking in Roman villa remains. And so it appears that, rather than arriving as warlike victors, the Saxons were invited by the British rulers and settled in a void in the landscape, perhaps a run-down Roman imperial estate. One Saxon cemetery stood apart from the others: Highdown in West Sussex, encircled by the ramparts of the Iron Age hillfort there. Perhaps this was a garrison, protecting the seaboard and coastal plain on behalf of a prosperous community of British landowners, and graves which might be those of British supervisors have also been found at Highdown. It was only during the sixth century that Saxon settlement advanced westwards across the downs from its early foci, although during the seventh century the Saxons became established in new settlements which became quite liberally scattered across the whole of the Sussex downs. At this point it could be argued that some new terminology is needed. While it seems reasonable and convenient to label fifth-century pagan settlers as 'Saxons', the name settles uncomfortably on the mixed communities of the later centuries.

Accounts that are now outdated by recent archaeological work heralded the Saxon invasion and ascendancy as the dawn of a brave new period of colonization, during which the 'vast, primeval forest' was rolled back and the outlines of the agricultural countryside were established. Nothing could be further from the truth. This was a time of desertion, dereliction and decay. Great swathes of countryside which had been productive farmland in Iron Age and Roman times gradually fell out of use, surrendering to weeds, bushes and then to forest. Shielded from our gaze by the impenetrable mists of the Dark Ages is a period of catastrophe, during which population levels must have plummeted and working countrysides have become wastelands. Many of the clues come from pottery scatters which mark the positions of lost Romano-British farmsteads, hamlets and villas. This pottery seems to be everywhere, showing that there was a dense stipple of rural settlements. Moreover, the Romano-British pottery frequently emerges when old woods are (regrettably) grubbed out, or in areas which are known to have been wooded during the Middle Ages.

The conclusion is obvious: the woodland which was being cleared or 'assarted' to create new farmland during the Middle Ages was not primeval woodland, as has been supposed. It was secondary woodland which had colonized areas that were farmed in the Roman period and abandoned thereafter.

Our detective work assumes a grimmer aspect when the question of population is investigated. I have said that the population of the Roman province could have numbered six million and was probably at least four million. Domesday Book of 1086 provides our first chance to estimate medieval population levels, and it is not easy to imagine that England supported more than three million souls at this time. And when Domesday was compiled, the population of Saxon England must have been growing for some centuries. However we look at the problem, there must have been a catastrophic fall in population during the murkier depths of the Dark Ages.

One cannot imagine that millions of cultivated British people allowed themselves to be butchered by a few thousand Saxon rustics. It is quite probable that the fourth-century collapse of towns and commerce and the traumas of local insurgencies induced a wasting of the population – but not on the terrible scale that seems to have been experienced. And so we are forced to search for other explanations.

Another contributory factor might have been the deterioration of an overworked environment. Roman rule gave a strong commercial boost to the already buoyant system of Iron Age farming. Perhaps the drive for greater agricultural production led to the destruction of life-giving soils – as had happened before, and happens today. Evidence may be found in the 'great silt-up' which has been detected in east Yorkshire and appears to have occurred in late-

Roman times. Dr Paul Buckland has described the severe soil erosion on sloping land that choked the rivers with silt. The erosion could have been caused by an excessive cultivation of winter wheat, which exposed the bare plough soil to the ravages of the winter climate.

The most credible explanation involves a sequence of plagues, comparable to the Great Pestilence or Black Death which exterminated about one third to one half of the English population in the years after 1348. Various plagues are certainly attested in the meagre Dark Age documents, and an unspecified epidemic ravaged the country in 664. *The Anglo Saxon Chronicle* records: 'In this year there was an eclipse of the sun on 3 May, and in this year came a great pestilence to the island of Britain. In the pestilence passed away bishop Tuda . . . and Eorcenberht, king of Kent, passed away. . . .' Three more kings died in the course of the next ten years, but their causes of death are uncertain. Bede also mentioned a pestilence which swept England in the seventh century. Historians argued that this could not have been the Black Death since black rats, which helped to spread the flea-borne disease, were not then present. However, the bones of this rat have now been identified in excavations of Roman wells in both London and York. So although the case for pestilence is growing and we know that the centuries following the end of Roman rule were a period of death, retreat and destruction, we cannot identify the culprits with any certainty.

While England endured its tribulations, life in the lands to the north and west continued on more tradi-

Devil's Dyke in Cambridgeshire, a mysterious and magnificent frontier-work barrier of the late Roman or early-to-middle Saxon periods.

tional lines. The essentially Iron Age societies of Ireland were largely unaffected by the centuries of Roman rule in Britain. In Scotland the prominence of Roman influence in the south of the territory had fluctuated, but most rural communities preserved the essential features of Iron Age peasant life. Although much has been written in praise of the 'Roman peace', here the Roman presence and occasional invasions may have disrupted rural life, and the problems caused by the retreat of the Empire were much smaller than in England. Wales had been effectively policed by the Romans; forts, camps, roads and a few towns were established, but on the whole the traditional Celtic way of life had survived. Throughout most of the Celtic fringes the circular homestead was still preferred to the rectangular Roman dwelling and small communities lived in scattered hamlets, tending their livestock, cultivating a little grain on the flatter, drier lands and scurrying for shelter whenever local tyrants were on the rampage. While Cornwall became nominally English, the traditional cultures of Scotland, Ireland and Wales survived, to be transformed by invading Normans rather than by Saxons.

2
Christianity — The Path Back to Civilization

The soul of man (says one councillor) is like a sparrow, which on a dark and rainy night passes for a moment through the door of a king's hall. Entering, it is for a moment surrounded by light and warmth and safe from the wintry storm; but after a short spell of brightness and quiet, it vanishes through another door into the dark storm from which it came. Likewise the life of man is for a moment visible; but what went before or is to come remains unknown. If therefore this new doctrine can tell us something about these mysteries, by all means let us follow it.

King Edwin of Northumbria is converted to Christianity. From Bede's *Ecclesiastical History of the English Nation*.

Breamore in Hampshire, one of Britain's loveliest Saxon churches.

Peering back into the Dark Age mists, we may think that we see Christianity at the close of the Roman period like a lamp glowing softly. Then the light flickers and fades, smouldering dimly in the darkest depths of the Dark Ages, but bursting back into life, burning fitfully at first, and then bathing the emergent nations of Britain in the pure, clear light of civilization. And perhaps it really was like this. Although we tend to regard the Dark Ages as a period of war, anarchy, invasion and destruction, when we explore the legacy of surviving monuments it is not the military creations which impress us, for they tend in the main to be modest and ambiguous. Rather, we find that the heritage is dominated by the Christian relics – the crosses, tomb slabs, Saxon churches and Celtic monasteries. Consequently, the proverbial Martian, who lacked any knowledge of the controversial literature of the period, might survey the Dark Age monuments and assume that this was a peaceful age of simple rustic piety.

Pagans and Converts

Christianity was introduced to Roman Britain sometime around the year 200. After periods when Christian worship could be a furtive or a potentially dangerous pursuit, the belief rose to become the principal religion of the later Roman Empire, although in the decades of trouble and urban decline during the fourth century there seems also to have been a revival of a spectrum of pagan cults, old and new, indigenous and imported. In Britain Christianity existed alongside the cults of the old Roman religion with its many deities. There were also the similarly pantheistic Celtic religions of the native pagans, with their nature gods and goddesses, sacred groves, holy wells and local deities, and also other Mediterranean and oriental religions. One of these was Mithraism, which had some similarities with Christianity and had a strong following in the garrisons. A number of monuments to the belief in Mithras were defaced, and it is possible that this was done by Roman Christians.

Once it was fashionable to believe that the pagan Saxon invaders extinguished Christianity in England, and that the religion only survived or reappeared in the remote fastnesses of the west and did not return to England until Augustine landed in Kent in 597 to begin the reconversion of the country. Now we are not so sure; the Saxon settlement was a symptom rather than a cause of the decay of the Roman world in Britain, while some humble form of ecclesiastical organization may have survived in England. Meanwhile, in the northern and western extremities of Britain, Christianity arrived and blossomed, so that the monastic Church of the Celtic lands gradually vanquished the pagan beliefs, or at least drove them to the brink of obscurity. A remarkable tradition of purity, devotion and evangelical conversions was established amidst the moist and misty backwaters of Atlantic Britain.

At the time of the Roman eviction from Britain, Christian belief seems to have been widespread, but by no means universal or supreme. Gradually, as the families who had supported small churches or worshipped at domestic shrines abandoned their villas or deserted the crumbling towns, vanishing from our view in the storm clouds of the Dark Ages, so Christian worship seems to have retreated towards sites which were endowed with a special sanctity. At these places, most of them now unknown, the religion may have survived. But while Christianity contracted in England, where the crisis of the imperial collapse was most keenly felt, in the lands to the west it might seem that Christianity came to provide a rallying point for the revitalization of communities which chose – perhaps surprisingly – to build their identity and beliefs around Roman values and biblical themes rather than around the traditions of their Celtic culture.

The religion of the pagan Saxon settlers in England seems, from the thin evidence available, to have had many facets. This is assuming that the newcomers *did* have a religion rather than a loose set of superstitions. The fact that corpses were usually provided with grave goods implies that there was a belief in the after-life – although this is not absolute proof. Saxons, in Britain and on the continent, seem to have recognized numerous gods, while their communities seem to have been frightened of all sorts of supernatural forces, like children lost in a forest. Woden was the supreme deity and other important characters included Frig, Thor and Tiw. As with several other contemporary pagan beliefs, each of the subordinate gods and goddesses had a special following and sphere of responsibility, with, for example, Thunor holding the brief in matters concerning thunder, while Tiw was the celestial minister of war.

Burial customs were diverse, and whilst most readers will know of the magnificent ship burial found beneath one of the Saxon barrows at Sutton Hoo in Suffolk and will have admired pictures of the priceless grave goods, such as the Swedish-style ceremonial helmet and the metal goods from Byzantium and Coptic Egypt, ship burials are only known from Sutton Hoo and from nearby Snape. They are by no means typical of their period. At Sutton Hoo, where an exciting new programme of excavation is currently in progress, there are around fourteen

Saxon barrows of the sixth to seventh centuries. These will have been built with burial chambers, though it is quite likely that tomb robbers have plundered most of their riches. Even here it is important to remember that the Sutton Hoo cemetery produces evidence of five other burial rites in addition to the celebrated ship burials. Also, while this was most probably the royal burial site of the kingdom of East Anglia, the excavations seem to be exploring a mixed community in which native British influences were strong; even the tradition of kingship seems to have been rooted in British rather than Saxon customs. It is important to emphasize the risk and folly of assuming that everyone who was given a Saxon-style burial, or whose remains have been excavated from a 'Saxon' cemetery, was a Saxon settler or descended from one. A corpse whose grave is not aligned according to Roman or Christian norms was not necessarily a Saxon. Detailed and difficult analyses of remains from Saxon cemeteries seem to suggest that a high proportion of the women and a considerable number of the men who were buried there were of native stock. With the decay and collapse of many Romanized societies in Britain it is not hard to imagine that many members of the indigenous communities would easily have adopted the less refined but presumably more confident culture of the newcomers. Female remains in traditional British-type cemeteries of the 'invasion' period seem sometimes to be disproportionately few, and one possibility is that the women took Saxon husbands and their remains lie in Saxon burial grounds.

Normally 'Saxon' corpses were either buried or cremated. The latter rite was most popular in the lands to the north of the Thames, while inhumations were most common in the areas to the south. After cremation the ashes of the deceased were placed in specially made bowls or urns which were then buried in designated cemeteries. Frequently, small possessions were placed amongst the charred relics. The provision of grave goods, which might sustain the departed on the road to the next world, be useful in the after-life, or establish the military, motherly or maidenly status of the deceased, was normal in the case of inhumations. Women were buried with their jewellery and domestic items, such as work-boxes or weaving implements; warriors with their weapons, while food, drinking vessels and animals were sometimes also provided. Occasionally it appears that wives or servants – excavation cannot make the distinction – may have been buried alive along with the deceased. In certain cases the grave might be marked by a prestigious barrow mound or encircling ditch, and a surviving Saxon barrow can be seen at Taplow

(Buckinghamshire) near Maidenhead. Standing some 4.5 metres (15 feet) high and with a diameter of 24 metres (80 feet), this mound must represent a very important burial. Frequently the simpler expedient of inserting the corpse in a ready-made prehistoric barrow was adopted.

Recently-excavated pagan Saxon cemeteries at Marden, in West Sussex near the Hampshire boundary, have revealed some interesting details. Some corpses were buried in rough wooden coffins, some were cremated, some burials or cremations were made under round barrows, and others later inserted into such mounds or into their surrounding ditches. Grave clusters and re-used graves may show that family burial plots existed within the cemetery. There are two adjacent cemeteries here, one of the sixth century and one of the seventh. Several of the graves were re-used, and in one the burial of a noble swordsman, who had been interred with his scabbard and a bucket, was disturbed when the grave was used for the corpse of a lofty spearman, who towered over 6 feet (1.8 metres) and was so tall that his head bent forwards in the undersized grave. The grave goods of the swordsman were then tossed back into the pit. By far the oldest of the discoveries was a set of belt fittings of the fifth century on the skeleton of a hunched old man, and it has been suggested that here might be one of the small and select band of original Saxon settlers.

We cannot know how devout and committed the Saxons were in the worship of their pagan deities, but there is much which implies a widespread terror

The contents of a Saxon inhumation burial are displayed at Bury St Edmunds Museum.

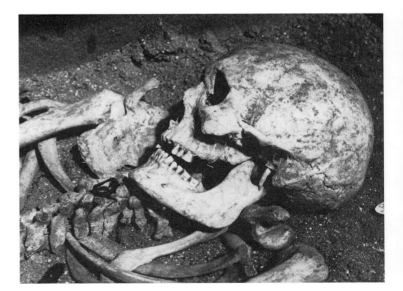

of ghosts. If we imagine life in decaying countrysides which were studded with the crumbling relics of Roman civilization, partly populated by the adherents of more deeply-rooted beliefs than those of the Romans, patterned by thickets of thorn and the youthful, tangled woods which sprang up and spread on the abandoned farmlands, then the eerie obsessions are more easily appreciated. There were no city lights to relieve the velvet blackness of night, and everywhere the wind sighed amongst the wreckage of the old order. To prevent more spirits from walking, corpses might be beheaded or weighed down with stones, while the popular cremation ritual itself may have been intended to provide a safe release for the spirit.

Of the organization of the pagan religion we know very little. There is scant evidence of a highly-organized priesthood or of imposing purpose-built temples, although shrines may have been quite numerous. Bede mentions pagan altars and idols and tells of a Chief Priest in the pre-conversion court of King Edwin of Northumbria (616–32). Occasionally excavations at pagan Saxon cemeteries have revealed traces of flimsy ritual buildings, while surviving placenames associated with pagan deities and which may denote the locations of their shrines are not uncommon. There are several Weedons in England, and the name includes the element *wig* or *wēoh*, an idol or shrine, and means 'holy hill' or 'hill of the temple, idol or shrine'. Wednesbury is 'Woden's fort'; Thunderfield, Thundersley and Thundridge all seem to indicate places associated with the worship of Thunor, while Tuesley in Surrey could be 'the sacred grove of Tiw'. In addition there are all the Harrow names, which may derive from a *hearh* or hill shrine.

In spite of the Saxon settlements, which introduced a substantially new pagan faith into countrysides in which a variety of other heathenisms must still have retained some vitality, it seems unlikely that the light of Christian worship was ever completely extinguished. It certainly did not end abruptly with the political break with Rome. The fifth-century *Life of St Germanus*, who was Bishop of Auxerre, records that the bishop visited Britain in 429 in order to assist sympathetic churchmen here in their campaign against the Pelagian heresy. (Pelagius, a late fourth-century Briton, had argued that God had provided Man with free will, so that Man had a considerable responsibility for his own destiny.) Clearly, the fact and circumstances of Germanus' visit show that Britain still preserved a vital and organized Church – although thereafter the continental references to the Church in Britain dry up.

Clues of a different type are contained in a number of 'Eccles' placenames. These names derive from the Latin *ecclesia*, which denotes a Christian church or community. In Welsh it becomes *eglwys*, in Cornish, *eglos*, and in many widely scattered parts of Britain it surfaces in placenames such as Eccles, Ecclefechan, Eaglesfield, Eaglesham, Exhall and Exley. These names seem to have originated in the fifth and sixth centuries. They surely indicate the continuing existence of actively Christian communities. Even so, it could be argued that the fact that such buildings or communities merited special designation in placenames shows that they had become rather unusual by this time. Whether the apparent contraction of Christian worship was caused by the advance of Saxon paganism, a revival of indigenous heathen cults, or simply by a general disenchantment with all brands of belief, we cannot know. But meanwhile Latin, the language of the Church, endured in Britain and its survival argues strongly for the parallel survival of communities of educated Christians. Latin appeared on inscribed stones, often erected in remote corners of Atlantic Britain in places which had been lightly touched or completely unaffected by Roman Christianity during the currency of the Empire in Britain. By Roman standards the carving may be crude and the Latin grammar unsound, but these monuments tell us that the erosion of Christianity in the south and east of Britain was accompanied by the establishment of the belief in places far away from the continental heartlands of the Church.

The 'Eccles' placenames seem to be older than any obviously surviving Christian church buildings, but it could be, as Professor Charles Thomas has hinted, that the places of worship used by one or more of the 'Eccles' communities would later emerge as the site of a 'minster', or mother church. These churches, which are described in more detail later in this chapter, were often situated on royal estates and built as the foci of administrative and seigneurial divisions; they served as the centres for ecclesiastical and evangelical activities in the period between the general conversion to Christianity and the establishment of flocks of 'field' or parish churches, which were conveniently placed to serve the needs of local congregations.

Christianity in England may have smouldered slowly, like incense, until the 'official' conversion of the Saxon communities following the arrival of St Augustine in Kent. The conversion poses many problems; in 600, on the instructions of Pope Gregory, Augustine arranged a meeting with the 'bishops of the British'. Although these bishops appear to have come mainly from Wales, where Christianity had probably been quite firmly rooted since Roman times, this event raises questions about the extent of an organized Church in England *before* the arrival of the saint and his mission. Just outside Canterbury the Kentish mission found a church which was quite serviceable, as Bede recorded: 'On the east side of the city stood an old church, built in honour of St Martin during the Roman occupation of Britain, where the Christian queen [Bertha was already a convert] . . . went to pray. Here they first assembled to sing the psalms, to pray, to say Mass, to preach, and to baptize, until the king's own conversion to the Faith gave them greater freedom to preach and to build and restore churches everywhere.' Had such a church stood empty and neglected since the end of the Roman Empire in Britain, almost two centuries previously, then it would surely have been a total ruin. A chancel which may quite possibly have been Queen Bertha's Church of St Martin has been explored by archaeologists, and parts of it certainly seem to have pre-dated the Augustinian mission. The earliest fragments incorporated in the church are built of coursed Roman tiles, but the Saxon adoption of Roman materials, the perpetuation of some Roman methods of building and the persistence of Roman techniques and motifs through the Saxon era all make it very difficult to disentangle the potentially Roman from the Saxon work.

After 597 the conversion of the English tended to be accomplished by the expedient of working on the provincial potentates in the expectation that their subjects' conversion – enforced or otherwise – would swiftly follow. In many ways the conversion was a swift and easy process, suggesting that the foundations were already laid and the kingdoms ripe for the change. In other ways, the Christian reconquest of England seems to have met with quite strong resistance. Within ninety years the respective monarchs were converted, although during this period a brief lapse into paganism or atheism affected almost every province. About thirty years after the conversion of Kent, missionary work in the north of England was under way and Augustine's disciple, Paulinus, was installed as bishop in York. In 633 he was forced to flee southwards and paganism very briefly returned to the fore after the death and overthrow of King Edwin. Shortly afterwards Christianity was restored, coming this time via Ireland, Lindisfarne (Northumberland) and Iona (Strathclyde) in the Celtic guise.

Although the missionaries and the literature of the period were mainly concerned with winning over dynasties, the records also tell of local difficulties.

Many rural communities seem to have cherished the old ways, as such communities so often do, or to have hedged their bets between the competing creeds. As late as 786 papal legates to Britain noticed the survival of heathen practices. In 685 Cuthbert became Bishop of Lindisfarne, and previously, as Prior of Melrose, he had, according to Bede, '. . . worked to rouse the ordinary folk far and near to exchange their foolish customs for a love of heavenly joys. For many profaned the Faith that they professed by a wicked life, and at a time of plague some had even abandoned Christian sacraments and had recourse to the delusive remedies of idolatory. . . .' On another occasion a large multitude of peasants, who were jeering on the shore as monks in small boats were being swept out to sea, told Cuthbert: 'May God save none of them! For they have robbed us of the old religion and nobody can cope with all these changes.'

If the strategy of conversion from the top downwards left many communities similarly confused and uncertain, eventually a single Christian kingdom would emerge in England which was strongly cemented by the establishment of a dense network of churches carrying the Christian ministry to every corner of the realm. In contrast, in the Celtic lands, the history of Christian conversion and worship pursued a rather different course.

The Early Church in the Celtic Lands

Each of the Celtic countries had its own conversion story, each spawned its own saints and Christian mythology. But these countries were also bound together by ancient sea routes, so that missionaries could circulate between the brave new worlds of Celtic monasticism, the new and the well-established footholds of Christian belief and the heartlands of paganism. In each of the Celtic territories the expansion of Christianity brought a strengthening of the infant civilization and a broadening of contacts – so that today folk who are brought close to despair by the tensions and complexities of the modern world and the peculiar qualities of its leaders might look back and regard the bright-eyed spiritualism and fortitude of Celtic Christianity as the hallmarks of a golden age. Golden ages tend to turn to dust when subjected to close historical or archaeological scrutiny. Even so, it is a source of wonder that Ireland, which lay beyond the furthest outposts of civilization when Rome and Britain went their separate ways, would within a few centuries be sending saints, learning and some of Europe's finest thinkers across the sea to work in areas close to the heart of the old Roman Empire.

It is difficult to imagine that organized Christian worship in Wales was ever completely extinguished during the centuries which followed its introduction amongst some Romano-British communities in the south of the country over a century before the Roman eviction. Cornwall, meanwhile, was a rather remote peninsula of the Roman world and was little affected by the activities of Roman Christianity. Yet most experts have thought that Tintagel, which was perhaps established around 475, emerged early during the Age of the Saints as possibly the first British monastery. Wine came here from the Mediterranean lands, and small boats may also have introduced the monastic ideal from communities established in North Africa and the Levant. Whether it was trade, missionary work, or the ideas returning with nameless Celtic pilgrims which sowed the seeds of monasticism on the sea-battered headlands of the west we may never know. However, the origins of Tintagel are uncertain, and it has recently been strongly argued that the earliest Dark Age community established here could more easily have been secular than religious.

The roots of Christianity in the south of Scotland burrowed more deeply and belonged to a different tradition of Christian organization. Around the time of the Roman collapse Christianity had penetrated Galloway, and the relics of buildings and a cemetery have been excavated near the medieval priory at Whithorn (Dumfries and Galloway). Carlisle may have been the episcopal centre from which Christianity was diffused into Scotland, and the enigmatic Ninian was perhaps the first bishop, despatched to serve the converts already established around Whithorn. Here the original organization of the Church was of an episcopal rather than a monastic form, that is organized in dioceses headed by bishops rather than around monasteries led by abbots. Of the fifth-century stones surviving at Kirkmadrine (Dumfries and Galloway), one commemorates three otherwise unknown bishops, the 'principal priests' Ides, Viventius and Mavorius. Ireland probably experienced the first conversions to Christianity at about the same time as Galloway. Saints, who are now the merest shadows, were active here before Pope Celestine despatched Palladius as bishop in 431. Perhaps a year, but maybe a couple of decades later, Patrick made his celebrated return to the island where he had been enslaved as a British captive and began his mission.

Although episcopal organization had been the norm in the Roman territories and lingered when the Empire withdrew from Britain, it was ill adjusted to the rugged realities of the Celtic environments which lacked towns or similar 'central places' that could serve as the foci of territorial bishoprics. Monasteries, often deliberately established in settings which would test the fortitude of their recruits to the full, became the bases for missionary work amongst the pagan Celts. In the latter part of the fifth century the eastern Mediterranean concept of monasticism (see p. 48), perhaps arriving via stepping-stones in south Wales or Cornwall, achieved its first footholds in Ireland. In due course, the vigorous idealism of the Irish monasteries and the asceticism and endurance of their charismatic missionaries brought Christianity to scores of scattered pagan communities in the northern margins of Britain. Although the Celtic missionaries proved sluggardly in taking their message to the English, Columba established his monastery on the Scottish island of Iona in 563 and – as an offshoot from this – Aidan founded a monastic community on Lindisfarne about 634. The Celtic mission to the Northumbrian mainland began just a couple of years after the flight of Paulinus in the face of the pagan revival following the overthrow of King Edwin. While one can have little but admiration for the stalwart missionaries of the Celtic Church, it may be worth remembering that what little we know of the conversions comes from sources such as the Irish annals which were recorded by monks. The pagans were not really literate, and we can know nothing of the conversion period as it was seen through their eyes. The Irish clerics had their own heroes to proclaim and their own Church to glorify – and history can be very unkind to those who have no indigenous literature.

The undoubted glory and purity of the Celtic Church – whose debts to continental Christianity were repaid many times over by monks renowned throughout the Christian world as theologians, teachers, indefatigable pilgrims and unrivalled illuminators of holy texts – did not save the Church from powerful critics. Being different can easily become a source of criticism, and in the eyes of Rome the Celtic Church came to be regarded as distinctly odd. It had no authoritative bishops, it did not have venerated martyrs but honoured a galaxy of obscure saints with strange-sounding names, it was fragmented among a swarm of autonomous monasteries, and it organized its affairs and observances in apparently idiosyncratic ways. The English, once they were safely in the Christian fold, seem to have resented the fact that the Christian Celts had seemed to spurn the pagan Saxons, who must surely have been good targets for conversion. In 664 the tensions between English and Roman Christianity on the one hand and the Celtic Church on the other were brought into focus at a synod called by King Oswiu of Northumbria (655–70) and held at Whitby (North Yorkshire). Although the specific issue at stake between Colman, Bishop of Lindisfarne, who represented the Celtic Church, and Wilfrid, Abbot of Ripon, who spoke for the Roman party, concerned the method of calculating the date of Easter, the Synod's decision in favour of the Roman position determined the religious orientation of the kingdom of Northumbria. Failure at Whitby marked the beginnings of the retreat of the Celtic Church.

In Scotland episcopal organization gradually advanced, although Celtic rites and ritual were perpetuated by the strict and ascetic Scottish order of the Culdees until their suppression early in the Middle Ages. In Wales the episcopal tradition was quite strongly rooted and some dioceses there dated back to the sixth century. Cornwall cherished its strong ties with the Celtic Church until being absorbed into the episcopal worlds of Wessex in the tenth century. In Ireland itself the story was sadder; internal challenges to the Celtic Church surfaced in the eleventh century. In 1155 Pope Adrian IV granted the overlordship of Ireland to the English king, Henry II (1154–89), and the rapacious Norman adventurers in Ireland were dignified by a papal benediction in 1170. As a result, Roman organization eventually extended a new form of unity across the Celtic world.

Holy Wells, Tombs and Crosses

The conversion of Britain took place around fifteen centuries ago. In many places it was accomplished by men with austere, ascetic ideals who worked in countrysides which were always quite poor or were ravaged by political uncertainties and economic decay. The early churches and monasteries which such missionaries established were mainly small and simple structures of timber, thatch, wattle and daub – buildings which would rapidly perish or would be replaced by more impressive and durable structures as the Church increased its influence. Leaving aside the northern parts of Scotland for the moment, it can be said that the initial conversion period is not proclaimed across the landscape by legions of imposing monuments. In Ireland, particularly, the rambler may find numerous pagan standing stones, many probably of a Bronze Age vintage, which have been Christianized by the addition of a simple cross symbol. Folklore and Christian mythology combine to provide their own colourful if questionable insights into the transition from the old to the new beliefs. Frequently the pagan holy places were deliberately

commandeered by the Christian missionaries. This pragmatic process can be recognized in the case of some of the holy wells which were destined to be venerated as places of pilgrimage and were associated with miracles and healing.

Weedon Lois in Northamptonshire is an interesting example; the Lois component must refer to the holy well of St Loy, which offered cures for blindness and leprosy. But the Weedon or 'temple hill' component suggests that the well was originally associated with a pagan shrine. In several cases the Celtic mythology seems to have its essence in pagan theology, for the themes of the shedding of blood, the renewal of life and miraculous fertility keep recurring in the associated Christian myths. At Holywell (Clwyd) in north Wales, for example, the legend connected with the well that gives the settlement its name tells of the murder of the Christian, Winifred, by her frustrated lover, the noble Caradoc. Her uncle, St Bueno, brought Winifred back to life, the earth opened to entomb Caradoc, and a stream bubbled forth from the spot where Winifred's head had fallen. Across the Welsh border in Shropshire, Stoke St Milborough takes its name from the holy well of Milburga, a seventh-century saint, and here there is a typical fertility legend. Pursued by her enemies, Milburga commanded her white horse to strike a rock with its hoof, and a holy spring gushed forth. It then flowed across a newly-sown field of barley, which instantly germinated, grew and ripened. The reapers were then told to tell the saint's pursuers that they had not seen her since the day that the crop was sown.

From the Pictish standing stones of northern Scotland the conversion story can be read as clearly as from a printed page. The problem is that the first half of the saga is inscribed in symbols relating to a narrative which we cannot understand. At the time when Roman power in Britain was waning, in the lands lying well to the north of the imperial frontier the tribal nation of the Picts was gradually consolidating. The culture of the Picts seems to have been archaic and the members of the nation may have spoken a tongue which was older than the Celtic settlement of Britain. Yet the Picts were far from being barbaric backwoodsmen, and in the fifth century they began to refine a style of art which combined human, animal and seemingly abstract motifs in an amazingly fluent style. Although the art may have been accomplished in wood-carving and also occurs in a few surviving articles of metal-work and on cave walls, its most familiar and striking expressions are displayed on standing stones.

The functions of these stones remain mysterious. They might be boundary-markers, tombstones or

The imposing medieval church developed at the site of St Winifred's (Winefride's) Well at Holywell, Clwyd, in north Wales. The well itself was surely sacred in pagan times.

ritual monuments. Nobody knows. The earliest of the stones, dating to the fifth or sixth centuries, belong to the pagan era in the Pictish lands, and they are emblazoned with elaborate, standardized, but as yet undeciphered symbols, with native animals, beautifully and economically expressed, and also mythical beasts. Next come the stones of the later sixth and early seventh centuries, dating from the times when Christian missionaries such as Columba were gaining access to the courts of the Pictish sub-kingdoms and welding Christian congregations in the countrysides around. Here, perhaps more graphically than in any other context, we can revisit the traumas and uncertainties which tormented societies at a time when one deeply-rooted religion was yielding to a new, vigorous, but untested belief. The Pictish stones of this middle order flaunt the old pagan symbols on one side of the slab, but the other is the preserve of an intricately-carved Celtic cross. Subsequently the stones carry the cross alone, for in the middle of the seventh century Christianity was supreme in the Pictish lands and around 843 Pictland was absorbed into the Scottish or Gaelic kingdom of Kenneth McAlpin. This marked the beginnings of Scottish statehood but also, apparently, the death of Pictish nationhood: the language of this enigmatic people vanished before it could be recorded and it may never be recovered. Yet in their standing stones the Picts left remarkable monuments to a talented, eccentric and now inscrutable nation.

Various Pictish stones still stand, and some of them at least must be in their original positions. A few have been incorporated in churches, others gathered together in museum collections, while many must have been broken and others moved and re-erected in new locations. Arguably the best single place to experience the majesty of this mysterious art form is the hamlet of Aberlemno, a few kilometres south of Brechin (Tayside). A small group of somewhat battered or eroded symbol stones has been gathered together at the roadside, one a fine pagan or 'Class I' slab bearing serpent, 'double disc and Z-rod', mirror and comb symbols. Standing in the nearby churchyard is a quite breathtaking Class II stone. The 'pagan' face carries symbols such as the 'Z-rod', but the eye is drawn first to the amazing pageant of Pictish cavalry – the army of a lost nation on the march and in battle, with the men and horses portrayed in a low relief that is superb. Although slightly eroded, the details which bring the Pictish age back to life can still be recognized. Walking round the slab one passes from the gaudy pagan world into the calm presence of Christianity, for here, standing in a background of twining mythical beasts, is a majestic cross with its panels writhing with vigorous decoration.

Whether a monument as magnificent as this should still stand exposed in this sad era of acid rain could be a matter for debate, while the threats posed by

BELOW *A detail from the battle or hunting scene depicted on the pagan side of the Pictish stone at Aberlemno near Brechin, Tayside.*

RIGHT *The Christian side of the Aberlemno cross, with the richly-ornamented cross flanked by panels with intertwined beasts.*

outrageous fortune can be studied on the Pictish stone at Lindores near Newburgh, Fife. Formerly it stood on a nearby hill, but when this land was cultivated the stone was uprooted and built into the wall of a roadside cottage. At some stage a sundial seems to have been set in the stone, while modern officialdom added its unfortunate stamp to this fragment of Scotland's heritage by carving a survey bench mark into the 'crescent and V-rod' symbol.

Stone crosses may be found throughout the whole of Britain and Ireland. They are the most prominent and numerous of the surviving Dark Age monuments, so that if the period were to be marketed in the modern manner, a cross would inevitably be adopted as the logo. A problem in understanding the heritage of crosses concerns the fact that the cross was a most versatile structure. It is generally assumed that crosses, once of wood as well as of stone, mark the places used for preaching in the days before communities acquired their parish churches. This must often be true, but crosses were also used to mark the limits of church property and other territories, were erected as accompaniments to existing churches where they watched over the churchyard, or were sometimes set up as tombstones or route marks, or provided to secure divine protection for a wide variety of places. Later, hundreds were erected at different medieval market locations.

Steeping ourselves in the spirit of the uncomplicated piety of the Dark Ages, we may fail to realize that the crosses sometimes seem to have been erected to bolster the image of an earthly mortal rather than to celebrate the Almighty. Often it was the son or grandson of the man commemorated who commissioned the cross, while the sentiments of the Sixth Commandment may be forgotten amongst the warlike scenes and inscriptions provided by the sculptors. This is demonstrated by the Pillar of Eliseg, the chieftain of Powys, which overlooks Valle Crucis Abbey at Llangollen, Clwyd. In 1779 a crude excavation of the cross mound revealed a burial in a stone cist, presumed to be that of the chieftain commemorated by the cross. The cross shaft carried a lengthy inscription, which was transcribed in 1696, before the ravages of time had obliterated the lettering. It told how Concenn, great-grandson of Eliseg, erected the stone to perpetuate the memory of the man who had struggled for nine years to annex Powys '. . . from the power of the English, which he made into a sword-land by fire. Whoever shall read this hand-engraved stone let him give a blessing on the soul of Eliseg. . . . The blessing of the Lord be upon Concenn and all members of his family, and upon the whole land of Powys until the Day of Judgement. Amen.' Of course, this all amounts to a glorification of the dynasty of Powys, and there is some dispute as to whether this is genuinely a ninth-century inscription or an eleventh-century addition to the cross. An element of mystery lingers around most Dark Age crosses.

Free-standing stone crosses did not become common until the era of conversion was quite well advanced, although they could have been preceded by generations of wooden crosses. Several other forms of standing stones existed at earlier stages in the Dark Ages. Memorial stones continued in use from the Roman period and carved cross symbols appeared on such stones after the sixth century. Depending on the time and place the inscription could be in 'Latin Majuscule' script, which was inherited directly from the late Roman Empire and continued to be used by communities in Britain in the fifth and sixth centuries. Such inscriptions can still be read with ease. Alternatively, stones might be

inscribed in the 'Irish' or 'Hiberno-Saxon' script, which evolved from the Latin script through a number of stages in the Near East, north Africa and the continent and then became common in Dark Age Britain from the seventh to the eleventh centuries. Finally, there was the ogam script, an alphabet which developed in pagan Ireland during the fourth century; its letter-symbols resemble the cuts on a stockman's tally stick and consist of different types of strokes which cut or touch a base line. Translation of Irish ogam, which is also found in Irish-influenced areas in Wales and Cornwall, has been facilitated by the fact that it frequently occurred in bilingual inscriptions, alongside a similar text in Latin. The eighth-century Pictish applications of ogam are, however, still to be deciphered.

Of the earlier surviving Christian stones, three were preserved in the much later church at Penmachno near Betws y Coed, Gwynedd. They include the Carausius stone of the fifth century, with the plaintively simple Latin inscription: 'Here lies Carausius in this heap of stones.' It is rather unusual in that the inscription is surmounted by the 'chi-rho' symbol (formed from the combination of the first two Greek letters of Christ's name). Another important group of early Christian stones is housed in the museum at Whithorn. It includes the fifth-century Latinus stone which, the Latin inscription tells us, was erected by 'the grandson of Barroradus' to commemorate Lord Latinus and his four-year-old daughter. Dating from the following century is the tombstone of Vortepor, one of six important stones preserved in Carmarthen museum, Dyfed. Here the

One of the early crosses preserved inside the church at Llanddewi Brefi, Dyfed.

inscription 'In memory of Vortepor the Protector' is surmounted by a cross, and an ogam translation is cut in the side of the stone. Almost all the churchmen, nobles and office-holders commemorated on such Dark Age memorial stones are otherwise anonymous figures, but Vortepor may have been descended from a 'protector' or trainee officer in the court of Magnus Maximus (383–88), the Roman usurper.

Vortepor may be known only to specialists in Dark Age history, but the medieval romance of Tristan and Iseult perpetuates the name of Tristan. He was probably the chieftain occupying the old Iron Age fort of Castle Dore in Cornwall, which was refortified in the two centuries following the Roman collapse. Tristan's tombstone has been re-erected 8 kilometres (5 miles) away, by the lodge gates of Menabilly: 'Here lies Tristan, son of Cynfawr.' Cynfawr was a sixth-century ruler of the Cornish Celtic kingdom of Dumnonia.

These and many other Christian memorial stones and tombstones with Latin inscriptions to the forgotten leaders of Dark Age society remind us how the Romanized communities of remote or peripheral provinces of Britain worked to keep alive the language, beliefs and institutions of the departed Empire. The memorials would seem crude and backwoodsish to any urbane and educated Roman. Even so, they remind us of the determination of dispersed Celtic communities to retrace the paths to civilization that the Romans had trodden.

A few very early Christian stones bore the chi-rho monogram, like the Carausius stone, or the fifth-century Selus stone in St Just Church, Cornwall. Long before the famous free-standing crosses appeared, much cruder crosses were pecked on unshapen pillars. Sometimes this may represent the Christianization of a pagan standing stone, perhaps a Bronze Age monolith, or, in Ireland, a pagan ogam stone. Crude examples of cross pillars are grouped with early Christian tombstones inside the church at Llanddewi Brefi, Dyfed. In the seventh or eighth centuries cross slabs appeared with the cross, now often exquisitely decorated, being carved in relief on a flat slab of stone. The 'Class III' Pictish stones are of this type, and the most magnificent is the ninth-century Sueno's Stone, which stands near the outskirts of Forres (Grampian) in northeast Scotland and towers to the exceptional height of 6.1 metres (20 feet). A splendid wheel-headed cross with panels of interlace decoration occupies one side of the slab; the Christian symbol is set in a pageant of Dark Age infantry, cavalry and casualties, and the stone may commemorate a victory over the pagan Norsemen.

Norse settlement in Ireland and the north and west of Britain introduced a runic alphabet, which had probably developed in Germany from the Roman script. Saxon settlers had already brought related runic alphabets to England, and after the conversion the runes appeared on a few crosses, such as the famous Bewcastle Cross (Cumbria) in the wild lands just to the north of Hadrian's Wall. The Norse settlers were soon converted to Christianity, and the arrival of the religion on the Isle of Man is commemorated on one face of the tenth-century Thorwald's Cross. Clearly the pagan myths were still being recounted, for Odin and the wolf, Fenris, also appear on the stone, to the right of this cross. This stone is preserved in Andreas parish church along with other Norse stones, including Sandulf's Cross with its runic dedication.

Since both faces of these cross slabs were decorated it is clear that the stones were intended to stand upright, often, we must assume, at the graves of the Christian notables whom they frequently commemorate. Other slabs of a similar antiquity were placed horizontally over the grave. An outstanding collection of Christian grave slabs can be seen amongst the ruins of the famous Celtic monastery of Clonmacnoise in Co. Offaly. They have been mounted on walls beside an avenue and so the visitor can easily explore the development of this form of sculpture from the eighth to the twelfth century. One has the name of the deceased, 'Colman', carved in Hiberno-Saxon script, but the ogam inscription beneath offers a little more: 'Poor Colman'.

Not all Dark Age gravestones were imposing, and most burials were not marked by stones. Recent excavations at Ardnadam, near the shores of Holy Loch, Strathclyde, explored the site of a Celtic monastery attributed to the Culdees. With characteristic disregard for the norms of the Roman Church, some of the graves here were aligned northeast–southwest rather than according to the east–west convention, and they consisted of shallow oval pits rather than the normal long cists of the early Christian period. In some cases, it seems that a cairn of turf covered the burial and a roughly heart-shaped stone was set at the top of the mound. In other cases, triangular boulders were placed at the head and foot of the grave. Some larger, diamond-shaped graves were outlined in quartz pebbles, a type of stone associated with rituals since the Stone Age, and these graves had headstones. Very few of the gravestones were carved in any way, although one had a crudely-pecked cross and faint letters, perhaps spelling *nomine*. Traces of the chapel associated with the Culdee burial ground are thought to belong to the ninth or tenth century.

The Isle of Man has a remarkably rich assemblage of Dark Age monuments associated with the Norse settlers. Pagan ship burials are still visible as mounds at Knock y Doonee and Cronk ny Arrey Lhaa, while Christian cross slabs embellished with runes can be found at Andreas, Braddau, Jurby, Maughold and Michael Malew. At Chapel Hill, Balladoole, there is a burial in the Danish manner which is marked by a boat-shaped setting of stones. This is an old hill-fort with a keeil nearby. The keeils are small chapels dating from the eighth to the twelfth century, often with associated burial grounds. Good examples include Balladoole, Maughold and Spooyt Vane. The domestic life of the period is represented by the two Norse houses, excavated and on display at Braaid.

Finally in this brief survey of Dark Age tomb-stones there is the hogback, a massive carved block of stone, arched like the back of a boar and with a shape similar to the roof of a simple thatched cottage. Two fine tenth-century examples can be seen inside the church at Gosforth in Cumbria. They may repre-

One of the two hogback tombstones which are preserved inside the church at Gosforth in Cumbria.

sent houses of the dead, and here the smaller example has roof-tile patterns running down from the ridge, while its neighbour seems to be 'thatched'. The hog-backs were incorporated into the foundations of the church here when it was built – or, more probably, rebuilt – in Norman times. Scenes of Dark Age warfare, men fighting serpents, Christ on the cross and an image which may represent one of the deceased nobles appear on the stones. Gosforth also boasted four Dark Age crosses. The heads of two of them have been incorporated into the walls of the church, while a tenth-century cross still stands intact in the churchyard. It is a quite remarkable monument, over 4.5 metres (*c.* 15 feet) tall, with a willowy shaft supporting the ring head, decorated in what may be scenes from the pagan Norse poem 'Voluspa', which foretells the end of the world.

Free-standing crosses first appeared around the seventh century. Although they tended to become more elaborate and imposing as time advanced, two of the most impressive examples are quite early. The Ruthwell Cross (Dumfries and Galloway) in the south of Scotland is a magnificent Northumbrian sculpture of the late seventh century, with biblical scenes carved in the panels of the shaft. Of similar inspiration is the Bewcastle Cross, which now consists only of a lofty, headless shaft. It is of a roughly similar date and has panels depicting Christ, John the Baptist and St John the Evangelist. The great majority of Dark Age crosses stand in churchyards or have been placed inside later churches. Sometimes the crosses have been moved from their original settings and very little may be known about their history. In other cases the cross may have sanctified a site which was used for preaching before the building of a church there, while often a churchyard cross will endure through many rebuildings of the adjacent church. The fine but incomplete cross at Bakewell in Derbyshire stands beside a church which has shed all its Saxon trappings in the course of different reconstructions, but at Masham in North Yorkshire the ninth-century cross shaft stands beside a church which contains fragments of earlier Saxon masonry.

Cornwall is a land of crosses, many of them hacked from slabs of uncompromising moor stone which might have been expected to dull any sculptor's enthusiasm. There are a few exceptional examples,

RIGHT *A richly-ornamented Saxon cross shaft in the churchyard at Bakewell, Derbyshire. This is not the more famous Bakewell Cross, which lurks in an enclosure nearby. The town seems to have been a centre for Mercian art, while visitors should also explore the fine medieval bridge, originally built for packhorses.*

the finest being the tenth-century cross beside the church at Cardingham, with twining strands of stone forming the circular cross head and ring-chain, running spirals and interlace decoration on the shaft. The mass of Cornish crosses are smaller and more simple and date from the tenth, eleventh and twelfth centuries. The duchy contains very little pre-Norman church architecture, and so the multitude of crosses provide the most visible link with Dark Age piety. Only a minority of these crosses can have been associated with early churches, and they must have served several other purposes which may now be difficult to identify.

Perhaps the best place in Britain to explore a succession of Dark Age crosses, all in a leafy and tranquil setting, is at the church at Nevern (Dyfed), near Fishguard. There are two ogam stones of the fifth or early sixth centuries which commemorate Maglocunus,

BELOW *This fifth- or early sixth-century monument to Vitalianus Emeretus stands in the churchyard at Nevern near Fishguard, Dyfed, close to the superb tenth-century cross which stands amongst the churchyard yews.*

ABOVE *The Carew Cross, at Carew near Pembroke, Dyfed, stands at the roadside close to the famous medieval castle. The shaft is decorated in fret and interlace patterns and there is an inscription to 'Margiteut, son of Etguin'. It dates from the late tenth century.*

son of Clutorius, and Vitalianus Emeretus; the former, with its well-preserved inscription, now serves as a window-sill inside the church. The most striking monument here is the wonderfully preserved and lavishly ornamented late tenth-century cross which stands beside the church in the shade of the venerable churchyard yews.

Surviving relics of the early Christian period on Iona are modest, with the exception of the trio of splendid high crosses, with dedications to SS Martin,

RIGHT *Muiredeach's Cross at Monasterboice in Co. Louth dates from around 840 and is one of the finest exhibits in Ireland's magnificent collection of high crosses.*

Matthew and John. St Martin's is the most complete and St John's is now a concrete replica, though its fragments, in the museum nearby, show how the jointing of the stone cross imitated carpentry.

Although Britain has a fine legacy of decorated Dark Age crosses, this tradition in sculpture was brought to its most glorious fruition by the sandstone carvers employed by the Celtic monasteries of Ireland. By the ninth century the ascetic monastic lifestyles were being modified, the foundations were becoming grander, while a reservoir of craftsmanship in the fields of building and sculpture was accumulating. Irish workshops began to reinterpret the magnificence of portable timber-and-inlay crosses in stone, applying the skills which stone carvers had acquired in the creation of cross slabs to the manufacture of free-standing high crosses. The wheel-headed form of the Celtic high crosses is thought to derive from the wooden predecessors, which had strengthening rings linking the limbs of the cross. Biblical scenes and panels of intricate, abstract ornament pack the panels of these crosses which, along with the enigmatic round towers, will tend to impress the visitor to the Celtic monastic sites more than the rest of the architecture and sculpture. Of the many quite spectacular examples which survive, space allows the mention of only a few, such as the West Cross and Muiredeach's Cross at Monasterboice, Co. Louth, and the Cross of the Scriptures at Clonmacnoise, all probably dating from the ninth century. Other examples are the Durrow Cross in Co. Offaly, the twelfth-century Doorty Cross at Kilfenora in Co. Clare, which depicts Christ as Abbot of the World, and the Moone Cross in Co. Kildare, which may date from the eighth century and displays a delightfully 'primitive' style of carving which contrasts with the sophisticated fluency of the later Doorty and Durrow crosses.

The Saxon Church

After fitful beginnings, the triumphal advance of the Saxon Church in England culminated in a landscape which was sprinkled with churches. This sprinkling was more generous than most people imagine, and in many places it amounted to a heavy stipple. Typically, these churches were quite small and unsophisticated buildings. They were sometimes of timber and sometimes of stone. Stone was laid in the rough textures of coursed or uncoursed rubble or the knobbly patterns of flint and conglomerate, with massive blocks of stone set alternately flat and upright as 'long and short work' in the quoins which supported the vulnerable corners of rectangular buildings. On the whole, Saxon churches tended to be rather taller and narrower and to have thinner walls than the churches of the Norman successors.

To our eyes, rather than those of their early congregations, the Saxon churches seem to be delightfully uncomplicated and homely buildings. And so it is very easy to fall into the trap of believing that Saxon worship and ritual were also simple and uncluttered. Rather, they were different. Just as the Celtic Church suffered for its individuality, which was perceived as unorthodoxy by influential outsiders, so the Saxon Church came in turn to be regarded as odd, particularly in its enthusiasm for venerating obscure saints. Were a modern visitor – Catholic or Protestant – able to join a Saxon congregation, then he or she would find the almost obsessive veneration of relics surprising, and would discover many unfamiliar features in the ritual and layout of the church. On returning, this time-traveller would find his or her doormat buried under scholarly invitations, for there is much still to be learned about the organization of Saxon worship. We will only fully be able to understand the church buildings when we can comprehend the form of the rituals which the buildings were created to serve.

The provision of churches in Saxon England passed through a number of stages. In the first flush of conversion, the royal families, who were invariably the prime targets for missionary work, often built (or rebuilt) churches for their own personal use. Bede tells us of the baptism of King Edwin of Northumbria in 627: 'The king's Baptism took place at York on Easter Day, the twelfth of April, in the church of St Peter the Apostle, which the king had hastily built of timber during the time of his instruction and preparation for Baptism. . . .' Edwin's conversion had already been followed by a renunciation of the pagan past and the Chief Priest, Coifi, volunteered to profane the altars and shrines of the old religion: 'I will do this myself; for now that the true God has granted me knowledge, who more suitably than I can set a public example and destroy the idols that I worshipped in ignorance?' Redwald in East Anglia had been less convinced, for in his temple the Christian altar stood side by side with an altar '. . . on which victims were offered to devils'.

Not all the earliest churches were built for the convenience of the royal dynasties, and in 635 King Oswald (633–41) renewed the cause of Christianity in Northumbria (following a brief pagan interregnum) with the assistance of Bishop Aidan: 'Churches were built in several places, and the people flocked gladly to hear the word of God, while the king of his bounty gave lands and endowments to establish monasteries.' The first generations of churches which were built to bring the Christian message to the countryside were not parish churches, and the creation of a close network of parish or 'field' churches came later. The early churches were almost entirely minsters or mother churches, staffed by a body of clergy who went forth to minister to the dispersed populations of the surrounding territory. Records which can identify early minsters are not easily found, but it seems that the churches were very frequently established on royal estates and at important centres for the administration of the realm. From the outset the churchmen had recognized the importance of having the kings on their side. In due course, the kings came to appreciate the practical advantages of the link with the Church. Administration lies at the core of kingship, and the relatively educated and literate minster communities provided the rulers with access to reservoirs of administrative talents. Brigstock in Northamptonshire is a good example, being situated at the heart of what was then a royal estate. Today the noble tower and stair turret survive from the imposing Saxon building, and, as is so often the case with Saxon churches, the tower is clasped by the nave and aisles of the medieval church.

The word 'minster' derives from *monasterium*, but when it is found in the old documents it most commonly relates to a mother church rather than to a conventional monastery. This is a reminder of an age when many monks combined the vocations of the missionary and the priest, while the group associated with a minster consisted of a priest and a religious community which could be monastic or secular. Some of the old minster churches have been transformed by later rebuildings and may now appear as quite undistinguished medieval parish churches, such as Horningsea in Cambridgeshire, where only unobtrusive fragments of the Saxon fabric survive. Some minsters exist only as ruins, such as those of the great church at Reculver in Kent, built inside the remains of a Roman Saxon Shore fort and with the relics dominated by the magnificent paired Norman towers. A few have been deserted by their village congregations and now stand alone, like the church at Fawsley in Northamptonshire, where the medieval village was depopulated by its cruel owners, the Knightley family. In other cases still, a larger-than-expected church may survive to whisper to the cognoscenti that the church and setting had former glories, as at Great Paxton in Cambridgeshire or Brixworth in Northamptonshire. Finally, there are the churches which almost certainly were minsters, even though the old documents have not survived to confirm our suspicions. Wing in Buckinghamshire is a good example.

As the Saxon period advanced, new 'field' churches were built to serve individual communities. They appeared on one estate after another, and were normally provided by the noble landowner concerned. And so eventually the ancient estates of the English countryside came to be perpetuated in their new guise as parishes, focusing on a particular church and supporting it with tithes. Churches of all kinds were built in sacred places which had been expropriated from the pagan religions. At Rudston in Humberside the church grew beside the towering Bronze Age monolith; at Knowlton in Dorset it was built inside the circular earthworks of one of the Neolithic henges there, and at Maxey in Cambridgeshire it stands on an ancient burial mound. Here, a Saxon settlement, which later migrated, originally accompanied the church; at Rudston a more durable village grew beside the church, while at Knowlton the church and the Saxon village (which was deserted in the Middle Ages) were always well separated.

Normally, however, the church was not built on a site that was thought sacred in pagan times, but on a piece of ground donated by the local lord. This plot might lie conveniently beside his hall, or occupy an impressive and prominent position, and it might or might not be in an existing settlement. Churches and villages seem to have materialized in the Saxon countryside at about the same time, and it is seldom possible to know which came first, but most though not all churches were closely associated with a particular settlement by the end of the Saxon period. By this time, too, churches had become numerous.

There are no records surviving to tell us just how many churches were established in Saxon times. There were certainly far more than ever found their way into the pages of Domesday Book of 1086, for research by Professor Darby shows that 159 places in Kent alone had churches which were not mentioned in that document. Today there are some 400 churches in Britain which are known still to preserve large or small components of Saxon masonry, despite all the many subsequent rebuildings. In fact the true figure may be much higher. Saxon walls were quite well built, and portions of sound wall will often remain after many bouts of fashionable or essential refenestration, the elongation of the nave, the addition of clerestories, the rebuilding of towers and so on – although walls built of rubble are extremely difficult to date. Even so, it is certain that thousands of Saxon churches have disappeared in the course of successive rebuildings or misguided 'restoration'.

It is easy to assume that a particular site would acquire just one Saxon church, yet the period of Saxon church building spanned some four centuries.

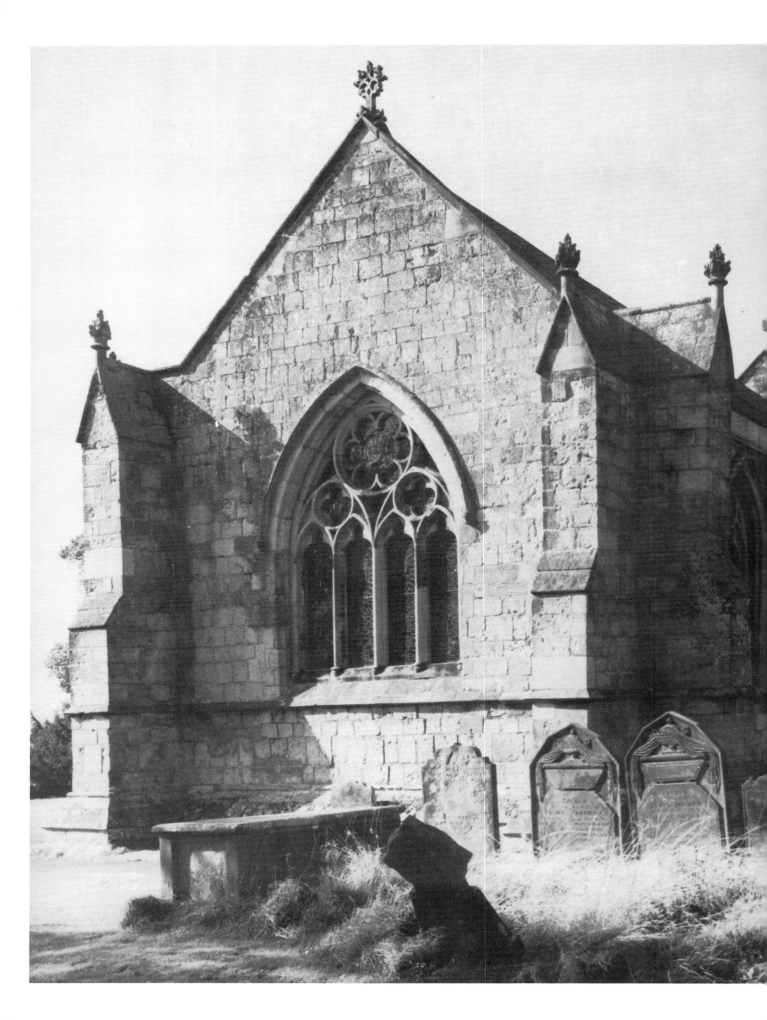

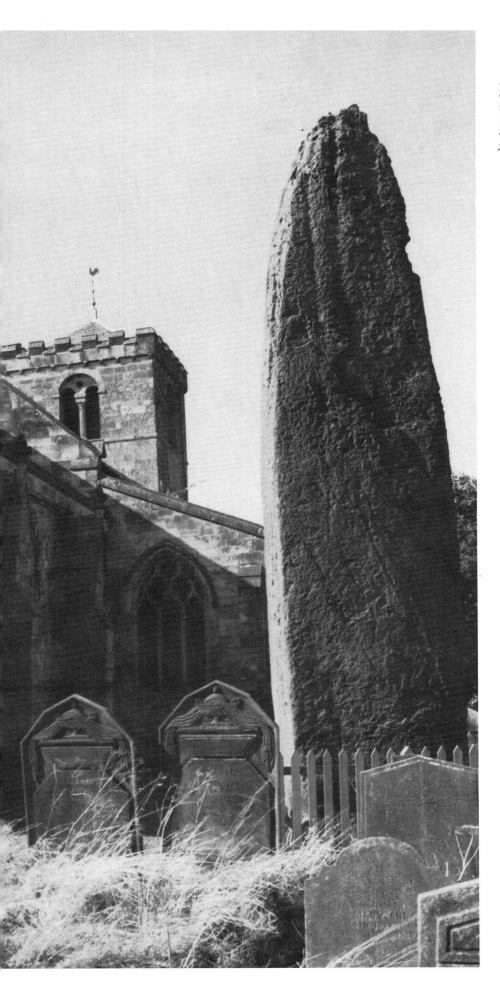

At Rudston in Humberside the Saxon church, rebuilt and enlarged during the medieval period, was sited beside the towering Bronze Age monolith, demonstrating how early Christians hijacked the pagan sacred sites.

Consequently a church might easily experience three or more cycles of renovation or reconstruction before the period had run its course. This Saxon evolution can be seen at many churches, such as the complicated structure (St Mary's Church) at Deerhurst in Gloucestershire. The west porch, for example, was part of a quite early church here, along with the nave and side chapels. It was subsequently raised to become a three-storey structure, and during the next reconstruction, probably in the tenth century, it was raised still higher and became the church tower.

The first generations of churches could be built of timber or of stone, depending on local circumstances. It may be that in some regions stone was provided as a form of largesse by the main ecclesiastical centres, for the extraction and distribution of stone was a much more challenging task than the use of timber. Edwin's baptismal church at York was '. . . hastily built of timber . . .', and Bede also records the story of the death of St Aidan in 651. When he died, the saint had been leaning against a post that buttressed the outside wall of a timber church. When the building was burned down by the Mercians, the wooden church perished, but Aidan's post remained unscorched. Later the church was rebuilt in timber, and burned down through carelessness. Again the post survived and was erected as a holy relic inside the third church built on this spot. While similar timber churches must once have been common, particularly in localities which had woods but no suitable local resources of stone, the nave walls of only one Saxon timber church survive. This is the famous building at Greensted in Essex, which is thought to date from as late as the tenth century. Here vertical oak logs still soundly wall the nave, although the remainder of the church is mainly of a late medieval vintage, and so it looks quite unlike the Saxon original.

It seems unlikely that the old Roman skills in the use of masonry could have endured in England until the conversion, and consequently the necessary expertise in the use of mortared stone must have been imported from the continent. Soon after Edwin's baptism at York, the king, under the instruction of Paulinus, built a stone church round the timber chapel, and many other original timber structures must similarly have been superseded. At first the use of stone was conditioned by the distribution of workable resources of this bulky and difficult material. The Saxons did not scorn humble materials and

Saxon oak posts still form the nave walls of the much later church at Greensted, Essex.

would use hunks of conglomerate and glacial boulders if these were all that was to hand, while the chalky downlands often provided flints. Where flints or river cobbles were employed, the masons were obliged either to import a stone to make strong quoins, or to experiment with cornerless structures. This latter alternative resulted in the construction of the East Anglian round towers, like the one at Beachamwell near Swaffham, Norfolk, and this tradition was perpetuated in the region by the Normans. In some places the church builders were lucky and quantities of dressed stone could be pillaged from ruined Roman buildings – the fine church tower at Little Ouseburn in North Yorkshire is built of such re-used stone. More commonly, the Saxons would scour ruins for supplies of russet Roman bricks or tiles, which could be used for general walling or for building the heads of arches. Sometimes they make an important contribution to the structure, as at Brixworth, or in the Norman walls of St Albans Cathedral.

Most of the churches which are billed as 'Saxon' – and attract many visitors as a result – really only display substantial fragments of Saxon work, as in the north and west nave wall and portions of the north transept at the gorgeous multi-period church at Stanton Lacy in Shropshire. Breamore in Hampshire has one of England's most beautiful churches, standing on higher ground some distance from the present village. Here more of the Saxon legacy survives and the nave, central tower and one transept date from about 1000; the head of a door carries a Saxon inscription which might be translated as: 'Here the covenant is manifested unto thee.' An élite handful of churches are still substantially Saxon or contain virtually complete Saxon components. They include the Chapel of St Lawrence at Bradford-on-Avon (Wiltshire), which is complete except for the south porch and may be mainly of the tenth century, Barton-on-Humber in Humberside, Wing and Great Paxton, with their superb naves, Brixworth, and Escomb near Bishop Auckland in Co. Durham, which retains most of its eighth-century appearance.

A fairly typical English church during the Saxon period would strike us as being rather small and austere, though without the oppressive aura associ-

ABOVE LEFT *Ruined Roman buildings were pillaged for the squared stone used in the Saxon church tower at Little Ouseburn in North Yorkshire.*

LEFT *Roman bricks were gathered and used to form the arch of this doorway at the magnificent Saxon church at Brixworth in Northamptonshire.*

ated with many small Norman churches. But the deceptively simple layout would not reflect the nature of Saxon worship and rituals, as the Church at this period included many influential cults and centres of pilgrimage associated with the relics of the numerous Saxon saints. Several cathedrals, such as Durham, Canterbury and Winchester, greatly enhanced their prestige by acquiring collections of famous relics.

The superb ninth-century apse at Wing in Buckinghamshire stands above an earlier crypt.

The church at Escomb, Co. Durham, little changed since the eighth century.

During the monastic revival of the tenth century, centres such as Ely (Cambridgeshire), St Albans and Glastonbury (Somerset) also became celebrated sites of pilgrimage, noted throughout the length of the land for their relics and the wonders which these performed.

The modern church-goer is accustomed to seeing the altar set against the east wall of the church. In Saxon times, however, the altar seems to have been free-standing. The priest may have officiated standing behind the altar and facing the congregation. Gradually it came to be accepted that the Mass was a private act of the priest and the altar was moved, though during the course of the Saxon period churches could acquire several altars, with the subsidiary ones being associated with a particular saint and relic cult. The chancel beyond the free-standing altar was often rounded to form an apse, around which priests could sit in a semicircle on the clergy bench, facing towards the congregation.

One of the finest surviving apses is at Wing, where the tall and impressive ninth-century structure stands above an earlier Saxon crypt. Sunken crypts feature in a number of Saxon churches. Recent excavations at Repton in Derbyshire have explored the crypt, which may have begun as a baptistery and which then housed the relics of St Wystan. Other recent excavations at St Oswald's, Gloucester, revealed an enormous crypt, some 8.2 metres (27 feet) square, which may have served as a pilgrim shrine of St Oswald or as the burial mausoleum of the founder of the late ninth-century church, Aethelflaed, Lady of the Mercians.

Frequently, subsidiary chambers or 'porticus' were attached to the sides of the main body of a Saxon church. Such porticus seem to have been used for a variety of functions: for private worship, as baptisteries, as burial chapels, or for Masses. Notables such as royalty or leading churchmen would wish to be buried as close as possible to any holy relics which might be lodged in an altar or elsewhere in a church. At first, burial within the walls of a Christian church was forbidden, but burial in a porticus, technically regarded as lying outside the church, could bring the deceased as close to the magical relics as convention allowed.

The plan of the Saxon church normally had two basic components, the nave and the chancel, with the frequent addition of porticus. Many churches were very small and consisted of just one room, but a few large examples had 'basilican' plans, similar to a Roman public hall, with aisles flanking the nave. The churches were built in a 'Romanesque' style, which involved the adoption of a variety of architectural features inherited from Roman times. Hallmarks of the Saxon manner of building include the use of rounded arches in the chancel (as can be seen at churches such as St Benet's in Cambridge, or Escomb), in the heads of windows and doors, and in the nave arcade where the church had a basilican plan (as at Wing, or Great Paxton). In the case of small window openings, a rounded head might be hewn in a single lintel block of stone, while triangular-headed windows were formed from angled slabs of stone. Pairs of round-headed windows were sometimes separated by lathe-turned stone baluster shafts, and windows of different types can be admired in the magnificent tenth-century tower at Earls Barton in Northamptonshire.

The Saxon architectural style evolved gradually, and since there were no revolutionary changes in building fashions the dating of a particular church can be quite difficult. On the whole, however, the churches tended to become more elaborate and ornamented as the period advanced. Most of the churches dating from the early part of the conversion period are found in Kent. They seem to be mission-ary churches, built in a modest way from available Roman materials to accommodate the small original congregations, though adopting basilican plans. It seems probable that Queen Bertha was worshipping in the church of St Martin at Canterbury before Augustine landed in Kent, while Bradwell-on-Sea in Essex, founded by St Cedd in 654, has lost its apse and porticus, but its typically tall and narrow nave has survived the test of time surprisingly well. Like several other early churches, it stands in the ruins of a Roman fort of the Saxon Shore: all later Roman forts will have contained plenty of re-usable building materials – and these were pillaged with gusto by the Bradwell builders – but it is also possible that some form of administrative importance still lingered at these crumbling citadels. The destruction of the Shore-fort church at Reculver by its vicar in 1809 allowed archaeologists to come to grips with the layout of the Saxon building. In the shadows of the Norman towers one can see the outlines of the seventh-century nave and apsed chancel, and also of the north and south porticus, which overlap the nave-chancel junction. Another early Saxon church is outlined in the turf at the Shore fort of Richborough.

In the course of the Saxon period many churches were rebuilt, enlarged and renovated. Towers and external ornamentation became increasingly popular, while the interiors of churches were apparently lime-washed or painted. Both the magnificent Earls Barton tower and the fine example at Barton-on-Humber are embellished with flat band or stripwork decoration, thought by some to mimic contemporary timber-framing. Where one existed, the tower was normally the least functional part of a church, but at least at Earls Barton it seems to have been used in a way which reminds us yet again of the peculiar nature of the Saxon church. The base of the tower seems to have served as the original nave of the church, to which a tiny chancel must once have been attached. The chambers in the tower above the nave were reached by the still obvious external doorways, and appear to have constituted the fortified residence of the noble family which built the church-cum-tower-house. Here we meet the church in its occasional role as a minor fortress, and at Earls Barton it stood on a steep hill spur which was guarded by prehistoric defensive earthworks that were partly re-cut in Dark Age times. At Barton-on-Humber the Saxon church was also much smaller than its medieval successor, consisting of the tower (whose base again provided a nave) and a small chancel attached to the east of the tower. There was a porticus, which probably served as a baptistery, attached to the opposite side of the tower.

ABOVE *A doorway of the Earls Barton tower.*

The remarkable Saxon tower at Earls Barton, Northamptonshire, constituted the greater part of the Saxon church.

In England the Church could have rich and powerful sponsors and easy access to the continental pace-setters in architectural affairs. Consequently the country acquired a generous endowment of Saxon churches, and a small but still impressive fraction of this legacy survives. In the Celtic lands, however, both wealth and congregations were more thinly spread, and the more imposing and durable architecture was reserved for monastic sites. The churches must have been small and box-like and lacking the distinctive Romanesque trappings which we associate with the English churches. The oldest, and in some ways the most interesting church in the far west of England, is – or was – St Piran-in-the-Sands, near Perranzabuloe in Cornwall, which is thought to have been an oratory (a cell or chapel) of a sixth- or seventh-century saint. In 1984 a surviving arch was pulled down by treasure hunters, whose utter idiocy matches the irresponsible naivety of those who organized a nationwide hunt for golden eggs and thereby caused a number of renowned archaeological sites to be vandalized.

A pair of impressive pre-Norman buildings survives in Scotland. First there is the St Regulus Tower at St Andrews, Fife, originally part of a monastery of the Culdees. It may date from the early eleventh century and has some architectural similarities with the much smaller but delightful Saxon church at Wharram-le-Street in North Yorkshire. Secondly, and much older, is the tower of Restenneth Priory near Forfar (Tayside). The lower part of the tower, perhaps originally a porticus, may date right back to the early eighth century and be the work of Northumbrian masons brought here at the invitation of a Pictish king.

In Wales, the minsters of England gained their equivalents in the tenth century with the emergence of monastic mother churches which were sustained by dues paid by the subordinate churches which they established. These ‘clasau’ appear to have been churches that were larger than normal, often with cruciform layouts (formed by the building of transepts resembling the short arms of a cross), and they were governed by an abbot and served by a staff of hereditary canons. Minster churches also appeared in Scotland during the later stages of the Dark Ages, and here the shift in emphasis from minsters to the ‘field’ or ‘proprietorial’ churches which were founded by local estate owners only became significant in the twelfth century. In Ireland recognizably Romanesque architecture only appeared in the mid-twelfth century and was not widespread, although the essentially indigenous tradition in monastic building had already had considerable achievements. While England can glory in its heritage of Dark Age minster and parish churches, the surviving legacy of monastic buildings is very modest. In the Celtic countries – particularly in Ireland – the situation is reversed, for it is the monastic legacy which sparkles.

The Early Monasteries

Monasticism originated in the bleak and solitary world of the eastern hermit, and the word derives from the Greek *monos*, meaning ‘alone’. In the third century groups of hermits began to form communities, following highly-regulated communal lives under the rule and guidance of a ‘father’, or abbot. By the middle of the fourth century monasticism had arrived in Italy and diffused westwards into Gaul. As a result of contacts which are as yet unknown, the movement reached Cornwall, south Wales and Ireland in the late fifth or early sixth century. In the Celtic countries the early Church was – or swiftly became – organized on a monastic basis. In the Saxon kingdoms of England monasteries were established in due course alongside the diocesan Church. The first English monasteries were created very soon after Augustine's arrival, and derelict Roman churches in Kent were restored as monasteries. Before his death and burial in the porticus of his church of SS Peter and Paul in Canterbury, Augustine had witnessed the establishment of monastic communities in a number of centres, including Canterbury, London and Rochester.

The early monasteries were often small and relatively flimsy conglomerations of buildings. Some were destined to perish in ninth-century Viking raids, while at those places which prospered, later sequences of development and rebuilding have masked and obliterated the original work. Some standing remains from the Saxon period can be seen in the church of St Peter at Monkwearmouth, Tyne and Wear. A monastery was founded here in 673 by Benedict Biscop, whose work was influenced by monastic architecture which he had seen in the course of his continental travels. Monkwearmouth and its twin foundation at Jarrow (Tyne and Wear) enjoyed considerable success, so that early in the eighth century the two houses had more than six hundred monks. The church at Monkwearmouth was altered on several occasions during the Saxon period, with the changes continuing into the eleventh century, when the two-storey porch was heightened to become a tower. Excavations have revealed something of the layout of the monasteries at Jarrow and Monkwearmouth: although the buildings of these foundations did not have the complexity and the

ABOVE *The reconstructed pagan Saxon village at West Stow, Suffolk.*

LEFT *Detail from the Saxon church at Earls Barton, Northamptonshire—a pair of round-headed windows separated by a baluster shaft.*

ABOVE *The Saxon church at Wharram le Street in the Yorkshire Wolds.*

The main street of the English burh *is still a through road at Stamford, Lincolnshire.*

ABOVE *The medieval castle at Corfe in Dorset (NT) towered over a busy quarrying village.*

The Jew's House at Lincoln, believed to have been the house of Jewish financiers in the twelfth century.

ABOVE LEFT *Carew Castle near Pembroke, Dyfed, a Welsh and then Norman stronghold that was enlarged in the thirteenth and fourteenth centuries.*

BELOW LEFT *The trend-setting castle at Framlingham, Suffolk, one of the first to be built with projecting towers set at intervals along the curtain wall to help keep assailants away from the wall base.*

RIGHT *The Norman great hall at Hedingham Castle in Essex. Halls such as this served as living room, dining-room, reception room and office, all merged in one large chamber.*

BELOW *The promontory which carried Dunnottar Castle near Stonehaven, Grampian, has probably been defended since at least Pictish times. English defences here were burned by the Scots in 1297 and 1336.*

Peveril Castle, a Norman keep overlooking Castleton in Derbyshire, a recently-planned settlement of the feudal era. The limestone gorge of Cave Dale enhanced the defences behind the keep.

OVERLEAF ABOVE *Eilean Donan Castle south of Dornie, Highland, stands on an islet which was defended in prehistoric times. The present castle was built around 1230, enlarged and then restored in 1912–32. It protected Loch Duich against Norse raiders.*

OVERLEAF BELOW *Rhuddlan, Clwyd, for long a centre of Welsh resistance, fell to the Normans and the work on the great Edwardian stronghold began here in 1277.*

regular organization that can be seen at many medieval monasteries, already the more disciplined use of space distinguishes these Saxon monasteries from similar sites in the Celtic countries.

At Jarrow, founded by Benedict shortly after Monkwearmouth, two early monastic churches lay very close together along the same axis. The larger church was demolished in the eighteenth century, while the smaller, probably dedicated in 684, serves as the chancel of the present church. Excavation has revealed the foundations of a pair of Saxon monastic buildings beneath the Norman ones which still survive. They stood in a line parallel to the churches and had the form of great rectangular halls, built in stone with glazed windows and roofs of stone tiles with lead flashings. The larger hall has been interpreted as a refectory, while the smaller was subdivided and may have contained a large chamber used as an assembly and writing place for the monks and a small private suite for the abbot. The two lines of buildings at Jarrow formed the opposite sides of a rectangle and at later sites the construction of cloisters and buildings enclosing a rectangle produced the characteristic medieval monastic layout, which can still be seen at scores of places. Such plans were introduced at Canterbury and Glastonbury during the tenth century and repeated again and again in the medieval monasteries.

The progress of the monastic movement in Britain suffered severe reverses. Jarrow fell victim to a Danish raid in 794, and in the early years of the following century a succession of monasteries perished in flames. Although the Church survived and was soon successful in converting the pagan settlers, its own vitality was sapped by laxity and corruption. King Alfred successfully extended his overlordship to territories occupied by the Danes, but enjoyed less success in his attempts to re-establish monastic life in England, even though he struggled for this goal until his death in 899. When it came, the strong revival of the Saxon Church was centred on Winchester and drew inspiration from the teaching of St Benedict.

Benedict was born around 480, founded the great abbey of Monte Casino in Italy and established the guidelines of the Benedictine order, by far the most influential of the Dark Age monastic orders. As a disciplined and centrally-controlled form of monasticism, the rule of St Benedict was promoted by Pope Gregory as a more desirable alternative to the austere, autonomous and 'unorthodox' form of organization associated with the footloose and fervent Celtic monks. Benedictine monks, though not usually outstanding for their missionary zeal, had formed the

Augustinian mission which returned England to the Christian fold.

Dunstan, who was of noble birth and took vows following an education by Celtic teachers at Glastonbury, established close contacts with the Benedictine abbey at Fleury on the Loire, and became Abbot of Glastonbury in 939. He was banished between 955 and 957, but returned at the invitation of King Edgar and in turn became Bishop of Worcester, Bishop of London and then Archbishop of Canterbury. He was responsible for the founding or refounding of monasteries at Bath (Avon), Westminster, Athelney and Muchelney (Somerset) and Malmesbury (Wiltshire). Oswald, who also had close links with Fleury, was responsible for taking the Benedictine reforms to other parts of England. He was Bishop of Worcester and Archbishop of York and succeeded in founding or re-establishing monasteries at Westbury-on-Trym (Avon), Ely, Peterborough, Ramsey and Thorney (Cambridgeshire), Winchcombe (Gloucestershire), Evesham, Pershore and Worcester (Hereford and Worcester), Crowland (Lincolnshire) and Abingdon (Oxfordshire). Perhaps surprisingly, these churchmen enjoyed more success in revitalizing the Saxon Church than did the three similarly motivated rulers, Alfred (871–99), Edward the Elder (899–924) and Lady Aethelflaed (c. 909–18), and together they were responsible for over thirty new or revived monasteries.

By the end of the tenth century a fine array of Benedictine monasteries had been established. Sadly, we know very little of the appearance of these places; no walls still stand and our understanding of their monastic architecture relies on the evidence of excavations. At Glastonbury Dunstan appears to have introduced the continental concept of the rectangular cloister to Britain. Measuring 55 metres by 36.5 metres (180 feet by 120 feet), the cloister here was embraced by ranges of buildings. Dunstan also lengthened the existing seventh- or eighth-century church, adding aisles and a tower. This disciplined claustral layout of specialized monastic buildings grouped round a courtyard provided the blueprint for many subsequent monastic complexes, but it is a great pity that we cannot visit sites where the model is still displayed in a Saxon form. The Saxon cathedral and cloisters at Canterbury, destroyed by fire and then redeveloped in the decade after 1067, must have been superb buildings.

Had monks from one of the quite imposing and neatly-set-out Benedictine monasteries been able to step back in time to explore an early Celtic monastery then they might have been impressed by the asceti-

cism and fervour of the monks that they met, but shocked by the simplicity and apparent disorder evident in the monastic buildings. In Ireland the attempts by early missionaries, like Patrick, to set up an episcopal organization were soon overtaken by the establishment of a flock of independent monasteries, founded in stark settings and offering only the most basic facilities and shelter. At a typical site a cluster of thatched and timber or wattle-walled huts served as cells. These were set within a circular enclosure, which also included a chapel, small cemetery and cross pillars or slabs announcing the Christian basis of the settlement. The austerity of such foundations echoed the traditions of the eastern monastic home-land, and by some uncertain means the movement had bypassed the more civilized parts of the continent to establish Christian footholds on its mysterious Atlantic extremities. But by around 600 Celtic monks from Ireland were actually introducing the monastic lifestyle to localities in France, Switzerland and even Italy, the old imperial heartland.

An impression of the appearance of a Dark Age Celtic monastery can be gained at a number of isolated sites in the west of Ireland which have escaped major redevelopments or destruction. One of the best is Skellig Michael in Co. Kerry, a rather inaccessible island site. Most of the remains stand on a shelf in the cliffs which is reached by daunting flights of steps. Six Dark Age cells survive intact in the form of clochans, square-based huts with thick, windowless dry-stone walls which batter inwards and become circular towards the roof. Two small chapels or oratories survive (although they are less impressive than the famous Gallarus oratory on the Dingle peninsula), along with thirty-one grave slabs and a cross pillar. The church standing at this site is of the thirteenth century and the monastic remains might be just a century or several centuries older, for 'primi-tive' and not noticeably Romanesque architecture was constructed at some Irish sites at all stages during the currency of the Celtic Church.

There are many other Celtic monastic sites which lie forgotten and overgrown. A favourite of this author is Annait on Skye, unsignposted but quite close to the B886 at NG 272527. Both flanks of the site are guarded by a deeply-incised burn and the modest monastic buildings were defended by a mass-ive stone wall which may possibly represent the reoc-cupation of an Iron Age fortress. Inside the defences

The round tower at Monasterboice, Co. Louth, has lost its cap but still stands to a height of 28 metres (92 feet). Near its foot is the beautiful mid ninth-century West Cross.

One of the many monastic grave slabs displayed at Clonmacnoise.

the earthworks of a rectangular chapel and three tiny oval cells can be recognized. When they visited the site in the course of their travels in the Highlands and Islands, Boswell and Dr Johnson decided it might have been dedicated to the Egyptian god, Anaitis!

It could have been during the ninth century that the more affluent of the Irish monasteries began to acquire lofty round towers: cylindrical structures of dry-stone walling, which may look to modern eyes for all the world like space rockets. These towers could be up to 34 metres (*c.* 110 feet) in height, but their function is still uncertain. They have been inter-preted as refuges for use during local conflicts and Viking raids. However, one would indeed have been foolish to hope for security in a chimney-shaped building with timber floors which invited the atten-tion of anyone travelling the land around. The towers, which could have been inspired by Italian bell towers, might have served as belfries or treasure

houses, although they could have been more symbolic than functional, like most church towers. Many fine examples survive, as at Monasterboice and Clonmacnoise, and Glendalough in Co. Wicklow. Less celebrated sites include Killala, Meelick and Turlough, all in Co. Mayo, or Kilmacduagh in Co. Galway, where the tower has a disconcerting tilt. There are just two examples of round towers on the Scottish mainland, reflecting ancient links with the Celtic Church in Ireland. These are at Abernethy near Perth and at Brechin in Tayside, where the tower gained an imposing extension, in the form of the thirteenth-century cathedral. A third round tower in Britain is attached to the Norse church at

LEFT *The Cross of the Scriptures at the early monastic site at Clonmacnoise in Co. Offaly dates from the beginning of the tenth century.*

BELOW *The elevated entrance to the round tower at Brechin.*

Egilsay, Orkney, and a fourth is on St Patrick's Isle at Peel in the Isle of Man. The Brechin round tower is of the tenth century, although its crowning spire is a fourteenth-century addition. Its entrance, accessible only by ladder in the normal manner, is flanked by carvings of bishops and crowned with a crucifixion.

The medieval centuries witnessed the construction of buildings which are still quite breathtaking, whether as ruins, like the abbeys of Fountains (NT) or Rievaulx in North Yorkshire, or as living buildings which survived the architectural carnage of the Reformation because they were designated as cathedrals, as in the case of Ely or Durham. The entrancing relics of Celtic monasticism in Ireland apart, however, the visible heritage of Dark Age monastic remains is modest. If a foundation proved successful and durable then its buildings disappeared beneath more elaborate and imposing constructions of the medieval period. If it failed or fell victim to pagan barbarian raids, then the buildings would decay in isolation. The Church of St Finan on Lindisfarne was built only of hewn oak logs, and at Iona the only visible relic of St Columba's monastery is that of the bank and ditch, or *vallum*, which defined the rectangular enclosure. On the island of Eileach an Naoimh (Strathclyde), a few kilometres across the waters between Mull and Jura, there is a little more to remind us of the simplicity and severity of early monastic life: the ruins of a small rectangular chapel, a trio of little beehive-shaped monastic cells and a simple seventh-century grave. Yet although the remains of this period are modest, the reputations of many of the sites are undiminished. The simplicity, fortitude and purity associated with the early centres of Christianity may offer as much (or more) spiritual inspiration as the spectacular architectural achievements of later ages, when the Church had become unimaginably wealthy and exceedingly influential.

3
The Dark Age Countryside: A Mystery Tour

My nose is pointed downwards; I crawl along
and dig in the ground. I go as I am guided
by the gray enemy of the forest, and by my lord,
who walks stooping, my guardian, at my tail,
pushes his way on the plain, lifts me and presses
    me on,
and sows in my track. Nose to ground, I move
    forwards,
having been brought from the wood, skilfully
    fastened together,
and carried on a wagon. I have many strange
    properties.
As I advance, on one side of me there is green,
while on the other my black track is clear. . . .

The Plough, a tenth-century English riddle
    translated by W. S. Mackie.

*Ancient countryside : a wonderful panorama of fields with rich,
winding hedgerows near Luppitt in Devon. Such fields are normally
at least as old as the Middle Ages, and many could be much older
still. This is the type of mature English countryside which the
agribusiness movement is rapidly destroying.*

The Unmaking of the English Landscape

In the course of the Dark Ages an ailing English countryside, which was sprinkled with decaying villas and declining hamlets and dappled by overgrown fields, was gradually revived and put back to work. Thickets were cleared, new hamlets and villages appeared and eventually the bare outlines of medieval village England were sketched on the rural canvas. In a manner quite contrary to popular belief, the Saxon settlers did not make the English landscape, though their very distant descendants did play a part in one of the most notable remakings of the countryside.

During the millennium between the Roman and the Norman landings, farmsteads and hamlets appeared, flourished and perished. Yet one important facet of the rural jigsaw does seem to have proved remarkably durable. This was the great estate. There must have been many such landholdings which might have begun as the fiefdom of a prehistoric noble, then become the property of a Roman entrepreneur or aristocrat, and have then passed to a British or a Saxon master whose descendants were eventually dispossessed by one of William's Norman adventurers. Known today as 'multiple estates', these great landholdings seem to have embraced a score of different resources and farming activities, so that each estate was self-sufficient in the essentials of life and produced some delicacies for its master. In the laws of Ine, King of Wessex, which were recorded between 688 and 694, the food rent of a large estate of ten hides is given. (The hide was not a standardized land measure, but is generally regarded as being around 50 hectares, or 120 acres.) The food rent included 10 vats of honey, 300 loaves, 12 'ambers'

BELOW *In a few places which have never since been ploughed, Romano-British and older field patterns survive as earthworks. This set of fields lies in the high limestone pastures above Grassington in North Yorkshire. Field patterns such as these, though living and hedged, will have been seen by the Saxon settlers, who did little to change them.*

Planned countryside : rectangular fields with straight walls or hedgerows, frequently the creation of Parliamentary Enclosure surveyors and often quite attractive. This is a panorama in upper Nidderdale in North Yorkshire.

of Welsh ale and 30 ambers of clear ale, 2 adult cows or 10 wethers, 10 geese, 20 hens, 10 cheeses, an amber of butter, 5 salmon, 100 eels and a quantity of fodder.

Perhaps the most telling evidence of the durability of old estate centres has emerged from the excavation of the deserted medieval village at Wharram Percy (North Yorkshire) in the Yorkshire Wolds. Beneath the footings of the medieval manor house the traces of an unidentified Saxon structure were found; beneath these relics lay the remains of a Roman villa which had itself been established on the site of an Iron Age stronghold. From these few square metres of ground, masters of different kinds and ages had dominated the surrounding countryside for countless centuries. The countryfolk meanwhile probably remained essentially the same, performing the same repetitive farming tasks, sharing the same sorts of gossip and grievances, and rendering their taxes and services to their lord.

Although the origins of these durable landholdings are hidden in the depths of time, the old estates may still exert a powerful influence upon the appearance of the living landscape. During the lifetimes of most readers, the grossly subsidized agribusiness movement has done its utmost to batter our glorious and personable countrysides into featureless prairies. Fortunately, the vandalism is still incomplete, so that there are many places where one can still distinguish between the different heritages of what have been called 'ancient countryside' and 'planned countryside'. Ancient countryside is a landscape of scattered

hamlets and farmsteads, with thick, winding hedgerows, jigsaw patterns of field and woodland and twisting leafy lanes. Planned countryside, in contrast, is characterized by plump villages which are quite widely spaced and is found in those areas where the medieval patterns of open field farming (see p. 206) are overlain by the geometrical hedgerow networks which were created by the Parliamentary Enclosures of the eighteenth and nineteenth centuries. At this point the reader might well ask what these two different kinds of countryside can tell us about the estates of Dark Age England?

The answers are uncertain, but it could well be that in the course of the Saxon centuries local accidents of inheritance coupled with political disruptions led to the progressive fragmentation of many estates. Planned countryside generally has its origins in the systems of open field farming which were introduced in the latter centuries of the Dark Ages, but these extensive patterns could only be imposed upon estates which were still sufficiently large to encompass the necessary extents of open field ploughland, pasture, hay meadow, common and woodland. Wherever the fragmentation of the ancient estates had gone too far, the older patterns

Fossilized field patterns near Appletreewick in Wharfedale, North Yorkshire. I have recently recognized a system of narrow lynchets which runs upslope here, while elsewhere in the dale similar fields are cut by medieval strip lynchets. This suggests that the vertical fields of the type shown here might date from the Dark Ages, and it is possible that small rectangular Roman fields (perhaps visible just behind the farm buildings) have been incorporated by the lower ends of the fields. More familiar medieval or later ridge and furrow ploughland can be seen in the bottom right corner.

58

of dispersed hamlets and small hedged fields and paddocks would persist. Consequently, anyone who wishes to experience the flavour of Roman or Saxon countryside must visit an area where the ancient type of countryside still survives. The Londoner need not travel to the English margins to enjoy the pleasures of such scenery, for Essex and Kent still have some to offer. There there are unspoiled corners where one can ramble the hollowed paths and byways and enjoy the intimate, verdant aura of lands which seem to have retained their essential character while two millennia have slipped by. But we still do not know just *how* old these ancient countrysides really are.

The Romans gained mastery of a land which was heavily exploited and highly productive. In certain places they must have increased the farmed area through their canal and drain-building projects, and the East Anglian fenland may have been exploited as a vast imperial estate. In just a few other places it is possible that the Romans may have reorganized the old field patterns. On the whole, though, they seem to have been content to leave well alone, erecting country mansions or villas in some of the choicest lowland places, but trusting to the indigenous farming skills and the incentives of market trading to yield a gushing stream of taxes and produce from the countrysides of England. In contrast, their British and Saxon successors inherited lands which were often ravaged by neglect following the decay of the Roman economy and the eruptions of pestilence, famine and skirmishing. In these conditions some British estate owners might have been pleased to receive groups of Saxons who could be settled on derelict lands to increase the labour force or provide protection against brigands. Whether they came as tenants, mercenaries or victors there is no evidence whatsoever that the new arrivals reorganized the old patterns of fields and farming in any way. In some places they will have brought old and overgrown fields back into production, while in many others the shrubs and woodland continued to advance across the derelict fieldscapes.

In areas of ancient countryside where the communal systems of open field farming were never introduced, change was a slow and gradual process, and in these places much of the flavour of Roman and Dark Age countryside will still persist. While the scenery has preserved its essential character, the settlements and some other facets of the Roman and Dark Age scene have been obliterated or buried by the endeavours of later generations of farmers, but there are some places where really venerable features still survive within the living scene. In the vicinity of Little Waltham in Essex, P. J. Drury discovered that a Roman road was cutting across a network of fields which was clearly older than the road itself. When the road had been driven across the fieldscape a number of field corners were detached, creating awkward little triangular enclosures. Here many of the ancient fields survived as living hedged enclosures until the very recent assaults of modern farming. At the time of writing, extremely important work by Tom Williamson at the University of East Anglia appears to be showing that great networks of pre-Roman fields endured in Norfolk until the modern blight of hedgerow removal. Again, the relationship between field patterns and Roman roads has provided the evidence. These prehistoric fields seem to have been set out in great blocks which are defined by long, roughly parallel tracks or drifts. The patterns seem rather reminiscent of some of the fossilized field networks of Wessex, so they might even be a legacy of the Bronze Age rather than the Iron Age.

In innumerable other places the controversial technique of hedgerow dating provides less certain evidence for the survival of ancient field patterns. Stated very simply, the theory holds that a hedge will gain one additional species of tree or shrub every century. To 'date' the hedges in a locality one must count the hedgerow tree and shrub species in a series of 30-metre (*c.* 100-foot) sections, and a section count of, say, ten species would, so the theory suggests, indicate a 1000-year-old hedge. Unfortunately, there are many problems associated with this technique. Nobody has been able to explain the precise mechanism by which a hedge should acquire a new species every century, while the basis on which the assessment should be done is not commonly agreed. Some authorities differentiate between blackberry and dewberry or count all the numerous varieties of wild rose individually; some accept honeysuckle or old man's beard while others do not, and so on. In addition there are complications such as 'elm invasion', for elm can penetrate a rich, old hedgerow and displace all other shrubs – and I believe that sloe (blackthorn) may similarly invade. Anyone with a crude impression of the theory might expect that a Roman hedge would now contain up to twenty species, while a Saxon one would have between ten and sixteen types of tree or shrub. In fact, a 30-metre (100-foot) stretch of hedgerow will hardly ever have more than twelve species, no matter how old it may be – there is just no space for any more.

In spite of all these problems it is true that demonstrably old hedgerows are normally rich in species, while young ones are almost always much poorer. Hedges with five and fewer species are likely to be younger than the first Elizabethan era; those with six to ten species will normally be medieval, and those with ten or more may be very old indeed. Having recently studied hedgerows in an area of ancient countryside in the Weald it is clear that here hedges with less than eight species are few, while those with ten or more species are normal wherever the hedge follows a road or a parish boundary. In places such as this one soon appreciates that the unspoiled countryside is a living museum, worth quite as much as any country mansion or art collection, yet enjoying hardly any protection.

Countryside is the creation of farmers – as anyone who lives on the Cambridgeshire prairies as I did knows only too well. The farmlands of the Dark Ages were worked from hamlets, farmsteads and small village settlements, and although there are no present-day settlements which even remotely resemble those of the Dark Ages, we cannot understand the period without exploring the origins of rural homesteads and what happened to them. The Roman countrysides were highly developed and well populated, and Christopher Taylor has argued that there were as many country dwellers in prosperous Roman England as could be found in the rural settings of Shakespeare's time. In any undulating countryside of reasonable quality one could have stood on the brow of a small hill and seen at least half a dozen native hamlets and farmsteads, all within easy walking distance. A diversity of settlements stippled the Roman fieldscape. There were the agricultural hamlets and farmsteads of the indigenous people; industrial villages churning out pottery, tiles and bricks, or the timber or metal products which the consumers now clamoured to buy; there were roadside market and service centres, which could be quite neatly planned or just rambling villages, and, in the more attractive areas, there were the villas, the fashionable estate centres and country seats of the 'county set', mainly occupied by native aristocrats and entrepreneurs who had prospered under Roman rule.

The fortunes of the villa rose and fell. During the fourth century a number of villas were built, enlarged and modernized, and for a while people and investment may have shifted from the ailing towns to the adjacent rural areas. But these highly organized commercial farms could not prosper in the decades to come, when the economy and law and order fell into disarray and families sought salvation in local self-sufficiency. In some places the villas were abandoned; in others occupation continued and the owners may have remained, encamped like squatters amidst the decaying grandeur of their lost sophistication. In other places, too, outsiders found shelter

Chilgrove Villa near Chichester, West Sussex, at the height of its prosperity in the first half of the fourth century (top) and (above) after its partial destruction by fire later in the same century.

within the Roman walls and built their homesteads amongst the ruins. Though goats may have browsed in the overgrown gardens, and shacks of timber and thatch replaced the grander buildings of stone, brick and tile, there will have been many places where the estate survived the decay of its command post, and others where the baton of leadership passed from the Roman villa to a Dark Age hall which was built amongst its debris.

One of the most interesting stories to emerge from recent excavations was put together by the archaeologist Warwick Rodwell during work at Rivenhall in Essex. Here the Saxon newcomers seem to have occupied the old, aisled barn of the abandoned

Roman villa during the fifth century, adopting it as a homely, aisled hall and building their hearth in the hollow left by the collapse of the Roman well. In due course a Dark Age manor and church developed here, and although no village ever formed, the site maintained its leadership over the surrounding countryside.

Other evidence has been excavated from the site of Barton Court villa in Oxfordshire. The villa was built around 270 and stood in a farmyard which contained a cottage, a corn drier and two wells. During the fourth century the decay of the farm is suggested by the silting up of the wells and field ditches, and although the villa was demolished (a little time after a hoard of worn late fourth-century coins was buried in its floor) and its stones were carted away, the nearby cottage remained in use for a while. About the time that the villa was demolished, settlers, including some Saxons, built their timber huts and halls round the old villa site, and in the sixth century four corpses were buried amongst the Roman debris. During this century the settlers' farmsteads were abandoned and the occupants moved to live at another site in the neighbourhood. Here, as in so many places, the Roman countryside had had little woodland, though a copse of oak and hazel was coppiced to produce essential supplies of timber. The villa stood amongst pastures and horticultural land, and after the harvest wheat, barley and flax were brought in from the ploughlands beyond. After the Roman collapse the gardening of exotic fruits and flowers ceased, and although the early Dark Age farmers continued to grow some flax and barley, shrubs were gradually advancing across the pastures.

It is easy, perhaps too easy, whilst regarding the villas and their associated dwellings as the homes of the Romano-British peoples to presume that the timber huts and halls, which appeared at the sites of their decay, were the abodes of Saxon invaders who displaced the British. Fragments of Germanic pottery are often associated with the fifth-century occupation of such sites, but these sherds do not prove that the newcomers were exclusively Saxons, and they certainly do not demonstrate the violent overthrow of the old order. The settlers might easily have been mixed communities of people tossed together in the chaos of the changing times – British farm workers and vagrants from the rotting towns as well as Saxon settlers and their British wives. There is little to suggest that the villas perished in flames as Saxon war bands rampaged across the countryside. Rather, we should see them as victims of the economic decay and uncertainty which accompanied the disintegration of Roman Britain. Some villas perished well before the end of Roman rule, some seem to have passed away along with the legions, and others survived for a while after the Roman eviction.

At many places the scenes of decaying grandeur attracted new, less sophisticated occupants. Sometimes the settlers stayed a while before drifting away to colonize new sites nearby, sometimes a farmstead sank stronger roots amongst the ruins, and in other cases still the villa re-emerged as a Dark Age manor and in due course a church and a village developed. At Totternhoe in Bedfordshire, at the site of a villa which had been abandoned before the departure of the Romans, the villa gate-house was demolished by settlers who used the materials to build a pair of cottages. These buildings were in turn abandoned around the middle of the fifth century. At West Stow in Suffolk, where the hamlet seems to have been established before the end of Roman rule, the various discoveries of Romano-British pottery and coins suggest that the settlers traded with their British neighbours. It could be that in this case the owners of a nearby villa settled a few Saxon mercenaries and their families in a neglected corner of their estate, in order to have protection against vagabonds and raiders. It certainly seems that the villa continued to be occupied for some decades after the establishment of a Saxon community on the neighbouring heath.

In general the picture that emerges is of small and vulnerable communities camping amongst the debris of Roman Britain. Perhaps those who had nothing to lose may have been better placed to survive in this rather awful age. The collapse of the economy removed the opportunities and incentives for commercial farming, so that peasants and landowners reverted to mixed farming in the quest for local self-sufficiency. But the problems were more than those of economics and politics. This appears to have been a period in which the climate was deteriorating too, so that the poorer and more marginal farmlands may have become unworkable, while other lands, which had been overworked when markets had clamoured for more and more production, may at last have had their fertility exhausted. But, as Chapter 1 suggested, to explain the full extent of the decline in the Dark Age countryside it may be necessary to seek more terrible and sinister causes, and a sequence of plagues of the scale of the Black Death epidemics in 1348–51 would seem to be the most likely explanation. Gradually, very gradually, the English peasants managed to stem the retreat and recreate the fabric of rural life. Yet a millennium and more passed before the populous prosperity of Roman Britain in its heyday could be equalled.

From Saxon Hamlet to Village England

Britain has been the destination of many groups of settlers from the continent, but no other immigrants have become the subject of so many deeply entrenched myths as the Saxons. They have been credited with all manner of achievements, not least the founding of thousands of English villages. Yet, as we have glimpsed, the early Saxon period was not a time of expansion and innovation, but one which witnessed the disintegration and decay of an efficient and finely-tuned system of farming. It was a time when a diverse array of settlements experienced abandonment and decline, and when the new settlements which were created tended to be small, spartan and ephemeral. However, the village has become a potent romantic symbol in the widespread disillusionment with the stresses and emptiness of modern urban life. We like to imagine that it represents a steady and wholesome alternative to the competitive frenzy of the town – and our sentimental attachment to these seemingly sleepy, neighbourly places is fortified if we can imagine that villages have endured since the times long ago when they were founded by the resolute pioneers of our Saxon 'ancestors'. In fact, villages are rather specialized settlements and will only form under particular favourable circumstances. The 'normal' form of rural settlement in Britain is the hamlet, and, like innumerable generations of country folk before them, the Saxon settlers in England and their immediate descendants were mainly hamlet dwellers.

In the course of this century a number of Saxon settlements have been excavated and they reveal variations in size and layout as well as in the buildings themselves. A few, like Mucking in Essex, were sizeable if disorganized places, but most were quite small and consisted of a handful of farmsteads set, in a seemingly random fashion, amongst associated paddocks and enclosures. The periodic rebuilding and re-siting of a few farmsteads can create the archaeological illusion of a more substantial settlement, so that excavators now take great pains to identify the sequence of building and rebuilding. At Cowdery's Down near Basingstoke in Hampshire, for example, pagan settlers established themselves on a site which had known many phases of prehistoric and Roman settlement. In the course of the Dark Age occupation here eighteen major buildings and two huts were constructed. The major buildings were built in phases, so that the hamlet or small village consisted succes-

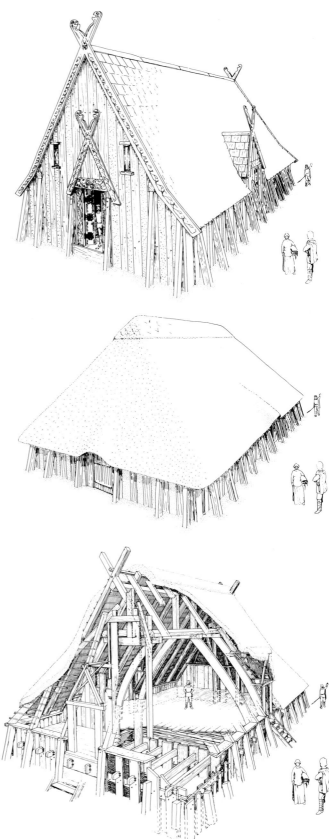

Alternative reconstructions of what is known as 'Structure C12' at Cowdery's Down, Hampshire, showing how different buildings could share the same excavated ground plan.

sively of three, six and ten such buildings, while in each phase the settlement had two enclosures or compounds, each containing some but not all of the buildings. In the first phase of Dark Age settlement here the hamlet may have been home to about twenty people, and in the course of the occupation the population could have grown to number over sixty. However, the buildings at Cowdery's Down were unusually large and substantial, so that the settlement might be interpreted as a noble centre which was occupied or visited by members of the local ruling class – in which case the population would have been smaller, and the various buildings more specialized in their function. In about 800, or perhaps a little before, when the cards of rural settlement were again being reshuffled and the outlines of Village England first began to be sketched on the landscape, the village at Cowdery's Down was abandoned.

Any attempts to describe a typical village or hamlet of the early Saxon period are bound to be undermined by the fact that as yet there are too few well-excavated examples to allow us to recognize exactly what was 'typical'. Each of the known sites had its own character, and while some excavations have revealed numbers of substantial rectangular timber buildings, other settlements apparently consisted of small and rather unimpressive huts. Also, it is not always possible to differentiate between buildings which were homesteads, barns, workshops or the hovels of labourers or serfs. But we can be quite sure that the Saxon hamlet or village looked nothing like any olde worlde English village which the reader may have visited.

Probably the typical settlement would be the hamlet-sized abode of an extended family, containing a few homesteads which variously accommodated the families of the patriarch and his children and other relations. These homesteads were rectangular buildings with gabled roofs of thatch and walls of upright planks which might or might not be separated by wattle and daub panels. Alternatively, the walls might have been of oak logs with daub panels filling the gaps between. These halls were scattered round the hamlet site in a seemingly haphazard manner and were attached to fenced paddocks or stock pens. The fences consisted of successive pairs of upright posts with rails or wattle held in the gap between each pair, and some of the hamlet buildings stood half inside and half outside the enclosures. Dotted about the site

were various subordinate farm buildings and workshops: the general aura of the settlement was more that of the farmyard than the village. In contrast to the medieval village, the dwellings were not set out along a road or round a green or market place, and the undisciplined nature of the hamlet was underlined by the muddy tracks which linked the homesteads, paddocks and rickyard.

One excavated Saxon settlement which does not really accord with this sketch is Mucking in Essex. Here there are traces of no less than two hundred small huts and probably several larger halls, though

Loose, hamlet-based settlements, comparable to this present-day pattern photographed in the north of Skye, appear to have been the norm in Dark Age Britain.

64

only some of these buildings would have been standing or occupied at any particular time. This settlement had a life-span of three centuries, and its nature is controversial. It is just possible that Germanic mercenaries were stationed here in late Roman times, on a site where they could survey the shipping moving up the Thames estuary towards London. Whether the settlement developed as a 'transit camp' – a reception centre for Saxon settlers from the continent – or was the seasonal abode of shepherds and stockmen, or was just an unusually large peasant village, we do not know. Chalton, near the present vil-

lage of this name in Hampshire, grew to be another quite substantial settlement, and the traces of almost fifty buildings have been recognized. West Stow is more typical – a group of some six farmsteads which were redeveloped over a period of two and a half centuries before the place was abandoned in the middle of the seventh century.

During the first few centuries of the Dark Ages England was essentially a land of hamlets, each hamlet probably the home of an extended family. The occupants of these hamlets could have been British or Saxon, and in many cases they would have

had mixed origins. Most of the settlements were destined for obscurity. In the north and west of Britain the hamlet was, and often still is, the fundamental rural settlement. But in most English localities, though a minority of hamlets would rise to greater glories as villages, the vast majority would survive only as solitary farmsteads or else vanish completely in the centuries to follow. In most of the parishes which are now dominated by a single village, the pastures and ploughlands are likely to hold the traces of upwards of half a dozen Dark Age hamlets.

The buildings which have been found at the settlement sites of the pagan period in England are of two types: rectangular timber halls and sunken-floored buildings. The latter are properly referred to as *Grubenhäuser*, and in informal archaeological chat they are called 'grub-huts'. It was the first excavations of settlements of grub-huts which tended to give the early Dark Age communities a bad name, for they gave rise to the impression that the occupants wallowed in mud and filth in the oblong pits or scoops which formed the bases of these poky little buildings. Grub-huts could be as small as 3 by 2 metres (*c.* 10 by 6 feet), and it seems likely that the floor pit would have been planked over, though its function remains obscure. In some cases, as at West Stow, the gabled roof was supported by a trio of posts placed at each end of the building and, according to different reconstructions, the thatch might have run right down to ground level or else have been carried on walls of split-oak planking. The function of the sub-floor pit is quite puzzling; it might have served for storage or drainage, and when a grub-hut was abandoned it could have been used as a rubbish pit. The grub-hut design seems to have been imported by Saxons from the continent. It is not certain that these little buildings were normally used as dwellings; they could often have been subsidiary structures built to serve as sheds or as workshops for weaving or pottery. Since we know very little about their above-ground appearance we can either imagine them as flimsy hovels – as represented by the reconstruction at the Weald and Downland Museum at Singleton in West Sussex – or as more substantial structures – like the West Stow reconstructions.

The rectangular timber halls were much more impressive buildings, which could measure 10 by 5 metres (*c.* 33 by 16 feet). These halls are likely to represent the homes of large families, and such buildings could just as easily have derived from prototypes built at native settlements during the Roman period as from designs imported by Saxons from the continent. Unfortunately, these more imposing structures leave far flimsier archaeological traces when

they decay. Various excavations show that halls and grub-huts were often close neighbours in the Dark Age settlements, but there must also be many other sites where ploughing has obliterated all traces of rectangular halls, although the evidence of grub-hut pits has survived. At Cowdery's Down, however, the excavators were more fortunate, and much evidence survived in the trenches which had held the bases of the walls. Forms of construction were revealed which are not closely paralleled in the surviving timber-framed buildings of the Middle Ages. Some halls had walls of strong and well-planed upright planks which were set in closely-spaced double rows, with the gaps between planks in the outer row being closed by the planks in the inner row, while the space between the two rows was filled with wattle and daub. Other walls consisted of single hyphenated lines of upright planks with wattle and daub infill panels. Excavation leaves many questions about the above-ground appearance of these buildings to be answered, but the excellent Cowdery's Down reconstruction drawings (see p. 63) show various possible interpretations of these quite impressive buildings.

Although the recognition of well-built timber halls has improved the image of Dark Age domestic life, the picture that is emerging of England in the early centuries of the Dark Ages is far removed from the visions of the historians, who conjured up the legends of bold pioneers. Where ancient pollen grains have survived in waterlogged places, scientists have been able to show how the well-manicured Roman countrysides were being colonized by shrubs and trees. Thistles, then thorns and then woodland will have crept across many pastures, and ploughlands will have surrendered to the tangles of weeds and briars which advanced from their hedgerow refuges. But the decay of the countryside could not continue forever, and slowly the tide was turned. In the eighth or ninth and the tenth centuries a revolution spread slowly across the English landscape. It seems to have had three components. On the religious front it was represented by the increase of estate or parish churches. In farming it saw large areas of the Midlands and parts of East Anglia transformed by the adoption of open field farming, while in settlements it was heralded by the appearance of small villages, which often proved to be much more durable than the old patterns of shifting, drifting hamlets.

While the mythical early-Saxon rural revolution has captured the imagination of generations of historians, this real mid to late Dark Age revolution has gone largely unnoticed. In the areas affected the changes were profound, and yet one cannot identify the estate owners who must have initiated the changes, or explain exactly how the revolution spread across the landscape at times when political power was often fragmented and fiercely contested, and when Danish raids and settlements were disrupting life in many localities. But it would be difficult to imagine that the establishment of thousands of new villages was unrelated to the ecclesiastical and agricultural changes. The transformation of a land of scattered hamlets into 'Village England' must have resulted from a process of settlement implosion, with the new villages sucking in settlers from a number of satellite hamlets. Inevitably, as the villages grew, many of the older hamlets withered. When living villages are looked at very carefully it is frequently found that they consist of two, or three, or four distinct nuclei, and some of the hamlets which lived through the changes must have done so by gradually merging – and so becoming villages. In parts of England one can find village-centred parishes which have small outlying settlements that are often known as 'greens' or 'ends'. Conventional wisdom tells that these places are 'secondary settlements' created by colonists from the mother villages during the medieval removal of the forest. More often than not, however, they are likely to be surviving fragments of the old hamlet patterns.

Villages existed during prehistoric and Roman times, but they were always in a minority, and tended to be abandoned after just a few generations of occupation. Many of the villages founded in the latter centuries of the Dark Ages are still living today. Two factors must have helped to stabilize these settlements. First, the creation of parish churches would often tend to anchor the village in the vicinity of its church, which was an enormously costly and important building – though whether in any particular place the church preceded the village or was preceded by it would be very difficult to discover. Secondly, the creation of a local system of open field farming made it more difficult for settlements to drift round the fields, and the most convenient place in which to live was always in a village rooted at the heart of the local empire of fields, meadows, pastures, woods and commons.

Towns are explored in Chapters 4 and 10, but here it is relevant to look briefly at the evidence for towns in the earlier part of the Saxon period. Ipswich was a town in the seventh century, one of the first post-Roman urban foundations in Western Europe, and also a large centre, covering some 50 hectares (120 acres). It was a trading port and industrial centre, importing wine from the continent and exporting the distinctive 'Ipswich ware' pottery throughout East Anglia and beyond. It flourished at a time when the network of country towns and market centres of the late Saxon and medieval centuries did not exist, and it must have been a very special type of town. Currently, experts (such as Keith Wade of the Suffolk Archaeological Unit) are proposing that it might be regarded as a sort of 'redistribution centre' which was closely linked to the East Anglian monarchy. It could have been founded by a king as a kind of personal trading centre: subjects could have paid the king in taxes, services or tribute, while the king rewarded his supporters with gifts which were produced in or imported to his Ipswich manufacturing and trading centre. Hamwith, the precursor of Southampton, may have played a similar role within the kingdom of Wessex. By the ninth century the urban system had been transformed; dozens of trading towns and markets had appeared and the redistribution economy had yielded to a system of market trading which all readers could easily comprehend.

Open field farming seems to have appeared in the later centuries of the Dark Ages, at a time when the tide of decay had been turned and the population was again beginning to grow. In places where the patterns and policies of estates allowed it to be adopted, the new system permitted an efficient integration of resources, with the concentration of the ploughland in two, three or more vast open fields maximizing the production of crops and releasing other land for the essential meadows and pastures. This new system was associated with communal methods of farming, and each community was obliged to develop intricate arrangements for the pooling of the oxen needed to draw their ploughs, for the control of grazing livestock, the use of commons, woods and meadows and the very detailed synchronization of farming activities. (A fuller description of the system is given in Chapter 10.) In the west, north and southeast, meanwhile, the patterns of landholding would not permit the adoption of open field farming; there the lands continued to be worked and held in severalty and more hamlets survived, though many were destined to collapse into solitary farmsteads. Even in supposed 'village country' in Hampshire, old farmsteads often stand amongst the earthworks of former hamlets.

* * *

Now let us meet the people who inhabited the Dark Age countrysides. It has often been suggested that after the Roman collapse England was colonized by free, 'democratic' Saxon peasants, and that the loss of individual freedoms occurred gradually, during troubled times when lesser folk were obliged to pledge themselves to warlords and nobles who could offer protection against raiders and aggressive neighbours. Yet there is no particular reason for imagining that countryfolk were ever free agents, from prehistoric times, when chieftains gathered tribute in their hilltop citadels, to the modern era, when we seem powerless to prevent the devastation of our countrysides by the barley barons. A system of bondage becomes recognizable at quite an early date in the Dark Ages, and the Laws of Ine, the late seventh-century King of Wessex, declare that: 'If a man departs from his lord without permission and steals into another shire, and is discovered, he shall return to where he was, and pay his lord 60 shillings.' In the later centuries of the Dark Ages, when more documentary evidence is available, we are able to recognize the emphatically hierarchical nature of society. Each man had his price, or *wergild*, which should be paid to his family by a murderer and the value of a man varied according to his status. In Kentish law the *wergild* of a free peasant was 100 shillings, and that of a noble was three times as much. In Wessex men were classed according to their *wergild* in shillings into 1200-men, 600-men, and 200-men.

Every man had a lord, and an enormous importance was attached to loyalty and the warrior's readiness to die in battle defending his leader. This is expressed in verse that was composed after the tenth-century battle against the Danes at Maldon in Essex:

> Here lies our lord, all hewn down –
> A hero in the dust; ever may mourn now
> He who thinks to turn from this battle-play.
> I am old in years: I will not turn hence.
> But I by the side of my lord,
> By so dear a man, think to lie.

Unlike their Norman successors, the Saxon lords were slave owners, although the conditions of slave life were not always hopelessly wretched. By the reign of King Alfred the slaves had acquired rights to own property and to sell gifts or craft goods and they were allowed holidays. In the reign of Cnut (1016–35) it was recorded that : 'All slaves are entitled to a Christmas feast and an Easter feast, and in harvest a handful of corn beside their dues.' Slavery could be a misfortune of birth or a punishment exacted on those who could not pay their fines.

Above the slaves in the rural hierarchy were peasants of different statuses who had varying obligations to their lords. They are recorded by other titles in the old records, but their descendants will have become the villeins, bordars and cottars of the medieval manors. They included the *gebur*, with his daunting burden of obligations, the *cotsaeta*, the forebear of the humble cottar, and the *geneat*, who occupied a more enviable position in the peasant hierarchy. The old documents often refer to the *ceorl*, or churl, a free peasant with a substantial landholding but also the obligations to go with it, including military service and attendance at the 'folkmoot' or district meeting. (A few moot mounds where such meetings were held can still be recognized, and many of them must have been re-used barrow mounds; examples include Mutlow Hill on Fleam Ditch in Cambridgeshire.) In the reign of Cnut a churl holding a hide at Hurstbourne Priors in Hampshire had to render: '40 pence at the autumnal equinox, and 6 church "mittan" of ale and 3 sesters of wheat for bread, and they must plough 3 acres in their own time, and sow them with their own seed, and bring it to the barn in their own time, and give 3 pounds of barley as rent, and mow half an acre of meadow as rent in their own time, and make it into a rick, and supply 4 fothers of split wood as rent, made into a stack in their own time, and supply 16 poles of fencing as rent likewise in their own time, and at Easter they shall give 2 ewes with 2 lambs . . . and they must wash the sheep and shear them in their own time, and work as they are bidden every week except three, one at mid-winter, the second at Easter, the third at the Rogation Days.'

The churl was not of aristocratic birth, but the next upward rung in the hierarchy was occupied by the noble landowner, known variously as a thane, *gesith*, or *ealdorman*. At the top of this social pyramid was the king, the giver of land and arms and granter of favours, who could demand the absolute loyalty of his noble subjects and the right to bask in the glory of their victories and achievements.

For all this, the royal residences of the Dark Ages bore scant resemblance to the glittering turreted castles of the Camelot myths. The palace of King Edwin of Northumbria at Yeavering (Northumberland) consisted of a small complex of buildings, which included a timber hall some 27 metres (88 feet) in length in which aisles were defined by the great posts which supported the roof, and with walls that were buttressed by rows of external posts. The hall stood between an unusual timber fort and a curving construction which has been interpreted as a grandstand – it might just have accommodated the audience when Paulinus preached here in 627. These and other buildings, including what appears to have been a Christianized temple, were burned, rebuilt and burned again as a result of Mercian raids. At Cheddar in Somerset the smaller palaces excavated here were used by the kings Edmund (939–46), Edwy (955–7) and Edgar (957–75), and possibly by Alfred too. Excavations have revealed a long, bow-sided hall which was replaced by a smaller, neater structure, possibly of two storeys, during the tenth century. This was among a complex of timber outbuildings, such as a fowl house, together with a stone chapel, all protected by a stockade and ditch. These palaces were really grander versions of the familiar timber halls; stone was almost entirely reserved for church-building works, although at Sulgrave in Northamptonshire stone was employed in a group of aristocratic buildings.

Although one may doubt whether all the laws and regulations enacted by the Saxon kings were always actually known and enforced, it is clear from the old documents that society was thoroughly stratified and that each man was charged with a heavy burden of responsibilities to his lord. The Normans hijacked a ready-made feudal system based on a galaxy of manors, each manor with its customs, each peasant with his onerous obligations and designated dues to lord and Church. The picture which emerges is that of a very conservative and regulated society, and this is mirrored in the writings of the time. The shepherd in *The Colloquies of Aelfric* of about 990 says: 'In the first of the morning I drive my sheep to their pasture and stand over them, in heat and cold with my dogs, lest the wolves swallow them up; and I lead them back to their folds and milk them twice a day; and their folds I move; and I make cheese and butter, and I am true to my lord.' In the reign of Cnut the shepherd also had certain dues: 'The shepherd's due is that he may have twelve nights manure at Christmas and one lamb and the fleece of a bell-wether and the milk of his flock for seven nights before the autumnal equinox and throughout the summer a cupful of buttermilk.'

During the seventeenth century and the later Romantic movement, in particular, the idea that a free and democratic Saxon society had been destroyed by the alien feudalism of the Normans circulated widely. Later such ideas were vigorously debunked by most historians, but at least where the place of women in society is concerned, the debunking seems to have gone too far. Recent researches by Christine Fell show that a degree of equality between the sexes existed in the English realm. The English bride, for example, received her dowry or 'morning-gift' herself, while under Norman feudalism she stood on the sidelines as it passed from the groom to her father or another male kinsman. The English produced a few quite daunting women leaders, like Aethelflaed, the Lady of the Mercians, a Thatcheresque figure who terrified all and sundry. Even during the Middle Ages, when noblewomen tended to become elevated beyond the realms of practical

affairs as the targets for courtly love, women often became tenants in their own right, and after the Great Pestilence large numbers of widows took over their husband's holdings.

Despite the rigid and autocratic nature of English society, the old documents and poetry also reveal an earthy, fun-loving community which was far from being impervious to the pleasures of good ale. This was also a remarkably artistic society, renowned throughout Europe for the delicate, naturalistic artwork of the 'Winchester school', and the more gaudy and vigorous decorative styles which resulted from the merging of English and Scandinavian traditions. In the course of the Dark Ages Britons and Saxons had met and mixed amongst the wreckage of the Roman order; eventually they had checked the decay of the farmland and begun the long process of recovery, launching a reshaping of the countryside which was to maintain its momentum into the early centuries of the medieval period. The scars of the Danish wars (see next chapter) were healing, and a unified kingdom could have looked forward to a brighter flowering of English civilization had not the defeat at Hastings in 1066 redirected the course of development for a nation which had still scarcely begun to gel.

The Celtic Rural Scene

In southern and eastern England it was the collapse of the Roman Empire rather than the arrival of a few thousand Saxon settlers that provided the setting, guidelines and starting point for Dark Age history. In the land to the north and west, however, the influence of imperial rule had been much lighter, while Cornwall, Wales, northern and western Scotland, Ireland and Cumbria were scarcely affected by the Saxon settlement. In these countries the traditional Iron Age lifestyle either continued to evolve through the Roman and Dark Age eras, or, in areas which had experienced Roman rule, the basics of indigenous life were easily revived following the departure of the legions. Although native dynasties may have competed for power, and Irish, and later Viking raiders, sometimes harried the coasts, the disruption of rural life was less in the Celtic lands than in the richer lowlands of England, where the influence of Roman civilization had been much more pervasive and its loss far more keenly felt. Some communities had prospered as a result of Roman policing and commerce, and one of the most impressive monuments on Anglesey is the Romano-British iron-working hamlet of Din Lligwy, which may have perished as a victim of Irish raiding. Intimations of the problems to come may have been recognized

ABOVE *A massively-built circular house of the traditional design stands within the defensive wall surrounding the hamlet of Din Lligwy on Anglesey, Gwynedd, which perished at the dawn of the Dark Ages, perhaps as a result of Irish raiding.*

LEFT *Defended farmsteads or 'raths' were largely, though not exclusively, an Irish phenomenon. Many thousands of examples were built between the Neolithic period and the Norman occupation, but most appear to belong to the late prehistoric and early Christian periods. This fine multi-vallate example, Ballycatteen Fort in Co. Cork, is more elaborate than most.*

when the Roman fort of Segontium near Caernarfon (Gwynedd) was evacuated around 385, and it could have been at this time that the rude stone buildings at Din Lligwy were surrounded by a pentagonal wall of boulders and rubble.

Enclosure walls of one kind or another are frequently associated with early Dark Age settlements in the west, and are part of a long tradition of minor fortifications. In Cornwall, lightly defended settlements often existed within circular walls or earth banks, and the earthworks of such rounds can still easily be recognized in several places. Here the native countryfolk had traded to obtain the attractive Roman wares while continuing to pursue their traditional ways of life. Trethurgy round was excavated in the 1970s; it originated in the third century as a handful of small, oval dwellings with paved floors and clay ovens, which were built within the encircling rampart grouped around a central cobbled yard. During the currency of the Roman Empire peasant farmers here bought pottery distributed by merchants from the Roman factories, but their lives may have been only lightly affected by the ending of Roman rule, and the round continued to be occupied until the sixth century.

The excavated footings of Norse long-houses at Brough of Birsay on Orkney.

In Wales and the West Country the overbearing hilltop citadels of the Iron Age experienced sporadic reoccupations of a non-military type during the centuries of the Roman occupation. Once the Romans were no longer able to police these areas it might seem likely that dynastic rivalries would have erupted and that there would have been wholesale refortification of the old hillforts. In a few cases, such as the Cadbury hillforts in Somerset and Avon (NT) mentioned in the next chapter, or possibly hillforts like Dinorben (Clwyd) in north Wales, a military reoccupation does seem to have taken place, but there is not yet the evidence to show that there was a general return of overlordship to the hillforts. In Ireland, however, the ancient Iron Age traditions of defence and raiding continued through into the medieval period, so that at the time when the Normans were establishing their castle-guarded footholds of conquest in the east, elsewhere in the country local land-owners were still occupying seemingly prehistoric ramparted

farmsteads or 'raths', and building simple stone-walled enclosures or stone forts in the rugged lands of the west. The occupation of the great majority of raths was between the sixth and twelfth centuries. Examples in state care in Northern Ireland include Rough Fort, Lisnagade and Lisnavaragh, all in Co. Down.

In Britain the tradition of enclosed or defended settlements gradually subsided in the north and west in favour of hamlets, which of one kind or another had always been the main elements in the mosaic of rural settlement. One might guess that in the course of the Dark Ages many sites would first be settled by a particular patriarch, and the addition of a couple of adjacent farmsteads to house members of the growing extended family established the foundations of a hamlet – which might perish in the centuries to follow or else endure as a farmstead or farmstead cluster to this day. Such an explanation would certainly seem to fit the Viking long-houses which stand beside the jumbled relics of homes of many prehistoric periods at Jarlshof on Shetland. Here, in the course of the ninth century, an original farmstead was enlarged and one and then another farmstead was added nearby. At Brough of Birsay on Orkney the footings of a hamlet or small village of boat-shaped Norse long-houses stand beside the site of an older Pictish settlement, resulting in one of the few Dark Age settlement sites visibly displaying much that might capture the interest of the casual visitor.

It would be wrong to regard the settlement of the Dark Age countrysides in the north and west of Britain as a purely casual affair accomplished by scores of independent pioneering patriarchs. Early-medieval documentary evidence, which has been painstakingly studied by Professor G.R.J. Jones, reveals a landscape which was divided between highly organized estates. Within these estates were hamlets which were often of a remarkably standardized size, some inhabited by free peasants and others by serfs, while each community had its own particular responsibilities to fulfil within the intricate world of the multiple estate. The estate could be the size of a parish or much larger and it would embrace a number of hamlets and their township territories. The master of the estate would reside permanently, or during his visits, in the chief settlement where his court was held, and around these little capitals was the demesne land, worked by bondmen who either lived in the capital or in satellite bond hamlets. The lord's reeve supervised the operation of the rural empire. The inhabitants of the surrounding hamlets each had responsibilities to provide particular rents and services; some might be charged with the upkeep, feeding and exercising of the lord's hunting dogs, others with the delivery of payments of eggs, honey, fish, ale, fodder or firewood, and so on. Although the descriptions of such estates were recorded in the medieval period, many in Wales seem to focus on an old Roman centre, and it may be that the origin of such territories is to be found back in the Iron Age. Similarly in Scotland, the multiple estates had a long if indeterminate history, and we can begin to recognize these units in the descriptions of territories granted to thanes at the start of the medieval period. Whether it masqueraded under the villa system, the clan system or the feudal system, the great estate had a long and powerful influence upon the countryside and its people.

When we peer back into the past we tend to see well-defined chapters, each one opening with a national or tribal conquest and titled the 'Roman', 'Saxon', 'Viking' or 'Norman' period. But perhaps our perceptions are wrong; it may have mattered very little to the average shepherd or ploughman whether his master spoke in Latin, Celtic, Saxon or Danish. He still had to deliver his rent, produce and labour. Perhaps he would have been more concerned with the state of the markets, the behaviour of the climate and the health of his family and livestock. Maybe we have erected our historical milestones in the wrong places.

4
From Camelot to Wallingford

The fort opposite the oak-wood –
Once it was Bruidge's, it was Cathal's
It was Aed's, it was Ailill's,
It was Conaing's, it was Cuiline's,
And it was Maelduine's –
The fort remains after each in his turn,
And the kings asleep in the ground.

                    From an old Irish poem.

At Earls Barton in Northamptonshire the strong Saxon church tower was built at the tip of a spur which was cut and defended by an older, perhaps prehistoric, ditch.

Visions of the Dark Ages are dominated by images of war. Looking through the distorting lenses of popular tradition we glimpse bands of British knights, their armour clashing and glinting as they ride forth from some turreted Camelot towards their ill-fated battles with the pagan invaders. The stage of the mind's eye has scarcely cleared before new epics with casts of thousands unfold as the Saxons – the patriots now – confront the terrifying Viking hordes. Finally, the Age comes thundering to its doom as the victors of Stamford Bridge die round their fallen king at Hastings. Nasty, gruesome wars certainly punctuated the history of the Dark Ages, yet where are the towered citadels and the crumbling Camelots which should survive as monuments to this blood-soaked era? They do not exist today; it is unlikely that they ever did. Eroded earthworks and a few modest and often ambiguous ruins make up the legacy of Dark Age fortifications. One might argue that there is only one really spectacular and imposing monument to the centuries of darkness. This is Devil's Dyke in Cambridgeshire, a monument which is surprisingly neglected by the public at large and whose creator, age and function remain mysterious. Yet I hope to show that the defence works of this period offer a great deal of interest. The historical importance of fortifications of the Dark Ages lies not in the magnificence and originality of the strongholds, but in the fact that the quest for security played a decisive role in the renaissance of the town.

Some strange process of hyper-inflation has conditioned ideas about the scale of Dark Age warfare. The armies of these times were probably far smaller than one imagines. Even so, a war band of just a few dozen warriors could cause considerable havoc and disruption when government was often ineffectual and when no kingdom could maintain a large, efficient and well-deployed standing army. The forces of the Dark Age kings seem usually to have been modest but remarkably mobile. Although the contemporary accounts sometimes describe battles with thousands of casualties, it seems that such figures were used in a boastful and rhetorical manner. Professor Leslie Alcock has quoted the Laws of Ine, which define an army as a force of more than 35 warriors, and he notes how Cyneheard, in 786, almost succeeded in capturing the kingdom of Wessex with a force of 85. On a grander but still hardly astonishing scale, he mentions how the Gaelic kingdom of Dalriada in the west of Scotland could muster 1200 or 1500 armed men, or around 1000 oarsmen. Most of the forces engaged in the wars of the Dark Ages must have numbered a few dozen to a few hundred warriors and, in England at least, members of the peasant majority will have had little part to play in such contests, except as the victims of looting and crop-burning. Such small armies will have demanded very little in the way of logistical support. Living off the land and travelling, if not fighting, on horseback they will have been able to launch surprise assaults on unsuspecting targets lying far from their homelands. Professor Alcock catalogues how, in 616, Aethelfrith (593–616) led his army from his capital at Bamburgh in Northumberland to a victory at Chester, a direct journey of 175 miles (280 kilometres), and how the army and British allies of Penda of Mercia travelled 250 miles (400 kilometres) to pursue Northumbrian troops to 'the city called Iudeu', which was probably Stirling (Central). Dynastic blood feuds and ever-shifting alliances ensured that there was plenty of opportunity for the aristocratic hot-heads of Dark Age society to demonstrate their military prowess and mobility.

In matters of defence the leaders of Dark Age Britain tended to look backwards in time. In the centuries following the Roman collapse this retrospection was reflected in the refortification of a few ancient and decrepit hillforts. At Cadbury Camp (NT), to the north of Congresbury in Avon, the Iron Age ramparted enclosure was divided into two parts by a new earth bank in the broad period 400 to 700, and at Maiden Castle in Dorset the eastern gateway was remodelled during the fourth and fifth centuries. Excavations in the 1960s at South Cadbury hillfort in Somerset have shown how, in the late fifth and sixth centuries, the Iron Age hillfort was more completely rehabilitated with the construction of a new rampart. This was built using a timber framework which was packed with rubble and revetted on both sides in stone. A metalled road entered the southwest gateway through massive double doors and a bridge probably carried the rampart walk above the gates. Here it appears that, during the slow decay of Roman civilization, a British chieftain or warlord who had the necessary resources of wealth and power to initiate a massive programme of refortification chose to create a citadel or capital. Perhaps he drew his tribute from the same area that had sustained the prehistoric citadel? At Cissbury in West Sussex a revitalization of the old hillfort was achieved by adding a turf capping to the slumping Iron Age ramparts and by widening the encircling ditch in the vicinity of the entrances, thus destroying the old counterscarp bank which lay outside the ditch.

Such activities could be regarded as marking a return to the ancient military traditions by the Romanized provincial leaders and communities, and there is little to suggest that the first generations of pagan settlers were particularly interested in the defensive potential of the old hillforts. Castle Ditch or Eddisbury hillfort in Cheshire was dismantled by the Romans, and the earthworks which survive today were built directly upon the slumped Iron Age defences in the period 912–18, when the site was redeveloped by King Alfred's daughter Aethelflaed, the Lady of the Mercians, as one of a series of fortified towns. The English attitude towards Roman towns and defence works is controversial, but there are records which suggest that Roman fortifications in stone at places such as London and Colchester were repaired in the ninth century. Later, in the reign of Ethelred the Unready (978–1016), an attempt seems to have been made to develop a defended town at South Cadbury and a mint was established which struck coins from 1009 to 1019. A final abortive attempt to refortify the site was made in the reign of King John (1199–1216).

In Cornwall, Scotland and Wales military thinking harked back to the ancient traditions, although the feats of the late Bronze Age and Iron Age communi-

ties were rarely equalled. Where explorations of the 'Camelot' capitals of the old Celtic kingdoms have taken place the discoveries have been unspectacular, and the general impression is one of modest garrison posts which may or may not have been permanently occupied by royalty, mostly built in places which a modern down-and-out would shun. At Castle Dore in Cornwall, the Iron Age fort had two ramparts and ditches; in the Dark Ages there was a slight refurbishment of the ramparts, a 'lodge' was built just inside the inner entrance and some large buildings were erected nearby. The principal construction was an aisled hall, some 27 metres (c. 90 feet) in length, and this has been interpreted as being possibly the fifth- or sixth-century hall of Cynfawr, father of the legendary Tristan. In Snowdonia excavations at the hillfort of Garn Boduan (Gwynedd) produced hints

Some Iron Age hillforts, like Castle Dore in Cornwall, were pressed back into service during the Dark Ages.

that a small fort, built on the summit inside and against the extensive Iron Age ramparts, might be of Dark Age date. The name, meaning 'Buan's home', could link the fortlet to a semi-historical figure who may have lived in the years around 600.

From the limited evidence available there are suggestions that Dark Age kings and chieftains in the Celtic kingdoms ruled from, or sought shelter in, hill-top strongholds such as Dunadd in Argyll (Strath-clyde), or Dinas Emrys in Powys. The list includes dramatic but inhospitable rocky islands and eminences like Castle Rock, Dumbarton (Strath-clyde), a British stronghold; the small Scottish citadel of Dunollie (Strathclyde), on a grim sea stack in Oban bay; the cliff-top Northumbrian fortress on Kirk Hill, St Abb's (NTS), near Berwick, or the fortress of the territory of Dalriada on Dundurn (Tayside), a bleak spur overlooking the valley of the River Earn. Excavations at the Mote of Mark (Dumfries and Gal-loway), a granite outcrop beside the estuary of the Urr in southwest Scotland, explored what proved to be the stronghold of a noble of the British kingdom of Rheged. The settlement was enclosed by ramparts of earth and stone which were laced with timbers and may have been 3 metres (c. 10 feet) in height and of a similar width. They were entered via a timber gate-way. Metal-working, glassworking, and the manu-facture of bracelets, beads and spindle whorls were practised within the defended area, and the remains of a modest circular hut with footings of pebbles and a gravel floor were recognized. The timber-laced ramparts were burned some time around 600, prob-ably by English invaders from Northumbria who then occupied the site briefly.

But not all the Dark Age constructions in the Celtic territories were of a fairly humble and unimposing nature. In 1808 work began on the demolition of an old fishing village and the construction of a new plan-ned townlet at Burghead (Grampian) on the shores of the Moray Firth. In the course of the building works massive amounts of rubble were removed, obliterating the three sets of ramparts which ran for just under a kilometre to cut the neck of the Burghead promontory. These ramparts had stood to a height of over 6 metres (c. 20 feet) and were up to 8 metres (c. 26 feet) thick, being built originally of sandstone slabs laced with posts and faced in a stone revetment which was pierced by the protruding tips of the tim-bers. Behind the ramparts the protected promontory was divided into two parts by another complex of great defensive walls, collapsed sections of which are still visible. Although apparently not mentioned in the contemporary records, this was a really impress-ive and formidable headland citadel and a major

capital of the Pictish territories. Radiocarbon dating gives the possibility that it originated in the period 120–560 or 400–820. Relics from the site span the period from the Roman to the Viking era, and a num-ber of incised Pictish stones have been found, includ-ing several which depict bulls. Occupation may have ceased following the burning of this capital in the ninth century. A second Pictish fortress capital has been recognized at Clatchard Craig near Cupar, where the ramparts incorporated re-used Roman masonry and where fragments of imported pottery have been found.

The retrospective nature of military thinking in England has already been described, with the revitalization of a few decaying hillforts, and outlooks were similarly conservative in the enthusiasm for frontier works. These took the form of 'linear earth-works', ditch-fronted banks which could run across the countryside for many kilometres. Such earth-works had an extremely long history. Some linear constructions seem to belong to the Bronze Age and could have been the successors to territorial boundaries that were marked by chains of barrows and alignments of upright posts. Others belong to the Iron Age and originated as frontier works, as the defences of ridges, as barriers cutting across route-ways, or as the outer defences of tribal capitals. Others still were built in the last turbulent decades of Roman rule to protect areas in the soft interior of the country against barbarian incursions. The best-known example is Bokerley Ditch, built in stages dur-ing the last half century of the Roman era, perhaps to defend an imperial estate. Linear earthworks are very difficult to date. They tend to have the same sim-ple quarry-ditch and dump-bank construction irrespective of their age, and since they are not settle-ment features any particular excavation may have only a slim chance of discovering datable artefacts on the old land surface which was buried beneath the bank.

The most impressive of all the Dark Age earth-works is Devil's Dyke in Cambridgeshire, which runs for more than 11 kilometres (c. 7 miles) from Reach village to Ditton Green. A distinctive feature of the flat prairie landscape, it still stands close to 9 metres (c. 30 feet) above the plain in several sections. It is frequently, though anonymously, seen on the television screen, since it forms the prominent divide between the racecourses at Newmarket, while one of the most attractive sections can be explored from the lay-by on the road between the villages of Burwell and Swaffham Prior. Despite the excellent state of preservation and the fact that it has been the subject of several excavations, the Dyke exemplifies the arch-

Devil's Dyke in Cambridgeshire ; this section, noted for its chalkland flora, forms the divide between the two famous racecourses at Newmarket.

aeological intransigence of such monuments, and it has only been dated to a period spanning several centuries between late Roman and middle Saxon times. As a result of the wide dating brackets several interpretations are possible. The most popular of these regards the Dyke as a massive frontier work built by the English of East Anglia against unwelcome incursions from the kingdoms of Mid Anglia or Mercia. It might, however, be a late Roman work, protecting East Anglian estates against attack from the west – as could have happened had there been an uprising of Saxons who were already established in Cambridge. One might even envisage the Dyke being manned by Roman garrisons from the East Anglian Shore forts to guard the isthmus against raiding parties which could have been active in the East Midlands – though this seems unlikely. Alternatively, the Dyke could have been built to secure Saxon-held territories against resurgent British forces following the apparent British victory at the mysterious battlefield of 'Badon'. Until the earthwork can be securely dated all questions about its builders and function must remain open.

Most linear earthworks have little to recommend them as straightforward fortifications; there would never have been the manpower available to garrison them effectively along their entire length. Rather, they should be regarded as flamboyant symbols of territorial control and as barriers against uncontrolled movement along selected routeways. Devil's Dyke is best interpreted as the grandest component in a complex of four dykes which controlled the ancient zone of thoroughfares which are known collectively as the Icknield Way. Of the others, Brent and Heydon ditches (Cambridgeshire) are seldom pronounced features of the modern landscape, although Fleam Ditch is still a prominent earthwork. It runs parallel to and about 16 kilometres (10 miles) to the south of Devil's Dyke, being most easily explored from the lay-by where it is cut by the A11.

Wansdyke in Wessex is more famous than Devil's Dyke, though by no means as spectacular. Again the earthworks seem to belong to the late Roman to middle Saxon period, and although the dyke runs from the margins of Savernake Forest in Wiltshire

LEFT *Wansdyke in Wessex, following the ridge of Tan Hill near Devizes.*

BELOW LEFT *Fleam Ditch in Cambridgeshire, a smaller relation of Devil's Dyke, but still fairly impressive. The two dogs are standing on the crest of the bank in one of the few more open stretches. Standing amongst prairie fields, the Ditch is now an important refuge for wildlife.*

RIGHT *Offa's Dyke near Llanfair Waterdine, Shropshire. The cattle are aligned on the crest of the bank and the continuing course of the earthwork is traced by the line of trees.*

to Maes Knoll in Somerset, there is a gap of about 19 kilometres (12 miles) in the earthworks which suggests that there are two separate and distinct frontier works, East Wansdyke and West Wansdyke. The absence of reliable dating evidence makes it impossible to know whether these works should be seen in the context of British resistance to Saxon incursions or reflect other squabbles between Dark Age dynasties, although East Wansdyke is sometimes regarded as the northern frontier work of Ceawlin's late sixth-century West Saxon kingdom.

Scattered round England there are also several lesser dykes which are attributed to the Dark Ages or which may be of this vintage. In and around the Vale of York, for example, there are Aberford Dykes, Becca Banks, Grim's Ditch and South Dyke. The Aberford Dykes could belong to the Iron Age, although Grim's Ditch and South Dyke may have guarded a fifth- and sixth-century British capital at Leeds and Becca Banks might be seventh-century defences of Northumbria against Mercia.

Names such as Grim's Ditch, Wansdyke ('Woden's Dyke') and Devil's Dyke remind us that these earthworks obtained their enduring labels in later Dark Age times after their true origins had been forgotten and when myth-makers invoked extraterrestrial creators. In contrast, Offa's Dyke was built at the command of the famous Mercian king (757–96), who reigned over what had become the most powerful kingdom south of the Humber. Our oldest historical reference to him comes from Bishop Asser in the ninth century, who recorded that recently in Mercia '. . . there ruled a mighty king called Offa, who struck all the kings and regions around him with terror. He it was who ordered the Great Dyke to be constructed between Wales and Mercia, stretching from sea to sea.' Offa's priorities are uncertain. The dyke might have been a response to Welsh raids into Mercia in 787, or it could have represented the completion of a grandiose scheme for Mercian frontier defences, anticipated by the shorter Wat's Dyke, probably built by a predecessor of Offa. And there is always the possibility that Offa was also seeking to emulate the deeds of a legendary namesake who, the sagas told, had 'drawn a boundary' in the north of Germany, When complete, Offa's Dyke ran from near Prestatyn (Clwyd) on the northern coast of Wales south to the estuary of the Severn near Chepstow in Gwent. The bank was around 15 metres (c. 50 feet) wide and might have carried a wall or palisade in some sections; and the ditch always lies on the Welsh side of the frontier work. Seen today, the dyke is seldom a really imposing feature and appears as a discontinous earthwork: some sections have been

ploughed out, and although it was thought that other gaps in the alignment were never embanked, recent explorations have found evidence of a bank and ditch in some of these stretches.

It is not the scale of the earthworks in any particular section of the dyke which will impress the modern visitor, but the extent and comprehensive nature of the monument as a whole. Fortunately sections of public footpath which follow the earthwork have been linked to allow long-distance rambles through some of Britain's finest countrysides. It is quite improbable that the frontier work was intended as a defensible line in its own right. It must, however, have fulfilled other objectives in a most telling manner. First, it proclaimed that Offa, as builder of such an extensive monument, was a mighty and magnificent ruler with the power to impose his will on the furthest reaches of his kingdom. Secondly, it established an indisputable frontier between the Midlands kingdom and the principalities of Wales, and thirdly, it left Welsh travellers in no doubt and bandits with no excuse when entering Mercian territory.

Although the Dark Ages tend to be regarded as a period of insecure kings and ineffectual authorities, creations such as Devil's Dyke and Offa's Dyke demonstrate the periodic existence of extremely competent, effective and powerful rulers: men who could exact the immense amounts of labour necessary to execute such schemes. It is likely that the earthworks were built in sections by gangs of impressed local labour recruited from the frontier districts. It has been calculated that Devil's Dyke embodies work sufficient to occupy 500 labourers for 400 days (or 250 labourers for 800 days, and so on).

King Offa was a real and important figure in Dark Age history – and also a man of whom most folk today know next to nothing. But everyone has heard of 'King' Arthur, who was not a king and may not even have been real. But woe betide the author who dares to omit Arthur from a Dark Age narrative! And yet, there is little of a factual nature and of any consequence that can be said about Arthur. His historical credentials are as good or as bad as those of a few dozen other figures who flit like grey moths in the shadowy areas between Dark Age myth and history. It is not hard to believe that Arthur existed, but impossible to know quite who and what he was, what deeds he performed and where. Several popular writers have taken the flimsy Arthurian 'facts' to ridiculous limits, and if we only stretch them to breaking point then Arthur might be presented as the last champion of Roman Britain who won a decisive battle against the Saxons around 495, but who was killed at the (mysterious) battle of Camlann in 515.

One of the weaknesses in the Arthurian historical cult concerns the fact that Gildas, who should have had plenty to say about such a prestigious contemporary, does not mention Arthur. (In fairness, he mentions very little indeed that is specific to real people and places.) Gildas actually places the Arthurian mantle on another leader, Ambrosius Aurelianus: '. . . perhaps the last of the Romans to survive, whose parents had worn the purple before they were killed in the fury of the storm.' The earliest mention of Arthur comes from 'Nennius', an even more dubious figure, reputed to be a ninth-century Welsh monk who gathered together a mass of old records and legends: 'I have made a heap of all I could find.' The probable non-person says of the possible non-person: 'Arthur fought against the Saxons alongside the kings of the Britons, but he himself was *Dux Bellorum*.' The title is interesting; in general it relates not to a royal personage but to a warlord and in particular to a Roman cavalry commander.

In the course of time Arthur achieved far more than any mortal could: he became all things to all men. To the Welsh he became the slumbering symbol of resistance who would one day awaken in the mists of Avalon and drive out the foreign overlords. To the French troubadours and strolling players he became a peg on which all manner of popular romances could be hung. To the nobles and courtiers of medieval Europe Arthur and his knights and ladies became the models for fashionable chivalry and courtly love, while kings sought to legitimize their dynasties by incorporating Arthur in their lineage. One even had a round table made. And today the Arthurian myths merge with ley lines, Glastonbury tosh, earth forces and UFOs in the mushy realms of nonsense frequented by those whose disenchantment with the modern world leads them to escapism rather than to scholarship or reform. Amusing times can be had observing the Gordian tangles which serious researchers and lesser lights contrive as they seek to link the Arthurian battle sites described by Nennius to real, recognizable places. In fact both Gildas and the Arthurian legends seem to be more at home in the North Country than in the traditional western locales. The great irony is that several of the prime 'Arthurian' sites – the medieval castle at Tintagel, the monastery at Glastonbury and the Wessex hillforts at Liddington (Wiltshire) and South Cadbury – are extremely interesting places in their own right. They could get on without Arthur very well. Arthur is easily debunked, and yet, once the modern nonsense and the medieval romanticizing have been swept away, it is quite possible to imagine that Arthur represents some heroic leader whose deeds and valour once gave solace to communities who found the decay of Roman Britain hard to face.

As yet one can do little more than Nennius, and when we 'heap together' what we find from a sifting of the archaeological and historical evidence then the picture which emerges is one of light Saxon settlement during the fifth century in a Roman realm which was already deeply in decline. For many decades the political situation will have been fluid, as provincial and regional dynasties struggled for ascendancy. This was the time when some hillforts will have been refurbished and when some linear earthworks must have been dug in attempts to 'hold the line'. Gradually, a pattern of kingdoms and principalities congealed from the political chaos. Some, such as Wessex, Mercia and Northumbria, proved to be durable, while others, such as Lindsey, Mid Anglia and Deira, were more ephemeral. Some were the bastions of various Celtic societies, such as the south Yorkshire kingdom of Elmet, the Cornish rump of the larger territory of Dumnonia, the Welsh principalities, and Rheged, Kyle and Dalriada in southern Scotland. Others are associated with Saxon dynasties, although Cerdic, the semi-mythical founder of Wessex, has a British name. The Arthurian wars are traditionally associated with the struggle between Saxon and British societies, yet perhaps the real picture was far more complicated, involving societies which were mixed at every level.

It is surely no accident that several of the 'Saxon' kingdoms seem to have had a remarkable similarity to the tribal territories of late Iron Age Britain, as the following comparisons suggest:

Iron Age tribal territory	Dark Age kingdom
Cantiaci	Kent
Regni	Sussex
Trinovantes / Catuvellauni	Essex and part of Hertfordshire
Iceni	East Anglia
Parisi	Deira (absorbed in Northumbria)
Brigantes / Votadini	Northumbria (Deira and Bernicia)
Carvetii	Kyle

It is also likely that the Dark Age dynasties inherited a system of tribute and taxation from the Roman Empire, with dues being paid in kind by the people of particular territories to regional administrative centres: Lindsey retained its Roman name, and like other territories, such as Kent, it appears to have existed previously as a discrete Roman administrative unit.

Conquest and inheritance reduced the numbers of Dark Age kingdoms, with Northumbria resulting from the absorption of Deira by Bernicia in 651, while Mercia sprawled across the English Midlands following the engulfment of older units, including East Anglia, Essex, Middlesex, Mid Anglia, Hwicce,

The Dark Age kingdoms of Britain.

Magonsaete and Lindsey. Ascendancy in the power stakes then shifted between the great kingdoms of Northumbria, Mercia and Wessex. Underlying the rivalries, dynastic feuds and conquests, however, there was also the lingering awareness of the existence of some sort of 'greater England'. It might have been rooted in legends of Roman *Britannia* or in post-conversion concepts of a single English Church led by Canterbury. By the time of Bede it is clear that some notion of an English nation, however abstract, had been established, and he also refers obliquely to a series of Dark Age kings who had 'held empire' over the territory of England. In the eighth century Offa claimed kingship over the English, although such a claim had little substance. It is impossible for us to know the course that the path to unity would have taken had the land been spared the agonies of foreign invasion.

The Wrath of the Northmen

Anyone living in the latter part of the eighth century might have had some cause for optimism. On the continent Charlemagne was welding together fragments from the old Roman Empire and Christianity was providing a new basis for unity between the scattered nations. Meanwhile the English kingdoms were enjoying a period of relative respite from the sapping dynastic struggles. Offa was now the magnificent leader of Mercia, and those who hoped for a deepening of European associations could take pleasure in the fact that the two great and ageing monarchs seemed to have patched up their former squabbles. In 796 Charlemagne wrote to his 'dear brother' Offa, expressing hopes for '. . .the bond of love and friendship formed in the unity between kings'. Sadly, however, the crucial historical omens were not to be found in these hopeful sentiments, but in events that had taken place some years previously.

In 787 a Saxon official of Beorhtic, the West Saxon king, was surprised and confused by the arrival of three shiploads of strange mariners: '. . . and then the reeve rode thither and tried to compel them to go to the royal manor, for he did not know what they were: and then they slew him.' Soon the people of Britain would be made only too well aware of the origins of such foreign raiders. In 793, with all the portents of lightning, famine and fiery dragons which seem to have been the essential accompaniments of the greater Dark Age melodramas, '. . . the harrying of the heathen miserably destroyed God's church in Lindisfarne by rapine and slaughter.' Alcuin of York, a scholar of the highest standing, wrote: '. . . never have such terrors as these appeared in Britain, which we must now suffer from pagans: it was not thought possible that such havoc could be made.' He demonstrated the clarity of his thinking when he wrote: 'An enormous threat hangs over this island and its people .... Yet the English people are divided, and king fights against king. ... Study Gildas, the wisest of the British, and examine the reasons why the ancestors of the British lost their kingdom and their fatherland; then look upon yourselves, and you will find almost identical causes.'

The Vikings were by no means a united people. Swedish Vikings had become active in overland conquest and trading throughout the eighth century, and these Varangians played an important role in the formation of the first Russian state in the lands through which they moved to trade with Byzantium, the city now known as Istanbul. Subsequently, although their spheres of activity often overlapped, Norse Vikings from Norway were associated with settlement in the northern Atlantic area and with raiding and settlement on the northern and western coasts of Britain and the eastern seaboard of Ireland, while Danish Vikings were largely responsible for the crippling raids on southern and eastern England and the continent. The meaning of the name 'Viking' is uncertain, although it could mean 'the people of the bays'.

A combination of push and pull factors must have been responsible for the eruption of Viking raiders on ninth-century Europe. The pull was provided by the easy pickings of piracy, slaving or raiding, which could be gained by plundering helpless merchantmen or attacking rich but defenceless monastic communities. The spoils from these adventures could be sold to Swedish merchants for redistribution via the land routes to the Orient. The push factors seem to have resulted from the limited resources of the Scandinavian homelands, which were unequal to the demands produced by a surge in birth rates. Very high rates of population increase amongst the communities of the fjords and Baltic islands appear to have produced a surplus of restless, landless youths, while the consequences of blood feuds and banishment added to the hordes of adventurers, thugs and desperadoes about to fall on the plump and civilized lands to the south. The Saxon migrations appear to have taken place during a phase of severe climatic deterioration, and although climatic conditions seem to have been better in Viking times, there is a possibility that a sequence of severe winters in the period 860–940 may have encouraged the migrations. Finally, the assaults on the Christian world were made possible by the evolution in Scandinavia of a line of light but seaworthy clinker-built ships. These had shallow draughts which enabled the Vikings to penetrate deeply inland along the river systems and pillage settlements lying many kilometres from the coast.

Once entrenched, any historical notion becomes a likely target for debunking, and over recent years a fashion for seeking out the more progressive and appealing sides of Viking culture – as exemplified by their vigorous artwork and remarkable achievements in commerce – has tended to gloss over the traditional perceptions of these sea raiders. The Vikings have received an exceptionally generous popular press. But the people who were on the receiving end of Viking raids were in no doubt that their assailants were unimaginably brutal and disgusting barbarians. The English and the Irish were far from being softies in matters of war and intrigue, but the records of the time proclaim a revulsion which goes far deeper than the conventional reaction to invaders. Alcuin described how the initial raid on Lindisfarne in 793 left the church of St Cuthbert '... spattered with the blood of the priests of God', but the sentiments of the Christian world were probably best expressed by the Irish chronicler, who described how: 'If a hundred heads of hardened iron could grow on one neck, and if each head possessed a hundred sharp tongues of tempered metal, and if each tongue cried out incessantly with a hundred ineradicably loud voices, they would never be able to enumerate the griefs which the people of Ireland ... have suffered at the hands of these warlike ruthless barbarians.' Recent excavations led by Martin Biddle at Repton in Derbyshire have underlined the brutality of the Danes. In a buried chamber were found the remains of 159 completely dismembered bodies. The Vikings had a winter camp here in 873–4, and the mutilated remains are thought to be those of the defeated Mercian army.

The Norse raids on the monasteries of northeast England at the end of the eighth century were followed in the first half of the ninth century by Danish raids of rising intensity on targets in southern and eastern England. The devastation culminated in 865 with the invasion of the Great Army and the collapse of all the English kingdoms except Wessex. Ironically, the pagan invasion and the partial conquest of England laid the foundations on which a united kingdom could be built. Alfred, the greatest English king of all times, his son and grandsons succeeded in stemming and then turning the Viking tide, so that eventually Eadred (946–55) could reign in his last year as king over all of England. The courage, dedication and leadership displayed by Alfred and his heirs established the house of Wessex as the ruling dynasty in England, although the contest with the

Vikings was not resolved until the Norman Conquest, and Viking invasions remained a threat for a while thereafter. For a brief period in the reign of Cnut England formed part of a Scandinavian North Sea empire, and her last king, Harold Godwineson, who died at Hastings, had a Danish mother.

In 878 the Danish leader, Guthrum, was converted to Christianity and the subsequent conversion of most of the Viking settlers removed a great barrier to improved relations between the English and Scandinavian communities. Peaceful Scandinavian settlement and trading and intermarriage with the English, evident in the excavations at York, gradually blurred the lines which divided the realm. At the end of the era Harold emerged from the divided loyalties and intrigues which characterized his family to stand as a great national patriot, his defeat at Hastings being in part a consequence of an impetuous dash from the field of battle at Stamford Bridge (now in Humberside), where the last great Viking host had been defeated.

The Roman and Norman invasions have left a spectacular and far-flung heritage of monuments – but where, outside the Isle of Man, is the legacy of the Viking conquests and settlement? It could be argued that the Viking contribution was of a destructive rather than a constructive nature, and should be measured in terms of the scores of religious foundations which were burned, pillaged or extinguished. There are a few crosses and hogback tombs, such as the ones at Gosforth, which display Scandinavian motifs, but these do not amount to a glittering collection of monuments. Then there are all the Scandinavian placenames, which are said to reveal the extensive nature of the Viking settlement. They include the -toft, -by and -thorpe names which denote farmsteads and settlements, and topographical names like -thwaite, a meadow, and -gill, a stream. Yet placenames are a constant tease – Cumbria, for example, is bursting with names which are conventionally associated with Dark Age Norse settlement, but it appears to have been a Celtic-speaking land until the twelfth century.

The Vikings' most significant impact on the landscape is to be found in facets of the townscape. There are several towns which were the creations of Viking settlers, warriors and merchants. These can be places where the townsfolk of today still have their trips to work, school or shop governed by the layouts of the original Viking streets and defences. In Ireland the Vikings were responsible for establishing the first recognizable towns, with the founding of fortified coastal trading centres at Clondalkin and Dublin (Co. Dublin), Annagassan (Co. Louth) and Arklow,

Waterford, Wexford and Wicklow (Co. Wicklow). The Viking world was bound together by trading routes and the northern seas were traversed by highways of conquest. In the British Isles new axes of movement and organization were established. The Norse conquest proceeded by a series of stepping stones linking the Norwegian homelands to Shetland and the new Viking power base on Orkney, and from there to the western Highlands and Islands, the Isle of Man, the eastern seaboard of Ireland, Anglesey and South Wales.

A stronghold at Dublin was established in 841, and in 866–7 the Great Army of the Danes took York and southeastern Northumbria. A new trading and slaving axis then developed between Dublin and York. The merchant centres were at first linked by long and rather perilous sea routes, but swiftly sea and land connections were forged via the Irish Sea and two main land routes. One followed the Roman road from Carlisle to York, while the more southerly route ran from Chester to Manchester and onwards via Ribblesdale and Wharfedale to Leeds and York.

Under the stimulus of Viking trading York, the old Roman legionary fortress and English ecclesiastical centre, expanded to the southeast of the Roman defences, emerging as Jorvik, the second largest city in England after London. The legacy of York's existence as a Viking focus – an independent Danish city which was taken by Norse Vikings in 919 and remained a Scandinavian base until the expulsion of Eric Bloodaxe in 954 – is still evident in the survival of many Scandinavian gate or street names, such as Micklegate, Monkgate and Walmgate. These Anglo-Viking streets were laid out across the old Roman alignments. In 1984 the opening of the remarkably imaginative Jorvik centre provided visitors with a colourful introduction to the sights, sounds and smells of life in the bustling merchant city.

Further south in England, in the area to the north and east of the Watling Street–Great Ouse–River Lea line which had become Danelaw following negotiations between Alfred and Guthrum after 880, a number of Viking settlements were established. These included the fortresses which would later become county towns at Cambridge, Huntingdon (Cambridgeshire) and Northampton, and the Five Boroughs: Derby, Leicester, Lincoln, Stamford (Lincolnshire) and Nottingham. In most cases some traces of the Danish layouts can still be discovered. At Cambridge, where the decayed Roman settlement lay just to the north of the River Cam, there are early references to 'Irishmen', who were surely Viking merchants. It may be that the spine of the Viking settlement is still marked by Bridge Street, which lies just south of the river and Roman nucleus and includes a church with the characteristic Scandinavian dedication to St Clement. However, in 1985 it was argued, quite plausibly, that the Danish borough at Cambridge was preceded by a Mercian *burh*, established nearby.

Of the Five Boroughs, Leicester and Lincoln were resurrected Roman towns, and although both still preserve many Danish street names, the Scandinavian contribution to their layouts is not obvious. Nottingham and Derby were new towns which seem to have absorbed existing villages. In Nottingham streets trace out the defences and divisions of the Danish borough in the southeastern quadrant of the walled medieval town to the east and west of Stoney Street. At Derby the evidence is less clear-cut, although there are hints of Dark Age defences in the street plan and the old market seems to have stood outside the defended area.

The most interesting of the Five Boroughs is Stamford. Here a river crossing of the Great North Road and a Saxon village lay just to the west of the area, on the north flanks of the River Welland, which was fortified by the Danes around 877 to create their stronghold and settlement. This borough had a somewhat coffin-shaped form. High Street still marks the axis of the Danish town, and Broad Street and a part of St Mary's Street trace out sections of the perimeter defences. In 918 Edward the Elder took his army to Stamford, gained the submission of the Danish borough and established his own fortified town just to the south of the river crossing and alongside the Great North Road. The road was then diverted to run down the spine of the English town, and in due course a bridge was built directly linking the Saxon and Danish boroughs. The towns eventually merged, but for centuries to follow travellers on the Great North Road had their journeys dictated by the events of Dark Age history, passing through the old Saxon town, across the bridge over the Welland, and then zig-zagging round the southwestern corner of the Danish defences to leave the town via Scotgate. Now that the Great North Road – the A1 – bypasses Stamford the modern visitor can really enjoy this fascinating and attractive old town.

In the initial phases of Danish attacks on England, the kingdoms had been helplessly exposed to raiders

This street in Cambridge runs down towards the river crossing and the Roman nucleus and Norman castle site beyond. It contains a church which is dedicated to St Clement, a favourite Viking dedication, and was probably an axis for the Danish borough.

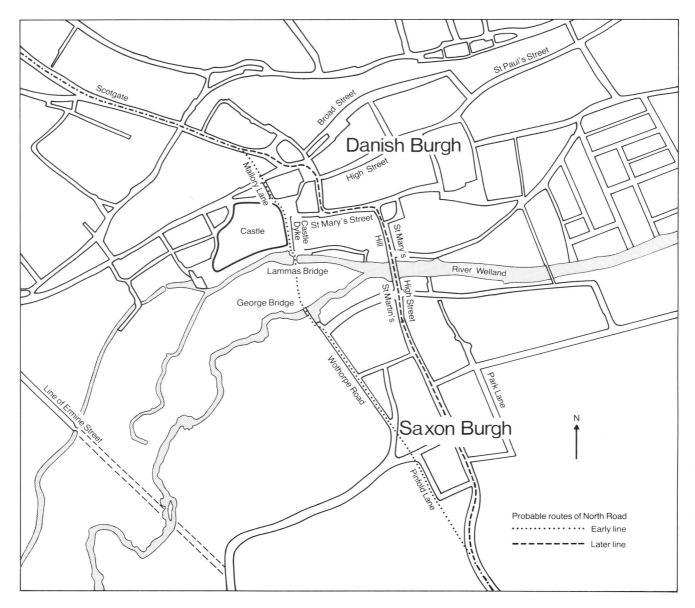

Stamford in Lincolnshire, showing the Danish burh, *the Saxon* burh, *and the lines of the North Road.*

who could emerge from the sea haze and river mists to strike swiftly at undefended targets. Alfred won a respite following his victory at Edington in 878 and was able to develop a strategy for the defence of the realm. He did not have to look far for a solution – it confronted him in the form of the fortified camps of his Danish adversaries. The process of establishing fortified settlements or *burhs* was perpetuated by Alfred's heirs, so that by the middle of the reign of Edward the Elder no Wessex community lived more than 32 kilometres (20 miles) from a little stronghold and the English kingdom had its first coherent defen-

sive system. The *burh* concept was swiftly copied in Mercia in the first decade of the tenth century at places such as Chester, Gloucester, Hereford, Worcester, Shrewsbury, Stafford and Warwick, many of them former Roman centres. The eastern and northern advance of English reconquest in the first quarter of the century introduced defensive centres such as Bedford, Bakewell (Derbyshire), Maldon (Essex), and Manchester. Thereafter, the future of the *burh* often depended on its ability to flourish as a commercial town.

A few *burhs*, like Eddisbury in Cheshire and perhaps Chisbury Camp in Wiltshire, were merely redeveloped Iron Age hillforts. Others, such as Portchester and Winchester, were revitalized Roman towns whose defences were refurbished and pressed back into service. At Winchester, although the Roman defences were re-used and the main axis between the eastern and western gates was retained, a completely new grid-plan layout of English streets was superimposed over the abandoned geometry of the Roman network. There were a few towns in England which pre-dated the *burhs*, one of which was the remarkably large Saxon Southampton. Its regular street pattern was planned around 700 and a population of perhaps four to five thousand lived here.

A number of *burhs*, such as Langport in Somerset, are now little more than villages; a few, such as Lyng in the same county, were unoccupied or swiftly abandoned during the Dark Ages, but many others, such as Oxford and Hastings, prospered as trading and administrative centres, so that all traces of the burghal layout were obliterated by redevelopment. In a number of places faint traces of the *burh* defences may still be recognized, as at Lydford in Devon or

at Shaftesbury, where a bank protected the steep ridge which carries the appealing town. The best of the *burhs* must, like Cricklade in Wiltshire, have had their designs inspired by the ruins of Roman camps and planned settlements, and they consisted of rectangular areas of *c.* 20 to 40 hectares (50 to 100 acres) in extent guarded by earth banks which seem sometimes to have been enhanced with stone facings. Inside these defences a neat gridwork of streets and lanes was established.

The *burhs* which now offer most to the historically aware visitor are the riverside towns of Wareham in Dorset and Wallingford in Oxfordshire. At Wallingford the near-rectangular *burh* had its eastern flank shielded by the Thames. It was guarded by a

Wallingford in Oxfordshire still preserves the street pattern and some of the defences of the Saxon burh; this street runs up from the crossing of the Thames.

rampart and ditch which still survives in some places, with a drop of some 6 metres (20 feet) from the crest of the bank to the foot of the outer ditch. Wareham was effectively moated to north and south by the rivers Piddle and Frome. Again a rectangular layout was used, although the defences follow the sweep of the Frome to the south. Some sections of the bank and ditch defences survive, with the bank standing *c.* 7.5 metres (25 feet) above the bottom of the fronting ditch. Originally about 3 metres (10 feet) in height

and faced with a timber revetment, the rampart was later heightened and faced with a stone wall.

It has for long been a corner-stone of historical dogma that the English did not have castles. In the late 1960s the suggestion that there might have been 'Saxon' castles produced an apoplectic reaction from at least one historian: castles were a feature of feudalism and as feudalism was only introduced by the Normans there could therefore be no Saxon castles! However, outdoor experience is an excellent cure for

dogmatism and archaeologists have produced Dark Age examples of what most normal people would be quite content to regard as castles. In fact, evidence of their existence is provided by an historical source: an eleventh-century document describes how a freeman might aspire to join the nobility and become a thane. He should acquire four hides of land, a chapel, a position in the hall of the king, a kitchen, a bell-house and a *'burhgeat'* – a 'castle gate'. It is not easy to know what such a castle gate should look like –

though quite likely that the excavations at Sulgrave in Northamptonshire have discovered one.

In the area around Sulgrave there are several manorial 'ringworks', doughnut-shaped earth banks with outer ditches. It has been suggested that such defence works were sometimes the predecessors of Norman mottes, though five are known to date as late as the twelfth century. At Sulgrave a Saxon tower was recognized, still standing 1.8 metres (6 feet) tall but engulfed in the bank of the later ringwork, which proved to be Norman. Inside the earthworks it was found that the hall of the French knight Ghilo was superimposed upon that of his dispossessed English predecessor. And so it was established that Sulgrave had been the home of a Saxon lord and that the hall had been accompanied by a free-standing stone and timber tower, although the evidence of the Saxon perimeter defences seems to have been obliterated by the construction of the ringwork. The tower was no great fortress, but it might easily have been used for defence. In the same county, the delightful church at Wadenhoe stands inside a puzzling and as yet unclassified defence work and the Saxon church at Earls Barton stands on a commanding spur which is cut and protected by prehistoric defences. The church consisted of little more than a massive tower with the nave in its base and domestic apartments above. So here too there are hints that Saxon military thinking included more than linear earthworks and *burhs*, although much is still to be discovered about the defensive uses of secular and ecclesiastical towers.

At the Saxon burh *of Wareham in Dorset the River Frome was an important component of the peripheral defences. Wareham was a Channel port from at least the seventh century, and the fifteenth-century tower marks the position of a church which has stood here since about 700.*

5
A Land Full of Castles

... and they filled the land full of castles.
They cruelly oppressed the wretched men of the
    land with castle works
and when the castles were made they filled them
    with devils and evil men
and they said openly, that Christ slept, and His
    saints.

The Anglo Saxon Chronicle, 1137.

The great Norman keep towering over the outer defences at Rochester, Kent.

The Norman Conquest of England in 1066 abruptly ended a fascinating and promising chapter in English history. Questions about the future course of English civilization were left unanswered and unanswerable. The consequences of the Conquest in England were far-reaching and severe, although it can be argued that the Normans played an even more forceful role in shaping the landscapes and development of Scotland, Ireland and Wales. In the years that followed the Norman annexation of Harold's kingdom, castles erupted across the length and breadth of the land. Initially many were deemed necessary to protect the conquerors against the conquered, but in due course the feuds and distrust which smouldered within the ruling classes argued for more and more, bigger and better strongholds. The castle was not only an essential symbol and instrument of the feudal order, it was also the hallmark of aristocratic status. Anybody who was anybody had to have one.

All those who believe in the value of awesome military hardware as a deterrent to war can gain in wisdom by studying the evolution of the medieval castle. The citadels did not impose peace, but became the foci for conflict. As the castles were improved and enlarged, so too were the offensive arts of siege warfare. The scale and the horror of war multiplied as the forces, effort and technology needed to crack the armoured monsters increased. Yet centuries of evolution failed to produce a single, demonstrably impregnable haven.

A Martial Society

Whereas the fortifications of Dark Age England had generally involved either the re-use of ancient defences and antique military concepts, or, in the case of the *burhs*, the reapplication of Roman practices (though not tactics, since at least the earlier Roman forts were not defences, but bases to be fought from), the Norman fortresses embodied fresh ideas brimming with potential for further development. It is, however, well worth remembering that the *burhs* were part of a national system of fortifications, while the post-Conquest castles were mainly private strongholds. No modern estate owner would dream of building a motte and bailey. He establishes his position and protects his interests in more subtle ways; his fiefdom is now garrisoned by accountants and lawyers. Similarly, it is of considerable importance to see the castle as a device and a reflection of the culture which created it. The English society of the later Saxon kings regarded defence as a problem which faced the whole community, just as the people and chieftains of the Iron Age had done. Norman-

dominated society, in contrast, placed the emphasis on private castles, which were not conceived as communal refuges but as the bastions of particular provincial dynasties. As a result, the royal castles of the time were not primarily disposed in such a way as to protect the nation against foreign aggressors, but were scattered amongst the private strongholds in order to assert the royal presence in areas where it might otherwise have been forgotten.

The castle must be seen in the context of a feudal society – even though the topic of feudalism is so fraught with pitfalls and controversies that the wary author might wish that it could somehow be avoided. The learned historians disagree about whether the system should be regarded purely as a Norman importation or whether it was rooted in Saxon (or Roman, or Iron Age) society. The lines of battle are defined in the pages of the academic journals, and from time to time the opposing generals will fall upon each other with all the fury of a Viking war band – their berserkers to the fore. And woe betide any 'popular' commentator who trespasses on the battleground.

Whether English society was feudal or not, the Normans introduced a new, more refined, pervasive and oppressive system. While it might be difficult to argue that English thanes – particularly those who were established in eleventh-century Scotland – were anything other than feudal lords, the English methods of organizing defence were rather different from those of the Normans. The nucleus of the English army was composed of the king's thanes – the greater nobles of the realm – and of his immensely loyal personal bodyguard of retainers, the housecarls. In times of war a form of conscription operated, and in each shire the king's sheriff mustered the fyrd. This force was led by its ealdorman and included the lesser thanes and the ceorls who were normally their (feudal) tenants. English society being what it was – more relaxed and inclined towards debate than that of the Normans – one could not always rely on an effective muster of the fyrd. People discovered vital tasks on the farm and important reasons for being somewhere else. In consequence, under Alfred the fyrd was divided into two parts, allowing the conscripts to alternate between farming and fighting. Wars between Dark Age armies in England did not normally involve fortresses. One force would make a stand on carefully chosen ground and form a shield wall. The opposing force, also generally fighting as infantry, would attack, and the armies would hack, slash and stab at each other with axes, swords and spears until either the shield wall broke or the attack was routed. It was a very bloody business indeed, more demanding of stamina and fortitude than martial prowess.

After the defeat at Hastings – where the old method of fighting proved crucially inadequate to alternating assaults on the shield wall by cavalry and archers – landholding in England was reorganized on a military basis. It has often been claimed that William I (1066–87) deliberately bestowed scattered holdings on his greater supporters in order to prevent regional concentrations of power. Equally, however, the carpetbaggers seem to have taken estates directly from dispossessed English landowners, suggesting that the pattern of noble landownership was already dispersed and fragmented. In any event, around 180 barons (not all of them William's companions-in-arms at Hastings) were allotted generous estates, dependent on their readiness to raise and train a force of about 5000 knights who would be made available to the Crown in times of war. The addition of knights raised by the leading churchmen put an armoured cavalry force of about 6000 at the new king's disposal. It has often been said that feudal society was a society organized for war.

Our visions of knights tend to be clouded by romance and by the growth of Arthurian cults of chivalry in the later medieval centuries. Most Norman knights had humble origins as servants and mercenaries, the supporters of a noble lord who rode with him to battle and garrisoned his castles. It is easy to imagine that no baron would want to have his cramped castle forever thronging with noisy, hungry knights, and it was far more practical to grant each knight a manor in return for the obligation to support his lord when summoned. In this way the knights could be kept out of the way until they were needed. The greater knights in turn could grant portions of their holdings to others, who would assume their martial responsibilities. Under the Normans the powerful bond of loyalty which had linked lords and tenants was superseded by more formalized obligations: rituals of homage extended down through the ranks of landowning society, linking the king to his tenants-in-chief and on through the hierarchy of tenancies down to the level of the lowest knight. In theory rather than in practice the convergence of oaths of fealty on the person of the king prevented clashes of loyalty and civil strife.

The core of the Norman army was composed of the aristocratic cavalry, and the placing of the military emphasis on the armoured knight created special demands. First, it was essential for the knight to obtain both a trained war-horse and the difficult skills needed to stay on it in battle. In addition, he needed a helmet, shield, spear, sword, and a very expensive

This wall painting in the church at Little Kimble in Buckinghamshire represents St George and provides a contemporary picture of the medieval knight. It dates from about 1300.

hauberk, or long coat of mail, which was composed of hundreds of individually forged and interlinked iron rings. The estate, benefice or fief allotted to a knight was presumed to be sufficient to yield the wealth of feudal taxes necessary to support, mount and equip such a warrior. But there must have been many little estates which had to be squeezed very hard to produce the wherewithal for knightly life, and scores where the knight himself was several stages of scruffiness removed from our ideas of a Galahad or Launcelot.

This then was the martial society which spawned and sustained the feudal castle. Initially these castles were needed to maintain and consolidate the conquest of the English after the main invasion force had dispersed, but before very long the king and the various members of the aristocracy began to discover that the castles would serve their own particular interests. Castles were needed to do rather more than impress the virtues of hard work and obedience on a few disgruntled peasants. William established his royal castles in the county towns, with the sheriff or a castellan to oversee the garrison of knights, while the barons established comparable castles on their estates. These private castles were – except in times of anarchy – licensed by the king, who claimed the right to install his own garrison in any castle on demand.

The Evolution of the Castle, from the White Tower to White Elephants

The most popular exhibit in the Norman arsenal of fortifications was the motte-and-bailey castle, consisting of a moated mound or 'motte' to which was attached a ramparted and ditched enclosure, the 'bailey'. This form of castle had experienced just a few decades of evolution in France and the Rhineland before it was introduced to Britain. A few mottes were built here just before the Conquest by the unpopular Norman favourites of Edward the Confessor (1042–66). They may not all have been identified, although the mound at Ewyas Harold (Hereford and Worcester) in the southern section of the Welsh Marches is a likely candidate. It was almost certainly built by Osbern, one of the Norman warriors introduced to help secure the Welsh frontiers in the 1050s, while the motte at Richard's Castle near Ludlow on the Shropshire border also dates from this time. Clavering in Essex is a third probable example.

Although most mottes were built in the century following the Conquest, excavations in both England and Scotland have shown that mottes sometimes represented a second stage in the fortification of a particular site, being preceded by ringworks of the type described in the previous chapter. This was the case at Aldingham (Cumbria) on the shores of Morecambe Bay. The motte, which was built upon a glacial mound or drumlin, is not a prominent feature of the undulating coastal landscape, but the fact that it was being undermined by the sea, exposing its internal structure, made it a prime target for archaeological excavation. The Normans were slow to penetrate this northwestern corner of the realm, and the Saxon Ernulf still held the site in 1086. But in the years around 1100 Henry I (1100–35) granted it to one Michael le Fleming. The early castle built here was shown to be a ringwork of 35 metres (c. 115 feet) diameter defined by a rampart 2.5 metres (c. 8 feet) high which protected the timber buildings built within it, and this fortification dates to the time when Michael commandeered the site. Around the middle of the twelfth century military fashions must have demanded sweeping changes, for the interior of the ringwork was filled with earth to form a low, flat-topped motte. In the middle of the following century there were plans for the mound to be heightened by

The motte at Berkhamsted Castle in Hertfordshire. This was one of the most important castles in Norman England and was granted by William the Conqueror to his half brother, Robert de Mortain. It was also a residence of Thomas Becket during his chancellorship under Henry II.

2 metres (*c.* 6 feet) and faced by a revetment of posts, although this work was abandoned incomplete.

A few other ringworks escaped such wholesale transformations. New Buckenham in Norfolk was built around or before 1140 as a great ringwork with a diameter of almost 122 metres (400 feet), which was positioned on the flanks of a new and rigidly-planned feudal town. The bank was subsequently heightened and a stone gate-house protected the drawbridge or turning bridge spanning the great wet moat. Were it not for the water which still fills the moat, the massive earthwork might seem to resemble an Iron Age hillfort. The ramparts may have been enhanced with a stone wall, although the most notable architectural feature of the site is the remains of the lower stages of a cylindrical stone tower lying on the eastern margins of the enclosed area – apparently the first round keep to be built in England. New Buckenham was a stronghold of the Daubigny family, as was the even more imposing Norman fortress at Castle Rising in the same county. There the stone cube of the squat hall keep and the Norman gateway have survived remarkably well, and they stand in the sunken centre of gigantic earthwork defences which echo the ringwork rather than the motte school of defences. There are other more distant echoes in the north of Scotland, where the impressive, although little visited, Peel Ring of Lumphanan (Grampian) was the bastion of the famous Durward family (Macbeth, the leader of the Celtic cause, was slain nearby in an earlier stage of the feudal era). Here a broad, flat-topped mound, which was once ringed by a stone shell keep, is embraced by the banks of a great ringwork.

The more conventional Norman castles were of the motte-and-bailey type, although the bailey was an

The fairly modest motte at Laxton in Nottinghamshire, a village much better known for the survival of the institutions of medieval farming. The motte of the de Caux family was an administrative centre of Sherwood Forest and a venue for the detested Forest Courts.

optional extra which was occasionally foregone. These castles varied enormously in size. Some mottes were gigantic constructions, like the monster at Thetford in Norfolk, a truncated cone with a height of *c.* 24 metres (80 feet), a diameter of *c.* 24 metres (80 feet) across its summit and one of *c.* 110 metres (360 feet) spanning its base. Other massive examples include Clifford's Hill in Northamptonshire, the only other British castle to equal the Thetford dimensions, and giants such as Ongar and Pleshey in Essex. Shrewsbury, built by Roger de Montgomery just after the Conquest, was constructed at the expense of some fifty-one dwellings which were removed to make way for the massive motte and bailey. Most mottes were much smaller, and some were very small indeed, doing little more than shield the base of the new lord's palisade should the site be attacked by a few resentful peasants. Recent excavations at Hen Domen near Montgomery (Powys) have revealed a bailey packed with buildings, though the poverty of finds suggests a community living at near-prehistoric standards of living.

Mottes were built of upcast material excavated from the surrounding circular moat, although in the case of the loftier examples additional supplies of earth and rubble were imported. Motte excavations are not very numerous, but it appears that the mound was sometimes built of alternating layers of rubble and rammed earth, and it might be coated in an icing of clay to stabilize the sides while making the slopes slippery and difficult to scale.

When built, the mound would be crowned by a rectangular tower or keep or ringed by a palisade of stakes; often both structures existed, as the excavations of Drum motte at Keir Knowe near Stirling (Central) have shown. These defences constituted a bastion which could be defended in the event of a serious assault. The first rounds of a conflict were normally fought at the ramparts and hedge, palisade or wall of the bailey, which guarded the lord's hall, stables and other outbuildings. The motte could have more than one bailey, and each could exist as a fortress. Sometimes the defences would loop outwards to embrace an entire village or townlet, as was the case at Pleshey and as can be seen on a grander scale at Castle Acre in Norfolk, where the settlement was protected by the outer bailey defences of William de Warenne's citadel. Normally a bridge or a drawbridge linked the bailey or inner bailey to the steps which ascended the mound, allowing defenders to retreat to the motte should the proceedings be going badly for them in the bailey.

The summits of the more important mottes supported towers, usually of timber but occasionally built of stone. Excavations on the motte at Abinger in Surrey revealed what was probably a typical layout. The flat top of the mound had a maximum diameter of *c.* 12 metres (40 feet), and in the middle of the summit stood a small timber tower, its base measuring only *c.* 3.5 by 3.5 metres (12 by 12 feet). Just inside the rim of the mound ran a timber palisade of upright posts which may have carried a rampart walk. In the century or so following the Norman Conquest thousands of such castles were built in Britain, although of course no examples in timber have survived, and so we can only imagine their above-ground appearance. Timber keeps might have been painted or embellished with carving, although their value as status symbols would always pale in comparison with a keep of stone. Stone keeps also had a distinct practical advantage: they were much less vulnerable to destruction by fire.

Castles of stone were costly to build and were very heavy structures. A few were built on mottes, either as parts of the original defensive plans or as replacements for earlier timber keeps. In either event they imposed heavy stresses on the motte, and at Clun in Shropshire the keep was built on the side of the mound. In a few cases the threat of slumping seems to have been avoided by heaping the motte round the completed base of the keep, as at Farnham in Surrey and Skenfrith in Gwent, or by sinking the keep deeply into the mound, as at Lydford in Devon. The keep could also exist as a free-standing castle: the motte was by no means essential. But it was always advisable to reinforce the bases of the walls, which were often thickened and splayed outwards to give more protection against engineers attacking the wall base. Scores of stone keeps were erected during the twelfth century and a number, based on prototypes in Normandy, were built within a couple of decades of the Conquest.

The earliest of these may have been the White Tower, now incorporated into the complex of fortifications which make up the Tower of London. It was begun by William I around 1078 as a great, three-storey, square tower which would combine the roles of stronghold and palace whilst serving as the centre of his government. It was originally entered at the level of the middle storey via a fore-building which has been lost; comparable fore-buildings can be seen at the keeps at Rochester and Newcastle-upon-Tyne. The keep at Dover Castle belongs to a much later stage in the currency of this type of fortress, being built by Henry II at a time when the rectangular stone keep was just beginning to appear a little outdated.

Although arguably the most formidable type of

ABOVE *Castle life involved repetitive and time-consuming journeys between chambers on different levels, up spiral stone steps like these at Orford Castle in Suffolk.*

RIGHT *The Norman keep is still a dominating feature of Richmond in North Yorkshire.*

stronghold so far seen in this country, the stone keep was a castle of a relatively unsophisticated design. It was a massive square construction with walls that could be more than 3 metres (10 feet) thick. These thick walls could contain small 'mural chambers', as at Dover, where they are honeycombed with small rooms, guard chambers and latrines. The larger keeps were normally built as three-storey structures, with storage in the lower level and the great hall above. Colchester has the most extensive ground-plan – *c.* 46 by 46 metres (150 by 150 feet) – though here the upper level is missing. Square corner towers normally guarded the vulnerable angles of the keep and housed the spiral stone staircases. Occasionally they did not project beyond the square of the walls, as at Richmond in North Yorkshire, or projected only slightly like buttresses, as at Hedingham in Essex. Most commonly they stood a few metres proud of the main body of the castle, as at Dover or Rochester, but occasionally they could be prominent and impos-

keep towers, which were cheaper to defend, while the greater members of the nobility opted for a curtain-wall design which enclosed a space large enough to contain a hall, chapel, stables, a cobbled yard or 'parade ground', and various storage buildings.

One type of castle which appeared before the Norman period had run its course might seem to represent a half-way house between the keep and the curtain wall. This was the shell keep. If the square keep is regarded as a replacement in stone for the timber motte tower (as it was sometimes but by no means always), then the shell keep could be viewed as a stone rendition of the motte palisade. Arguably the finest surviving example is Restormel in Cornwall, built by Robert de Cardinham about 1200. The shell keep could be a very formidable structure, as exemplified by the fortress at Castle Acre. Here the summit of

Round keeps never obtained the degree of popularity in England that they enjoyed in Wales and the Welsh Marches. This is Longtown Castle in Hereford and Worcester, built about 1180.

the great motte was encircled by the thick flint walls of the shell keep, which were crenellated, reinforced with shallow buttresses and pierced by arrow slits. Inside the wall, however, the arrangements were most unusual, for excavations have shown that the stone dwelling house was converted into an enclosed keep by adding great thicknesses of masonry to the inner faces of its walls. Another unusual variant is exemplified at Berkeley Castle in Gloucestershire and Farnham Castle in Surrey, where the great stone shell keeps were not built around the top of the mottes, but round their bases to serve as revetments to the mounds.

If the bailey defences were replaced by walls at the same time that a shell keep superseded the motte palisade then a much improved stronghold would result, and normally the stone curtain of the bailey was brought up the motte to link with the shell keep. Launceston (Cornwall), Totnes (Devon), Carisbrooke on the Isle of Wight and Pickering (North Yorkshire) are all good examples. At Launceston the bailey contained a small town, and a cylindrical keep

was built on the narrow summit of the motte, just inside the walls of the shell keep. A few curtain walls were built early in the Norman era, and at Peveril, Ludlow and Richmond such defences appeared in the eleventh century. At Richmond the gate-house in the curtain was developed as a square keep in the twelfth century. A far more sophisticated version of the curtain-wall concept was introduced at Framlingham Castle in Suffolk in 1190–1200, setting the stage for a host of fresh developments. The great problem with keeps was the difficulty of keeping assailants away from the wall base, and this problem

still existed with curtain walls. It was answered in a way that harked back to the artillery bastions added to the Roman forts of the Saxon Shore: projecting towers were set at intervals in the curtain to provide flanking fire to sweep the walls clear of attackers. Such mural towers appeared firstly at Dover (c. 1179–91). At Framlingham they were built square, in the manner of the old keeps, but soon, and for similar reasons, they were superseded by round and polygonal forms.

East Anglia must have been a seedbed for innovations in castle design. New Buckenham may have been the earliest example of a round keep in England, while Orford in Suffolk, built as a royal castle around 1165–7, was regarded with particular pleasure by its proud owner, Henry II. It had the unusual form of an eighteen-sided polygon with three buttressing towers. Further refinements in the design of round

OPPOSITE *The restored round keep at Caldicot Castle near Newport, Gwent, a splendid little castle where the additions from later phases of castle building are also preserved.*

BELOW *The magnificent shell keep of Restormel in Cornwall, begun about 1200.*

keeps produced Conisbrough Castle in South Yorkshire about two decades later, a cylindrical tower with a splayed base reinforced by six massive buttresses. Other superb examples include Pembroke (Dyfed), which was constructed around 1200, and Skenfrith (NT) and Longtown in the Welsh Marches, the last two examples being built on motte mounds. The keeps at Pembroke and Skenfrith, where the round keep and round towered curtain date from 1220–40, show that the initial concept of the keep as the ultimate bastion which could still be defended after the outer defences had been overrun still commanded some support. The retention of mottes was more open to question, since the positioning of the tower on an earthen mound could only be welcomed by the sapper. The Norman innovations were imitated by chieftains and princes in the Celtic territories, Dolbadarn in Snowdonia (Gwynedd), for example, being a Welsh round keep.

While the castle was built to serve in the context of a society at war, it was generally a fortified residence and a crucial symbol of feudal lordship from which government was dispensed. In a few cases, the castle will have been a relatively comfortable home. About a third of Henry II's expenditure at Windsor was devoted to domestic amenities and comforts: the king had a garden within the castle and furnishings were brought from London. At Winchester Henry had a falconry and hedged garden, as well as the normal chapel, kitchen and residential apartments. In general, however, there was a spartan quality to castle life and it was normal for a great lord to spend much of his time circulating round his estates with a large retinue, moving from one manor to the next and consuming the production of each estate in the course of the progress, dispensing 'justice' and decisions, while spending much of the time hunting. Right through until the time of Elizabeth I (1558–1603), the monarch was the most footloose member of society, constantly on the move around the realm, since it was very important for him to see and be seen in these times with no electronic media, telephones or newspapers. Lavish preparations were necessary for the entertainment of the king and his great retinue of nobles, officers and servants whenever he was about to descend on a royal or private castle.

An historian once estimated that in England alone some 1500 medieval castles were built, with seven-eighths of the total being, so far as could be deduced, foundations of the eleventh and twelfth centuries. Presumably he was only counting castles with some masonry and the greater mottes, for up to 6000 castles of earth or stone are now thought to have been constructed between 1066 and 1100. The improvements in castle design which had been adopted in the twelfth century were subject to further sophistication and refinement in the thirteenth century. Although free-standing keep towers were still built by the lesser lords, in the grander castles the emphasis shifted towards the curtain wall. This was designed to allow archers and crossbowmen to command the entire vicinity of the castle, while the enclosed courtyard within offered ample accommodation for living quarters. As we have seen, the curtain was strengthened at regular intervals by strategically-placed mural towers. The rectangular towers of the Framlingham type were soon superseded by round, polygonal and D-shaped towers. At Conisbrough, where the curtain and its round mural towers were built early in the thirteenth century, the towers were solid drums of masonry, like the bastions of the last of the Roman forts. In later examples they were built to be entered from the courtyard and rampart walk and provided additional accommodation. Then each interval tower was developed as a keep in its own right, an independent stronghold which could be defended should the remainder of the castle fall. Pevensey Castle (East Sussex), Goodrich and the outer curtain at Dover all have fine examples.

The most vulnerable part of a castle now lay where the curtain was breached by the entrance gateway, and the strengthening of the barbican defences guarding the entrances resulted in a new shift in emphasis from the keep or mural towers to the heavily armoured gate-house. This in turn became an independent fortress of last resort. Pevensey of around 1250, Dunstanburgh (NT) in Northumberland of 1314, Kidwelly near Carmarthen, the early thirteenth-century gate-house at Chepstow (Gwent), Criccieth in the north of Wales of 1220–40, and Edwardian castles such as Harlech all present excellent expressions of the gate-house concept. At Kidwelly the main gate-house, placed by the angle of the D-shaped outer ward defences, developed in the early fourteenth century during an updating of the old castle and it absorbed the original angle tower, which can be seen as a bulge in the flank of the gate-house. The notion of concentrating the defensive

Dover Castle occupies a site which has been defended since prehistoric times. The celebrated Norman keep was built in the 1160s, and in the course of the twelfth and thirteenth centuries concentric rings of outer defences were developed. In 1216 French forces almost succeeded in breaching the gateway in the outer curtain, and the entrance was moved and protected by these formidable defences.

Goodrich, Hereford and Worcester, is one of the finest medieval castles in Britain. The nucleus is provided by a Norman keep (just visible between the central and left towers). The castle was granted to the royal champion, William Marshall, early in the thirteenth century and was then considerably enlarged. The view of the castle as it rises from its rock-cut moat conjures up a medieval world.

might of a castle in its gate-house maintained its appeal until well after the period covered by this book, and it finds expression in late castles such as Donnington in Berkshire (1385) and Saltwood in Kent (1383), as well as in the delightful fortified manor house of Bodiam (NT) in East Sussex, also built around 1383. Bodiam has elaborate entrance defences: a gate-house set between square towers fronted by a bridge pit and a moat, with an outer gate-house and bridge pit at the margins of the moat.

Whereas the builders of keeps and motte-and-bailey castles had often sought to place their castles in commanding, elevated situations, the success of mining operations tended to lead to a preference for low-lying sites which facilitated the construction of wet moats. Not only did the moat present an additional barrier to attackers approaching the castle, it also provided the means of flooding tunnels. One of the most dramatic and effective moats is at Caerphilly Castle (Mid Glamorgan) in south Wales, where revetted outworks, lakes and a fortified dam provided an incomparable complex of land and water defences

The impressive barbican defences at Helmsley in North Yorkshire emphasize the shifts in medieval military architecture. The curtain wall is surrounded by unusually deep double ditches, though a Norman keep, currently being restored, formed the older nucleus of the castle.

which had to be negotiated before the castle walls were reached.

As the castles evolved, so too did the offensive technology. Sappers' mines still remained a worrying threat, while great timber penthouses or cats appeared on the battlefield. At night the castle moat might be filled with bundles of brushwood and rubble on which the cat could be propelled across to the wall on rollers, where the miners and engineers hidden inside the engine would begin their work. The bestiary of siege engines included the bear, a lofty tower housing archers who swept the ramparts with their fire. Then there was the ram, a great swinging beam with an armoured head which was used to batter the masonry of the wall base, while the smaller mouse was used to prize open crannies in the wall, enabling engineers to lever out larger blocks of stonework. The artillery weapons which were available to both sides in a siege included devices like the arbalast, a giant crossbow, and various monstrous slingshot and catapult engines such as the trebuchet and mangonel. Castle builders responded to the gathering of unwelcome visitors who might be found hard at work round the wall base by developing projecting battlements or machicolations, from which missiles, boiling oil or pitch and other nasties could be showered on the heads below. Good examples of machicolations can be seen on the gate-house at Cooling in Kent. But the most fearsome weapon of all was the simple longbow, now appearing in immensely powerful forms which could propel an iron-shod arrow clean through a suit of the best armour at a range of 650 ft (c. 200 metres).

The remarkable improvements in castle design which were accomplished during the thirteenth century culminated when the medieval fortress was brought to perfection in the concentric castle. These leviathans of the feudal world were mainly royal castles and were conceived as the lynchpins of the great Edwardian strategy for the final conquest and subjugation of Wales. In the course of his Welsh campaigns of 1277 and 1282 Edward I (1272–1307) appointed Master James of St George from Savoy to serve as 'Master of the King's Work in Wales'. Although each of the castles devised by Master James was individually designed and carefully tailored to its geographical setting, each one also embodied a wealth of hard-learned experience and the latest continental concepts in castle design. Most were planned according to a concentric theme, with towering inner ward defences which were ringed by the lower curtain and mural towers of the outer ward. The first of the Welsh concentric castles was Caerphilly, begun not by the king but by Earl Gilbert in 1271 on the site

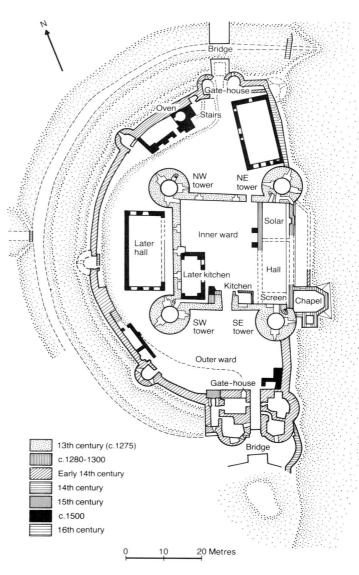

Kidwelly Castle, Dyfed, showing several typical phases of enlargement and alteration.

13th century (c.1275)
c.1280-1300
Early 14th century
14th century
15th century
c.1500
16th century

0   10   20 Metres

The early medieval castles of the Celtic countries tended to be much smaller and more impoverished than their English counterparts. This is Caesteal Maol or Castle Moil on Skye, a small thirteenth-century keep which is said to have been built by a Norse dynasty to exact tolls from ships passing through the strait between the island and the mainland. It commands Kyleakin harbour.

of a Roman fortress and of a new castle recently destroyed by the Welsh prince, Llewelyn. It is possible that Master James of St George was involved in the design of this amazing fortress, with its square inner bailey studded by four large towers and two massive gate-houses, each tower and gate-house a citadel in its own right. The inner bailey is ringed by a lower curtain with the great moat and outworks beyond.

Though never entirely completed, Beaumaris (Gwynedd), which embodied an investment of a then stupendous sum of around £14,000, is regarded as the most perfect example of a concentric castle. Other magnificent expressions of the concentric ideal can be seen at Harlech and Rhuddlan (Clwyd). In each case (apart from Harlech), a fortified plantation town was included in the military package. Caernarfon, by

far the most expensive of all the Edwardian castles, diverged from the concentric model and consisted of two adjacent wards enclosed by a somewhat keyhole-shaped wall which was punctuated by eleven great towers. Conwy (Gwynedd) also had a single curtain, with its eight great towers providing ample accommodation and storage space. Flint (Clwyd) was the most individualistic member of the series. Here a rectangular bailey has corner towers in three of the

ABOVE *Grosmont Castle in Gwent. Note the great thickness of the wall base and also the chimney – a most unusual survival.*

RIGHT *The enclosure at Conwy, Gwynedd, a reminder of the sterner qualities of castle life, although an unusually impressive array of domestic facilities were provided here in the shadow of the walls and towers.*

ABOVE *A section of the massive curtain at Kildrummy in upper Donside, Grampian, the most northerly castle of* enceinte.

LEFT *Caernarfon, Gwynedd, the most costly of all the Edwardian castles. An accompanying plantation town formed an additional part of the pacification measures.*

angles and a gigantic moated and detached round keep guarding the fourth angle.

Wales did not have a complete monopoly of the great castles of the late thirteenth century. Kildrummy Castle (Grampian), glowering over upper Donside in the north of Scotland, became the most northerly example of a castle of *enceinte*. Its plan has strong echoes of both Harlech and Coucy Castle in France. Two other Scottish castles of this period should also be noted. Bothwell in Strathclyde was built in the closing decades of the thirteenth century. It served as an English stronghold in the Scottish Wars of Independence, fell to the Scots after a fourteen-month siege in 1298, and was retaken by Edward I in 1301, when soldiers stormed the walls, erupting from a great siege tower or 'belfry'. It was captured by the Scots and retaken by the English

Tantallon Castle, Lothian, stands on a rocky eminence overlooking the Firth of Forth. It was the medieval stronghold of the Douglas Earls of Angus, who were variously heroes and traitors of the cause of Scottish independence. The main curtain guards only two sides of the courtyard, since the other sides stand above formidable cliffs. The fourteenth-century fabric comprises the gate-house and the East and Douglas Towers.

OVERLEAF Bodiam Castle (NT) in East Sussex was built after 1385. By this time private strongholds had become redundant and the emphasis was shifting towards coastal castles for national defence. There would also be a trend to retain the outward trappings of defence, while increasing domestic comforts and abandoning more serious attempts to defend the dynastic seat. Bodiam was a forward-looking castle in that, though private, it helped to defend a southern strip of country which was exposed to French raids, while including more sophisticated domestic accommodation.

*In Scotland and the troubled area of the Borders, castles and tower
houses retained their viability long after they had become redundant
in the lands to the south. Langley Castle in Northumberland –
restored about 1900 – is a fine example of a fourteenth-century
tower house.*

again in the following century, though during the occupation by the forces of Robert Bruce, the vast great tower which dominated the other towers of the enclosure was split in two and the masonry was thrown into the Clyde. Caerlaverock near Dumfries was built in the 1290s with a concentric arrangement of moats and ramparts to guard the citadel, though whether this was originally an English or a Scottish stronghold is uncertain. This castle was also destroyed under the Bruce policy of depriving the English of Scottish power bases. Although rebuilt, it was again demolished by Scots in the 1350s, so that the ruins which are seen today belong to a fifteenth-century rebuilding.

Other castles were converted into fashionable concentric forms by the addition of an outer curtain, as at the Tower of London and Kidwelly, which acquired its great gate-house at the same time. By this stage the castles of the top rank had become exceedingly formidable structures which incorporated millions of tons of expensive masonry. Their approaches were guarded by moats while the curtain and towers of the outer ward were dominated by the lofty battlements of the even tougher inner ward, studded with towers and gate-houses, each one more difficult to crack than a large Norman keep. Movement within the castle was controlled by a series of portcullises and guard chambers, so that each passageway became a potential killing ground for attackers.

And at this point the castle began its slow decline. Beaumaris was begun in 1295 but was never completed. Thereafter no gigantic citadels were built, whether as royal strongpoints or as private fortresses. Wales was now conquered and held in the strong grip of the Edwardian castles, and the sixty-three royal castles which are known to have been held by the king in 1322 were apparently deemed sufficient to hold down his realm. So long as the kings were able to impose their will upon the country then the nobles had less cause to fear each other or the revolts of the peasant classes. Also, the concentric castles had evolved to such a degree of size, sophistication and cost that scarcely anybody but a king could countenance the construction of a credible modern stronghold. (Edward I, who had built several such castles, was regarded as the grandest king in the whole of Christendom.)

This was all in marked contrast to the situation in Norman times, when provincial magnates like de Clinton at Kenilworth, Daubigny at Castle Rising, de Warenne at Castle Acre, or de Vere at Hedingham could erect strongholds to equal or surpass anything that the king might build.

Those of a martial outlook now sought to display their prowess in the stage-managed tournaments, which had become very fashionable and elaborate during the vogue for chivalry which flourished in Edward's reign. Meanwhile, and for many years to come, the castle remained an essential prop of aristocratic status. Nobility demanded the trappings of castle life, but such a life could be led more comfortably and at much less expense in a building which looked – more or less – like a castle, but which lacked the excesses of masonry needed to withstand a full-scale siege. The drift from minor castle to toy fortress and on into the world of fantasy began with defended manor houses such as Stokesay in Shropshire of 1291 and rather grander strongholds such as Nunney in Somerset of 1373, and it culminated well after the close of our period in elegant and delightful sham castles, such as the brick 'palaces' of Herstmonceux in East Sussex of 1440, or Oxburgh Hall (NT) in Norfolk of 1482. The king himself was party to this drift, for the incredibly costly developments at Windsor during the two decades following 1350, which were sponsored by Edward III (1327–77), almost entirely involved the provision of luxurious apartments. The kings and nobles may not yet have been able to sleep easily, but at least they could now slumber in comfort.

Many old castles were hastily pressed into service on different occasions, most notably during the Wars of the Roses and the Civil War. Even so, whether or not many people realized it at the time, by 1300 the first division of English castles contained an array of monstrously expensive white elephants.

6
The Medieval House

Wretched is the hall . . . each day in the week
There the lord and lady liketh not to sit;
Now have the rich a rule to eat by themselves
In a privy parlour . . . for poor men's sake,
Or in a chamber with a fireplace, and leave the
        chief hall
That was made for meals, for men to eat in. . . .

Langland, *The Vision of Piers Plowman*
(*c.* 1362).

Though mainly of the early sixteenth century, the hall at Cotehele (NT) in Cornwall echoes a tradition which disappears into the Dark Ages.

The house is a collection of ideas and traditions. Its layout and construction can tell us about what the people of the time expected that a home should be and what the current building technology would allow. As manners of living change, a few old dwellings may endure through the transitions to serve as reminders of how people once lived and what they believed a house should contain. Some features survive to remind us that the folk of long ago were very much like ourselves. Today the Joneses of suburbia may announce their social status by building a barbecue and a swimming pool. Their medieval equivalents dug moats around their homesteads – just so that people would know that they were folk of some standing and substance. But in other ways differences in society and the priorities of domestic life ensured that the medieval house bore little resemblance to a prehistoric or a Roman dwelling, and was also far removed from the modern ideas of home. Like the castle and the church it was the creation and the mirror of a particular society. The family of today would find it very difficult to adjust to life in such a house. Of course there would be no electric gadgets, but even if the house were quite grand and substantial the lack of privacy or special-purpose rooms and the change to living and (for at least a part of the household) to sleeping in a single, vast and semi-public room would cause distress. There would be very little furniture, the cooking facilities would be thought primitive and the sanitary provisions – such as they were – would seem positively barbaric. Each generation has its own ideas of the ideal home, and a long sequence of important changes separates us from our medieval forebears.

Should a foreign visitor ask for a tour of a well-preserved medieval house, then this could easily be arranged. Boothby Pagnell in Lincolnshire, Stokesay in Shropshire or Old Soar Manor (NT) in Kent would do very nicely. And yet, our visitor would depart with a very lop-sided view of medieval domestic life – in just the same way that a drive around the 'better' areas of Purley is scarcely an apt introduction to the broad spectrum of living conditions in modern Britain. It is unlikely that a single wall of a medieval peasant hovel is still standing anywhere in Britain, even though the peasant classes constituted the great mass of the population. Meanwhile, throughout much of the period the top people in society were living in castles, although they would periodically reside in manor houses on their various estates. So the houses that survive are those of a narrow section of the community, including knights of the middle or lower ranks and affluent merchants.

A minority of the houses occupied by people at this level in society were built of stone, and a minute fraction of these dwellings has survived in a recognizable form. More were built of timber-framing, and in the course of time these houses have either burned down, or have been dismantled and the bits incorporated in newer buildings, or have been partially rebuilt. A large number of only moderately modified houses of the fifteenth and sixteenth centuries survive and there is a thin sprinkling of fourteenth-century houses, but timber-framed houses dating back to the thirteenth or twelfth centuries are very rare. Occasionally portions of such buildings can be recognized, encased in the fabric of later houses. The discovery of an eleventh-century timber-framed house would be a wonderful thing indeed, although it is quite possible that timbers of this date may still be standing unsuspected as components of a younger building. In this chapter our gaze is largely confined to England. No slight on the Celtic countries is intended and it is simply the case that, apart from the evidence found at castle sites, there is virtually no surviving domestic architecture of the eleventh to fourteenth century to be found in these old lands of relatively youthful buildings.

The Norman nobles had a very clear idea of what a house should be. They agreed with the English tradition in regarding the hall as the core and centrepiece of the house. This was a living room, dining room, reception room and office all merged in one large chamber. The Norman stone houses which survive are typically 'first-floor halls', sometimes known as 'hall-and-cellar houses'. The best example is probably the one dating from around 1200 which stands in the grounds of the private manor house at Boothby Pagnell. The hall is situated at first-floor level and is reached by an external stone staircase. It has a late twelfth-century fireplace in its west wall and stands above a basement, or undercroft, consisting of two cellars, one larger than the other, which must have been used for storage. A doorway leads from the hall into the solar, a private sitting room used by the lord and his family. This arrangement of rooms was quite typical and standardized, so that for all his power and privileges the average Norman lord would inhabit just two rooms – and one of these had to serve as a semi-public chamber where the business and hospitality of the estate were conducted.

From the evidence of the sagas, excavations and old documents it seems likely that the pre-Conquest English lord would normally have lived in an aisled

The steps leading up to the domestic level at the Norman first-floor hall at Boothby Pagnell, Lincolnshire.

The domestic range at Manorbier Castle, near Tenby, Dyfed, is Britain's best surviving example of twelfth- to thirteenth-century living accommodation. Vaulted undercrofts support the rooms, including a great hall, in the middle of this range, which is flanked by solars. A chapel standing above a crypt forms the left-hand end of the range.

hall of timber, a building which was open up to its rafters and which had its roof supported by rows of aisle posts, rather like the piers in the nave arcade of a medieval church. (A few two-storey English dwellings must have existed, for *The Anglo Saxon Chronicle* records how, in 978, the council of the Witan was unceremoniously precipitated into the basement when the floor of the meeting chamber collapsed, leaving Dunstan perched on a beam.) Members of the 'squirearchy' of medieval England often occupied more evolved forms of the aisled hall, while the hall of Oakham Castle (Leicestershire) – a fortified manor house of about 1190 – presents an expression of the aisled-hall concept in durable stone. The twelfth-century features here include the six cylindrical piers and the two-light window openings.

A number of stone town houses survive from the Norman period, and these were generally the homes of affluent financiers and merchants. They are often known by the name of 'Jew's Houses', and some of them probably were occupied by Jews. (Christians were not allowed to practise usury and the occasional riots against Jews – sometimes stage-managed by their leading debtors – encouraged the choice of a strong stone-built abode.) The most celebrated example is the Jew's House at 15 The Strait, Lincoln, built as a first-floor hall around 1170–80 and believed to have been the home of Jewish financiers. Originally the house may have been entered at street level along a passage leading through its storage basement, and access to the domestic level could have been via a wooden staircase ascending from a kitchen annexe. Adjoining this house is the rather later and more modernized Jew's Court. Also in Lincoln is Aaron the Jew's House of about 1170–80 (now consisting of 46–7 Steep Hill and 1 Christ's Hospital Terrace) and Deloraine Court, divided into houses on James Street.

Some Norman and slightly later dwellings are incorporated in private houses, but other buildings which are accessible or visible to the public include: the manor house built about 1183 which is absorbed into The National Trust's Washington Old Hall, a Jacobean house in Tyne and Wear; the guest houses at Fountains Abbey (NT) in North Yorkshire, dating from around 1147; Burton Agnes Old Hall in Humberside, a first-floor hall of 1170–80 with a superb vaulted undercroft; Moyses Hall beside the market place at Bury St Edmunds, an important hall and solar house built about 1180; 'King John's House' of about 1150 and 'Canute's Palace' of about 1180, both in Southampton; the School of Pythagoras in Cambridge of around 1200, and in Norwich Isaac's House at 167 King Street dating from around 1175

and the Norman undercroft beneath what was once the hall of Jurnet the Jew and is now Wensum House. Some remains of domestic buildings can be explored at castle sites. The late twelfth-century Scolland's Hall at Richmond Castle in North Yorkshire is situated in the southeast angle of the castle wall, with a solar to its east which was much altered in the thirteenth century. Similarly, Pudsey's Hall at Durham Castle was built about 1170, but the finest example of a range of twelfth- and thirteenth-century domestic buildings can be explored at Manorbier Castle near Tenby in Dyfed.

The range is important and unusual because Manorbier escaped the demolition or redevelopment which took place at most medieval castles, with the result that, as Margaret Wood has described: 'The domestic range is an untouched example of early medieval accommodation and shows the improvement of comfort and privacy from the late twelfth to the thirteenth centuries.' The first-floor hall with its solar was built above semi-circular barrel vaults against the southwest curtain wall of the castle during the twelfth century. Around 1260 the level of comfort and amenities was improved by adding a second solar to the other end of the hall, and from this solar there was access to a chapel and to the garderobe or lavatory, which was built over the moat. Today one can explore the barrel vaults of the undercroft – presented as dungeons – and then ascend the external staircase to the hall, solar and chapel level. Although the hall and one of the solars are now roofless much of the atmosphere of medieval castle life survives.

The early medieval aisled-hall type of timber manor houses of the rural areas and the stone-built first-floor halls were not vastly different from what are generally thought of as 'typical' medieval houses, which had probably evolved by the start of the thirteenth century. In these dwellings the hub and the dominating feature of the house was still the hall, a spacious and lofty room which was open up to its rafters. These houses are sometimes described as being of the H-plan type. The hall forms the bar of the H and the (stubby) uprights of the letter are represented by separately-roofed two-storey blocks built at either end of the hall. One block, set behind the lord's dais in the hall, contained a solar on the upper floor with a parlour or cellar beneath. The other end of the hall was closed by the screens, a wooden partition shielding it from draughts from the entrance to the house, which opened into a passage-

The School of Pythagoras in Cambridge dates from about 1200.

LEFT *The solar at Old Soar Manor, Kent (NT); the doorway leads to the small chapel attached to the corner of the solar block.*

BELOW LEFT *The roof construction at Old Soar Manor, with the roof structures supported by king posts standing on cambered tie beams.*

RIGHT *The great hall at Stokesay Castle, Shropshire, arguably the most remarkable component in our legacy of medieval domestic buildings.*

way placed just behind the screens. The block immediately beyond the screens passage housed the buttery, pantry and kitchen, while a private bed chamber might occupy its upper level. As the years rolled by the hall remained the central component of the house, but additional accommodation was obtained by expanding both the cross wings to produce a more markedly H-shaped layout, or by lengthening just one cross wing, to create an L-shaped plan.

The increasing flexibility in the design of houses is beautifully demonstrated at The National Trust's Old Soar Manor in Kent. The surviving part of the house was built in Kentish ragstone around 1290. The original aisled hall is now represented by a private house of the eighteenth century, and the medieval section, which is open to the public, comprises the solar block. The solar stands at first-floor level above a barrel-vaulted undercroft and is reached by an internal staircase. From one corner of the solar there is access to the room containing the garderobe – which may seem primitive to modern eyes, but which was doubtless a great refinement on what had gone before. The room approached from the other corner of the solar is a small and simple private chapel, once reached by an external staircase. Although the hall and solar layout was quite in keeping with twelfth-century thinking, the chapel and garderobe are quite novel, existing as virtually detached small rectangular blocks which only join the main body of the house at their corners.

A visit to Old Soar Manor provides a splendid introduction to the home of a medieval knight at the height of the age of chivalry. The roof is still supported by the two original kingposts carried on cambered tie beams, and the absence of furniture underlines the spartan nature of medieval life, when a table, benches, a couple of chairs and cots and a few storage chests were just about all that was needed to furnish a home.

Anyone familiar with one Norman aisled or first-floor hall would have been pretty well able to find their way around them all, even if blindfolded. But during the thirteenth century the house became a delightfully discordant agglomeration of buildings. Rises in the standards of living, growing demands for comfort and convenience and the consequently increasing pressures to keep up with neighbours all wrought important changes. In modern decades countless dwellings have been enlarged by extending them in one direction or another. It was just the same in medieval times – except that there were no planners, architects or building regulations. Nor was there any perception of the house as a compact,

coherent and balanced entity. It was a collection of rooms, bays or blocks which were often of different ages and which were tacked on to one another in whatever way seemed most convenient at the time. As a result it was often only possible to move round a house by making periodic detours through outside corridors. Various external staircases might be used, and sometimes these would culminate in an 'oriel', a small projecting chamber or landing with a large window. Some houses were revamped to meet new demands. The Treasurer's House (NT) opposite the church at Martock in Somerset was a thirteenth-century first-floor hall, the hall of which became a solar when a new hall was built beside it in the fourteenth century to produce an L-shaped plan.

Yet for all the changes the hall still retained its pre-eminence, not only as the main living room of the household, but also as the focus of the estate. Aristocratic life demanded a great deal of feasting and entertainment as well as a measure of largesse towards those who were deemed worthy of hospitality. And so the status of the hall was assured. It was needed for dining and public gatherings; served as the conference centre and administrative headquarters of the estate; provided the venue for the manor court, and, when the court had recessed, the business was done and the feasting was over, it became a dormitory for the servants.

During the thirteenth and fourteenth centuries the aisled hall very gradually became redundant as improved building methods made it possible to roof a large span without recourse to aisle posts. A superb example of a thirteenth-century aisleless hall still survives virtually intact at Stokesay. Were I allowed to take a visitor to just one English building, then Stokesay might easily be the choice. An almost unbelievably delightful building, Stokesay is a fortified stone manor house standing within a moat and reached via a sixteenth-century gate-house. The fortified north tower is of the twelfth century but is crowned by a timber-framed upper storey of the seventeenth century. The late thirteenth-century hall and solar block are linked to this tower, with a polygonal tower of similar date adjoining the southern end of the range. Everything about the manor house is magnificent, but pride of place must go to the hall. This has internal dimensions of about 16 by 9 metres (c. 52 by 30 feet); it is a construction of four bays

Stokesay Castle, showing the twelfth-century north tower which is crowned by timber-framed structures of the seventeenth century, with the sixteenth-century gate-house to the left.

and is crowned by an arch-braced collar beam roof (as illustrated on p. 135).

In 1950 Margaret Wood estimated that England contained some seventy surviving thirteenth-century houses, about half of which were very good examples. Most are of stone, for the timber-framed houses of the time have perished or tend to be incorporated in later houses in such a way as to be scarcely recognizable. A fair proportion of the enduring thirteenth-century houses are private homes, but a number are visible to the public. Longthorpe Tower near Peterborough in Cambridgeshire is an early fourteenth-century tower which was added as a solar to the mid thirteenth-century first-floor hall. The 'Forester's Lodge' at Upper Millichope in Shropshire is a very interesting building of the late thirteenth century, now part of a farmhouse, comprising a first-floor hall and undercroft. Acton Burnell Castle in the same county was a 'palace' of the Bishop of Bath and Wells who was also Chancellor to Edward I; it dates from the late thirteenth century. Sutton-at-Hone Chapel (St John's Jerusalem) in Kent was a chapel of the Knights Hospitallers, once attached to a manor house which has been demolished. It dates from around 1234 and is a National Trust property. The 'Abbot's Lodging' at Netley Abbey in Hampshire is a first-floor hall of the thirteenth century, with a solar block and chapel forming projections from one of the long walls.

During the fourteenth century the directions of development which had begun to transform the home in the previous century were pursued with gusto. Houses became even more rambling as additional ranges were linked to the traditional hall and solar nucleus. Often it was convenient to arrange the buildings in the form of a hollow rectangle, thus embracing a courtyard. Thrusting individuals of less than castle-owning rank would seek to ape their social 'superiors' by adding showy fortifications to their houses. Such status-claiming ambitions provided good business for the Crown, since the right to build towers and battlements was only obtained by purchasing a licence to crenellate from the king. Greys Court near Henley in Oxfordshire, which is owned by The National Trust, is a fine manor of the sixteenth century. There are, however, also the fragmentary remains of the mid fourteenth-century manor house built for Sir John de Greys after 1347. Sir John's house consisted of a rectangular walled enclosure with towers at each corner and a small square 'keep'.

Moats were still considered to enhance one's standing in society, so the ranges of buildings surrounding a courtyard were in turn often embraced by a rectangular moat to create a very impressive package. One might further mimic the castled classes by adding a gate-house. Usually these defensive trappings were mainly for show, though occasionally, in areas threatened by Welsh or Scottish raiders or difficult neighbours, they had more practical advantages. All these developments are excellently demonstrated at Markenfield Hall near Ripon (North Yorkshire),

The ruins of the manor house or tower house at Greys Court (NT), near Henley, Oxfordshire, built in the mid fourteenth century as a house which was fortified by towers at each end.

where John de Markingfield bought his license to crenellate in 1310. Set within a rectangular moat and guarded by a gate-house, the main building ranges form an L-shaped plan. One arm of the L consists of a first-floor hall, still reached by an external staircase, and the other included the chapel, with the chambers at ground-floor level being used as a kitchen and storage rooms. The other buildings around the courtyard include fifteenth- and sixteenth-century replacements for earlier buildings.

In exploring surviving medieval buildings it is just possible to hop from one temporal stepping stone to the next and so understand the evolution of the home of the rural knight. But what of the homes of the rustic masses? Nothing remains. The excavations at deserted medieval village sites like Wharram Percy in North Yorkshire show that peasant dwellings were so flimsy and shabby that they needed a total rebuilding about every generation. All peasants lived in 'modern' houses! The most popular arrangement was the small long-house, a single-storey building divided into two chambers – one for livestock and the other for the whole family. There were probably no windows and the thatch above was scarcely visible through the smoke haze swirling up from the open hearth in the middle of the earthen floor.

Probably the best place to experience the appearance of a medieval peasant dwelling is at the Weald and Downland Open Air Museum at Singleton in West Sussex. A fine selection of later medieval houses has been re-erected here, while the 'Hangleton House' is a reconstruction of a thirteenth-century peasant dwelling based on information from two excavated houses at Hangleton near Hove in East Sussex. It is not a long-house, but a single semi-partitioned room with low walls of flint rubble which are (conjecturally) roofed in straw thatch. Something of the flavour of peasant domestic life in the Middle Ages can be gleaned by visiting the black houses of the Scottish Highlands and Islands. Examples of these houses, which have either been reconstructed or stripped of later alterations, are displayed at Col-

bost, Luib and Kilmuir on Skye, Arnol on Lewis, and at the folk museum at Kingussie (Highland). Such dwellings are specialized regional developments of the ancient long-house tradition and they echo the ethos if not the finer detail of medieval rural life as lived by the masses.

A yawning social chasm separated the cottars, bordars and villeins from the knights and greater

An impression of the open and spartan nature of medieval house interiors is provided by the 'Winkhurst House', re-erected at the remarkable Weald and Downland Open Air Museum at Singleton, West Sussex, and possibly dating back to the fourteenth century. This is the view from the hall, with its open hearth, to the entry, with the solar reached by a staircase and projecting above the entry end of the hall.

aristocrats. Occupying the social middle ground were the yeomen farmers and the merchants and tradesmen of the towns, comprising the nuclei of a middle class which would gradually swell in importance. Such people normally lived in timber-framed dwellings which were far superior to the cramped hovels of the peasant classes, and which had layouts that echoed those of the grander houses. Each region developed its own particular style of timber-framing, although two basic traditions were involved. The cruck-framing technique was based on the use of pairs of massive, slightly curving timber blades which were linked at their tips to make A-shaped frames. These were then used to form the gable ends and bays of dwellings. Although a roof line could be heightened by setting the bases of the blades on a raised stone plinth, the height of such a dwelling is constrained by the lengths of timbers available for cruck blades, so that cruck-framed dwellings are generally quite small. Where the alternative technique of box-framing was employed the framework of the house consisted of a box composed of oaken posts, sills and wall plates which was reinforced or tensioned by timber studs and braces.

The origins of both forms of building are controversial. Cruck-frames were certainly being built in the thirteenth century and the style could go back to the Dark Ages or beyond; certain forms of box-framing were employed by the Romans, although the pedigree of the medieval box-framed dwelling is not yet established. Whichever style was employed, the spaces between the wall timbers were sealed by a mud concoction of daub which was plastered on to a wattle of woven twigs, or on staves or laths. Roofs were normally thatched, although shingles, weatherboarding and plain tiles were also employed. Because most of the older timber-framed houses have experienced many phases of alteration, it is seldom easy to assign a date to a particular dwelling. Dwellings which pre-date the Black Death can sometimes be recognized by the survival of a low 'catslide' type of roof of the kind used originally to roof an aisled hall, or by the existence of elements of an old H-plan layout and the absence of projecting upper storeys or jetties. A few thirteenth-century town houses seem to have been built with jetties, but these only became common features in the fifteenth and sixteenth centuries. In York, Lady Row, Goodramgate, is a block of early fourteenth-century jettied houses, while at Newgate in the same city there is a jettied row belonging to the following century.

The development of medieval buildings from the early aisled and first-floor halls onwards shows a fascinating blend of conservatism and innovation.

The Dark Age and medieval tradition persisted in some places into the eighteenth century, producing simple little dwellings like this one, near the foot of Pen-y-ghent in North Yorkshire.

The period had ended before the boldest trend-setters felt ready to evict the great hall from its pre-eminent position as the centre-piece and social focus of the home. Even today it lingers on as a humble entrance lobby. Gradually, however, the austerity of the early medieval houses gave way to a certain measure of opulence. Clearly associated with this transition was the notion of special-purpose rooms, so that the later medieval dwellings became rabbit warrens of several ranges. These encompassed servants' quarters, storage rooms, public rooms, offices, private sitting rooms and bedchambers for the various members of the family. Finally, the demise of the castle allowed the current ideas about domestic life to be adopted on the grand scale by the top families of the realm. This at last produced the stately home. At this point it is worth remembering that the medieval period spanned several centuries. A Norman knight let loose in Oxburgh Hall would have felt as overwhelmed and as out-of-place as would a yokel from Yetminster transported to London's Barbican Centre.

7
The People at Prayer

... if a priest neglect the shaving of beard or of
   locks;
if a priest, at the appointed time, do not ring the
   hours, or sing the hours;
if a priest come with weapons into a church;
if a priest misorder the annual services of the
   church, by day or by night;
if a priest misconduct an ordeal;
if a priest enwrap his tonsure;
if a priest love drunkenness, or become a
   gleeman or an 'alescop' ...
if a priest forsake a woman and take another, let
   him be excommunicated.

Law of the Northumbrian Priests, *c.* 1020.

Staverton – They say that Master Walter, the
Vicar, beareth himself well and honestly, and
teacheth them excellently in spiritual things;
not is there, as they assert, any defect in him.
Of hidden mortal sin they know nought. And
his Vicarage, as they assert, is worth ten marks.

Register of Bishop Stapledon of Exeter, 1301.

*The church at Barfreston in Kent, small and simple in plan but
with exceptionally lavish decoration.*

OPPOSITE PAGE

ABOVE *The fortified stone manor-house at Stokesay, Shropshire, where a superb example of a thirteenth-century aisleless hall survives virtually intact.*

BELOW LEFT *Both moats and gatehouses enhanced one's standing in medieval society, although those at Markenfield Hall, North Yorkshire, pictured here, probably also had more practical advantages, as the house lay within the range of Scottish war parties.*

BELOW RIGHT *Roche Rock in Cornwall carries the ruins of a medieval chapel which has the cell of a hermit hacked into the rocks beneath.*

The massive Norman tower nave at Fingest, Buckinghamshire, echoes the older English tradition seen at Earls Barton. The twin saddleback roof is a later addition, probably dating from the seventeenth century.

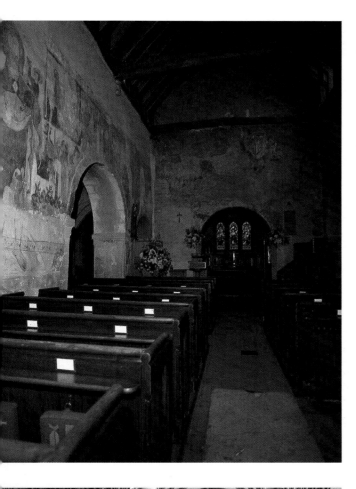

FAR LEFT *The west front of Lincoln Cathedral.*

LEFT *Beautiful medieval wall paintings in the church at Little Missenden in Buckinghamshire. The figure of St Christopher carrying the Child Christ may be of the late thirteenth century.*

BELOW RIGHT *The splendid Norman interior of Peterborough Cathedral.*

BELOW LEFT *The magnificent interior of Lincoln Cathedral.*

ABOVE *At St David's, Dyfed, the rectangular space west of the ambulatory was originally open to the sky and the fan vaulting was inserted in the sixteenth century, when the area became the Trinity Chapel. The remains of St David rest here.*

RIGHT *Bolton Priory in North Yorkshire, founded by the Augustinians. This order had more than two hundred establishments by the time of the Black Death.*

ABOVE *Fountains Abbey (NT), North Yorkshire, a magnificent Cistercian house founded by a breakaway group of Benedictine monks. The superb Perpendicular tower was built by Abbot Marmaduke Huby in 1494–1526.*

RIGHT *The impressive ruins of the Cistercian abbey of Rievaulx, North Yorkshire, seen from The National Trust's Rievaulx Terrace.*

ABOVE *The deserted medieval village of Castle Camps, Cambridgeshire, where the church stands inside the bailey defences of the Norman castle.*

RIGHT *Some of the most delightful and imposing of all the rural medieval buildings must be the great barns, the cathedrals of medieval agriculture. This fine example is at Lacock in Wiltshire, where The National Trust owns the village and the Abbey.*

In the course of the medieval period most communities gained a new church. Some of them gained several. Throughout most of England and much of Wales these were not the first churches to occupy the sacred ground, but in many places the old pre-Conquest church was so comprehensively rebuilt that it virtually disappeared. With periodic pauses and bursts of new activity this process of enlargement, titivation and replacement continued right through the Middle Ages. Structures were adapted and embellished to allow for growth in the congregation, to accord with changes in the ritual of worship and to express the new fashions in ecclesiastical architecture. Eventually, in most places where the latest turns in the cycle of rebuilding were less than comprehensive in their effects, the church emerged as a delightful architectural confection incorporating the tastes and efforts of many different ages of church building. Although it is often inspected and appraised according to the merits and originality of its architecture, the church should essentially be seen as the spiritual focus of a particular community. It was a magnificent and domineering building which embodied much of the wealth created by toil in the surrounding ploughlands and pastures. It was usually far grander, more expensive and more elaborately furnished than the houses of any of the local lords. It soared like a stately palace above the sordid homes of the village peasants, as if to underline their squalor. It provided unchallengeable answers to all their questions of good and evil, life and death.

The period covered by this book spans two great styles of architecture, the Romanesque and the Gothic, as well as the transitional phase which links them. Both the Saxon and Norman building styles belonged to the Romanesque tradition and were rooted in vaguely-remembered classical inspirations. Yet the styles were different, even though they met and merged in hundreds of churches of the eleventh and twelfth centuries. That of the Saxons had at first borrowed some continental ideas, but had then become more thoroughly insular. That of the Normans was heavily influenced by the developing Romanesque idioms of Western Europe. In most respects the Norman Conquest marked a sharp and often a painful break with the past, but this reorientation is less apparent in the parish churches. The impact of the Conquest swiftly became evident in the ecclesiastical first division of cathedrals and abbeys, but it was only after about 1120 that the building of Norman parish churches had gathered momentum. Even then the old ways of building were still being followed in the backwaters, so that many of the churches of around 1100–50 appear more Saxon than

Norman. Perhaps the time lag between the Conquest and the acceleration of parish church building reflects the disruption and, in places, the devastation wrought by the Norman victory and its aftermath. Landowners were still the main providers of churches and perhaps they needed some time to secure and reorganize their estates.

While styles which thoroughly expressed the Western European Romanesque movement blossomed in the new cathedrals and abbeys, in the countryside there was more blending of old and new. This diluted the original Norman style – not necessarily a bad thing – and allowed the development of a more insular Norman architecture. The conquerors had reintroduced the apse in their grander churches, and apses also featured in some smaller ones, like Kilpeck near Hereford and Copford in Essex – but soon the anglicization of Norman architecture brought the abandonment of the feature. The Saxon influence is evident in the layout of many parish churches in England, with the tower nave at Fingest in Buckinghamshire, the church with a central tower but no transepts at Stewkley in the same county, or the lovely church at Barfreston in Kent (ornately embellished with carving but still a simple nave-and-chancel building) all echoing English traditions. Even so, there are a number of distinctive features which distinguish most Norman churches.

The most obvious of these concerns the introduction of a completely new portfolio of decorative motifs used to embellish the mouldings in the heads of windows and around doors. The most popular was the repeated chevron and others include the beak-head, lozenge, cable, billet, chain, scallop and pellet. In the more humble churches the ornamentation might be confined to an arc of chevrons above the door. In other cases, such as St Peter's in Northampton, or Stewkley (where the chancel arch has lavish beak-head decoration), the ornamentation is more opulent, while in a few quite small country churches, such as Iffley in Oxfordshire, Barfreston and Kilpeck, the display of decoration is staggeringly profuse. The contrast with the most modest of Norman churches – like the Heath chapel, now alone on a deserted village site in Shropshire, or the church of Winterborne Tomson near Bere Regis in Dorset – is extreme. At Kilpeck the door is surrounded by grotesques and devils, and fertility symbols sprout from the tops of the walls. It is often said that gargoyles and other blatantly pagan symbols represent demons driven out of a church at its consecration. However, fertility symbols in the form of 'green men' can be discovered inside churches of various medieval dates, prominently or in hidden places, and

ABOVE *Norman blind arcading decorates the church tower at Stewkley in Buckinghamshire. Built around 1140, this church has unusually lavish Norman decoration.*

RIGHT *Exceptionally fine Norman carving surrounds the door of the church at Kilpeck, Hereford and Worcester. Note the pagan fertility symbol of the green man (just below centre), with vigorous vines sprouting from his mouth.*

LEFT *This beautiful carving in the interior of Kilpeck church captures the austerity and intensity of early medieval religious values.*

they show no signs of being shooed away. Perhaps the churchmen tolerated such devices so long as the congregations believed they would assist the church in its vital task of sustaining the productive farmland.

A second characteristic of Norman churches concerns the way in which the masons often seem to have had less confidence in their abilities than their predecessors, so that walls were generally more massive than before. They could be 4 feet (*c.* 1.2 metres) thick, with flat buttresses that were too shallow to offer real support placed at intervals. In the grander churches walls and piers tended to be built of rubble which was faced with an ashlar skin of squared stones. Any reservations which the masons may have harboured concerning their engineering capabilities were sometimes soundly based, for such walls periodically collapsed.

Thirdly, there were changes in the proportions of the churches, which tended to be more squat, with broader towers. The larger churches were often built with transepts, allowing extra altars to be included

and providing a more symmetrical appearance than had the porticus of the Saxon churches. Long arcaded naves with a clerestory above the nave became fashionable. The western location of Saxon towers was sometimes superseded by the central tower, with the body of the church pressing against it like rocks clasping a lighthouse; South Lopham in Norfolk is a good example. Such central towers could cause difficulties, particularly during attempts to enlarge the arch between the nave and the chancel which helped to support the base of the tower. Where the resources and available skills permitted, there was also an increased emphasis on the use of stone rather than carpentry; sometimes this involved the con-

RIGHT *The splendid Norman central tower at South Lopham in Norfolk is surprisingly little known.*

BELOW *The minster church at Stow in Lincolnshire demonstrates the cruciform plan which was characteristic of the more important minster churches.*

struction of a stone-vaulted roof over the chancel, or even over the whole church, as at Elkstone in Gloucestershire. At the magnificent Saxon minster church at Stow in Lincolnshire the old chancel was vaulted, and so it remained until a fire brought down the vaulting. Then, during restoration in 1850, an excellent reconstruction of the Norman vaulting was installed.

A final characteristic of Norman parish churches, recently recognized by Hugh Richmond, reveals the high degree of standardization which underlay the apparent diversity, for it seems that the naves were set out to the dimensions of two adjoining squares. The measurement of the body of the church therefore makes it possible to recognize Norman buildings even after all the diagnostic round-headed window and chancel arches and mouldings have disappeared in the course of rebuilding and refenestration. When the various Norman preferences were combined in a single substantial church, then the building could

The reconstructed Norman vaulting at Stow.

appear as a church with a long nave with arcaded aisles and a central tower with north and south transepts, producing a cruciform plan. Examples include Melbourne in Derbyshire, Hemel Hempstead in Hertfordshire and Old Shoreham in West Sussex, although Melbourne and Old Shoreham have lost the apses of their transepts and had square ends added to replace the apses of their chancels. The elimination of apses partly reflected the anglicization of the Norman architecture, but it also resulted from the need to lengthen the chancel in order to provide space for the increasingly elaborate ritual of the church.

At its best Norman architecture can be monumental and imposing, and at its worst it seems crude, dark and overbearing. Apart from the problems posed by the collapse of some poorly designed or executed buildings, the Romanesque style imposed severe limitations on the dimensions and appearance of churches. During the twelfth century a number of experiments gave birth to a completely new style. They were carried out in the greater churches, although masons working in parish churches may have contributed some ideas. This new Gothic or pointed style was a European development which found its first great expression in the Abbey of St Denis in Paris after 1140. England played a part in pioneering the innovations, for pointed arches had already appeared in the nave vault at Durham Cathedral, and other versions of an early Gothic style were introduced by the Cistercians, who had strong links with the continental centres of learning and innovation. During the last quarter of the twelfth century elements of the new style made their debuts in Cistercian abbeys, such as Fountains (NT) and Kirkstall (West Yorkshire), and in the cathedrals at Canterbury, Worcester, Lincoln, Ripon Minster (North Yorkshire), Wells (Somerset) and Chichester (West Sussex).

In the parish churches the masons seem to have been more stolid than radical, so that the new architecture tiptoed in, a Gothic moulding or capital here and a pointed arch there. The transitional architecture was not really a style in its own right but a cautious picking and choosing between building habits and innovations. Different facets of the style can be glimpsed in the nave arcades and capitals at Castle Hedingham in Essex or Woodford in Northamptonshire, in the 'cushion' capitals and pointed arches at Polebrook in the same county, or in the clustered shafts forming the piers in the nave arcade at Deeping St James in Lincolnshire. It was only around the second decade of the thirteenth century that an undiluted Gothic architecture was adopted in the parish churches of England. Meanwhile, in the

The humble Norman church at the deserted village of Heath in Shropshire, unusual in being an unaltered survivor of a type of 'field' church which was very common in the Norman realm.

remoter parts of the Celtic countries simple rectangular churches continued to be built, generally without any fashionable or obvious stylistic features.

Underlying the changes in the larger churches there were compelling engineering arguments, although these operated with less force in the case of the smaller churches. Masons working in the Norman style had sought to bear the downward and outward thrusts of roof vaulting along the whole length of massive walls. The adoption of the new style of building involved concentrating the thrusts at specific points, where they could be borne on buttresses and piers. In this way the intervening sections of wall were lightened and could be pierced by large window openings to brighten the interior of the church. Elongated and pointed lancet windows were adopted, sometimes appearing singly but often grouped in twos, threes or fives under a single hood mould – the beginnings of the familiar traceried window. Most parish churches were roofed in timber rather than having a more prestigious stone vault inserted below the carpentry of the roof, so that the load-bearing advantages of the innovations were less obvious than in the more majestic cathedrals and abbeys. The new pointed arches and window openings, though often foregone in parish churches built during the transitional period, were stronger and were particularly effective when combined with roof vaulting.

The first Gothic style is known as Early English, and its serene but studious and rather austere qualities tend to be most conspicuous in the northern abbeys and in cathedrals such as Lincoln and Salisbury. In the parish churches the architecture was usually simple and restrained, although more adventurous applications of the style can be seen in churches such as Stone in Kent, West Walton in Norfolk and Warmington in Northamptonshire. In some regions of England the arrival of the Early English style was proclaimed by the appearance of spires, and as each parish attempted to surpass its neighbours the skylines were transformed, as though a race of subterranean giants were seeking to prick the clouds with needles of stone. Previously some pointed tower coverings had developed, including saddleback structures as at Wadenhoe in Northamptonshire, Rhenish helm caps as at Sompting in West Sussex, and pyramids as at Climping in West Sussex. The development of the spire may have involved the rapid attenuation of these structures, although a very early example of a broach spire appeared in an evolved form at Barnack in Cambridgeshire around 1200; the Chartres cathedral spire of 1165 may have provided a distant inspiration to the masons working in England. The broach spire, adopted with great enthusiasm in the East Midlands, was a complicated structure with triangular masses of masonry and internal arches bridging the intervening space between the square of the tower and the

octagon of the spire. Developing skills in English masonry came of age in the countryside with the ability to build such beautiful, durable but – if only to modern eyes – almost completely unfunctional creations.

Other developments in church architecture were of a much more practical nature. The population was growing rapidly and the older churches were not only unfashionable but were also unable to accommodate the swelling congregations. Where Saxon or Norman walls had endured they were often transformed by the insertion of bigger and brighter windows. Naves and chancels were lengthened, chancel arches and nave arcades heightened as a considerable portion of the wealth of the countryside became fossilized in a glistening array of costly buildings. The outside of a church was normally rendered and then limewashed. The interiors were also rendered and limewashed or painted in bright hues, while expanses of bare wall were decorated with paintings of the Last Judgement, biblical scenes and saints. The woodwork in the rood screen that stood between nave and chancel was also often brightly coloured and the glittering glass added to the carnival of colour. It is ironic that while we today may delight in the subtle shades of stone that naturally mimic the colour of the breast of a dove or a newly-shorn sheep, the designers of churches normally intended that the masonry would be invisible beneath the limewash or gaudy paint.

The Gothic innovations had by-passed the structural limitations of the Romanesque style so that the church had become an elaborate and sophisticated building. The engineering problems being solved, the next stage in its evolution, apparent at the end of the thirteenth century, placed the emphasis on the decorative embellishment of the building. The church was now a stone framework of a complicated design, thrust met by counterthrust. Upon this stable skeleton were carried star bursts of vaulting, torrents of carving and vast windows with vibrant glass and twining tracery. The grander churches, like Patrington in Humberside and Weobley and Ledbury in Hereford and Worcester, became magnificent palaces, blossoming with intricate decoration – although there were many more humble parish churches where the decoration was minimal and the craftsmanship indifferent. Meanwhile the broach spire, always rather regional in its adoption, was yielding to the more widespread enthusiasm for parapet

The remarkably early broach spire at Barnack in Cambridgeshire dates from about 1200.

spires. These dispensed with broaches and rose from within the pinnacled parapet of the tower, with ornate flying buttresses sometimes providing arching links between the spire and the tower that bore it.

Although the Decorated style was superseded, the Gothic manner still had one more important card to play. This book ends with the ghastly national catastrophe of the Great Pestilence of 1348–51, and the appearance of the new Perpendicular style in parish churches lies just beyond it. However, as the Perpendicular produced a number of coherent and spectacular new churches and as most medieval English churches display something of this style, it deserves a mention here. Some churches were comprehensively rebuilt in the late fifteenth century, others acquired a soaring tower or one of the now fashionable guild or family chapels, while a remarkable number were refenestrated with Perpendicular tracery with its vertical bars leading upwards to flattened arches. In England the Gothic style came to fruition in this new and largely insular architecture which represented the ultimate solution to the long-established quest for buildings which were taller and lighter and pierced by more massive window openings. Building in the Perpendicular style had a strong vertical emphasis and the eye would often be carried further skywards by a soaring battlemented tower. The structural basis for the innovations was provided by the use of flatter roofs above depressed arches, which carried the thrusts of the masonry directly to the piers and buttresses. In one respect the Perpendicular represented the natural culmination of experience gained by masons seeking to exploit the possibilities of the arch and buttress. In others the style must somehow have been influenced by the social disasters and the new economic order which rolled across Britain following the tides of the Pestilence. The Plague years brought a halt to church building, and when work resumed a numerous and completely different generation of churches was born. The changes are clearly displayed at Patrington, where building began in the Decorated manner, was halted by the Pestilence, and recommenced in the Perpendicular.

Brief architectural descriptions such as this are all very well, but they cannot provide a proper introduction to the medieval parish churches of Britain. Over the years scores of authors have trodden the same path, and most of us topple into the pit of misinformation by spreading the assumption that 'model' churches are typical. And yet West Walton is far from being typical of the parish churches built when the Early English style was current, and Patrington is a magnificent building but quite unrepresentative of the run-of-the-mill Decorated churches. There was, in truth, never such a thing as a 'typical' church, for any individual building was affected by a number of factors apart from the prevailing architectural style. First, the resources of finance and skill were seldom sufficient to allow a particular architectural vogue to find its fullest and most elaborate expression in an ordinary parish church. Secondly, superimposed upon the national building trends there were many regional whims and fancies, always there to assert the individuality of the provinces and prevent the creation of stereotyped buildings. A third factor was linked to the first, for in the absence of unusually generous patrons a partial redevelopment was normally preferred to a wholesale rebuilding. Only in the rare cases where churches have been excavated do we discover the remarkable sequences of such works. As often as not eight or more really significant phases of alteration will link a surviving church to the original building. Of these, less than half may actually be discernible in the visible fabric. It may be anybody's guess whether the actual walls, standing silently as windows have been inserted, removed and replaced again, are Saxon, Norman or later.

In some parts of the north of England and many parts of the Celtic countries the lack of funds and the coarse and ancient building stones did not encourage those with a taste for vaulting, tracery or carving. In Wales many of the country churches are simple, two-celled box-like structures of the thirteenth century – and probably look little different from their Dark Age predecessors. Scattered thinly amongst them are a few larger cruciform buildings in identifiable medieval styles. Their transepts, some still standing but others demolished, suggest the extra altars associated with a community of clergy, and such churches often seem to have originated as the *clasau* or minster churches described in Chapter 2. Yet the legacy of

The beautiful church with a parapet spire at Weobley, Hereford and Worcester. This large church was built mainly in the Decorated style, but note the single and grouped lancets.

medieval churches in Wales is not without variety. Perhaps the most striking contrast is between the small rubble buildings of the rural backwaters, which are towerless and display only a simple bellcote, and the churches of the Norman-occupied territories in the southern margins of the country. To the south of the 'Landsker' or military frontier are the delightful churches of what was Pembrokeshire (now part of Dyfed), with tall narrow towers which are said to have served as look-out posts standing guard over villages which may still perpetuate the names of their Norman founders.

The exploration of regional differences in the parish churches of Britain can be fascinating. Some of them are easily traced to the geographical characteristics of the regions. The transport of building stone was an exceedingly costly affair, and while the expense might be tolerated in order to obtain top-grade materials for a cathedral, most parish churches display the products of a humble nearby quarry. In this respect those who built on the Jurassic limestone belt in the Cotswolds and Northamptonshire were highly favoured, while the chalkland parishes in East Anglia normally had to make do with flint and imported dressings from the Barnack quarries near Peterborough, with perhaps local chalk 'clunch' for the protected internal masonry. And yet there were many local fancies which seem to be quite unrelated to geology and the dictates of the purse. It is not easy to see why Yorkshire folk – when they could afford it – particularly favoured a long, low building with a battlemented clerestory and pinnacled tower, why clerestories found so little favour south of the Thames, or why it was that along the long southern strip of England aisles were generally provided with their own gabled roofs.

The regional variations in building styles, though often inexplicable, appeared in scores of different forms. Detached church towers are not uncommon in the West Midlands, as at Richard's Castle and Pembridge (Hereford and Worcester), but are rare in the east, where Long Sutton in Lincolnshire and Elstow in Bedfordshire seem most unusual. The variations are also apparent in church interiors and in their furnishings. Timber wagon roofs, resembling the inside of a barrel, found favour in the west but were matched by the elegant hammer-beam roofs of the eastern counties. Fonts with four lions around the shaft or the seven sacraments depicted in panels around the basin were an East Anglian speciality, while in Buckinghamshire the localized style of Aylesbury fonts, so elegant as to seem like neo-classical creations, appeared in several churches. And so the story continued throughout the realm as local

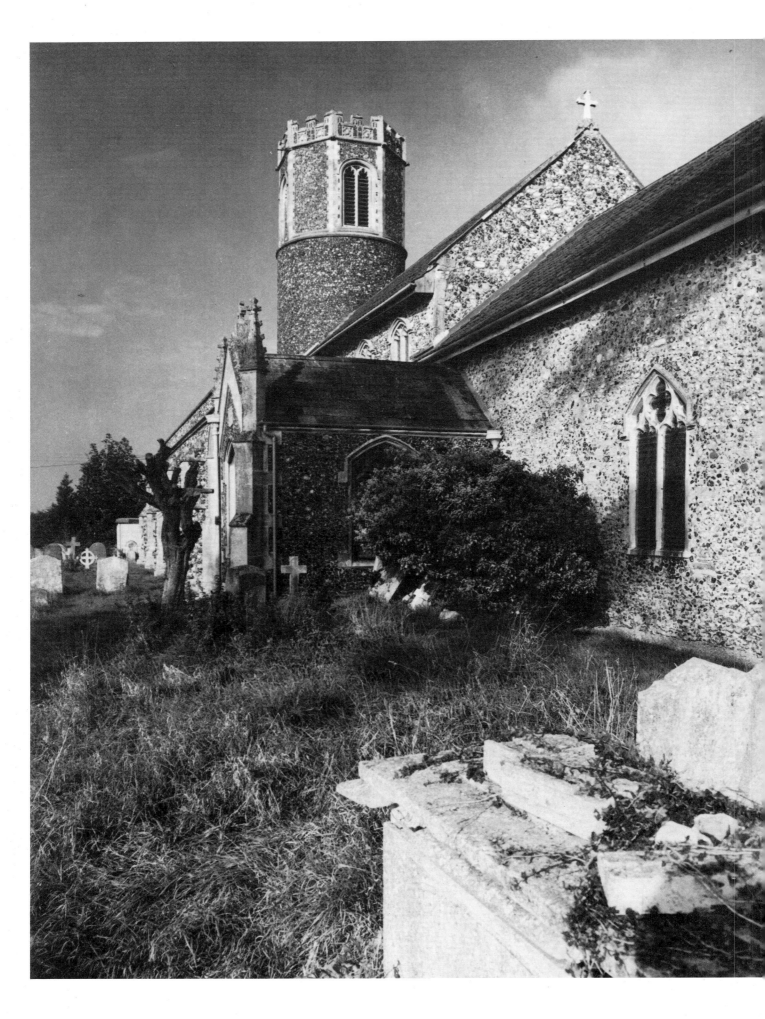

LEFT *Saxon and Norman round towers are common in the chalk and flint country of East Anglia, but seldom seen elsewhere. The use of flint and the shortage of good building stone for quoins encouraged a cornerless form of construction. This example, later heightened with an octagonal addition which was possibly inspired by Ely Cathedral, is at Roydon in Norfolk.*

RIGHT *Whittlesey in Cambridgeshire. The superb mid fifteenth-century vaulted spire crowns a tower and church rebuilt after fire damage in the thirteenth century. The imposing church is a reminder of the prosperity of the medieval Fenland.*

BELOW *Aylesbury fonts are one of the many local specialisms to be found in the parish churches of Britain. They are restricted to the surroundings of Aylesbury and this superb Norman example is in the church at Great Kimble, Buckinghamshire.*

craftsmen perfected their skills in ways that have ensured regionalism will live as long as the old churches survive to shame the cut-price 'international' styles of modern building.

The regional aspect of British churches is further underlined by the fact that great surges of rebuilding – often accompanying local phases of prosperity – took place in different provinces at different times. In East Anglia there was a great deal of rebuilding to accommodate the swelling congregations in the thirteenth century, while in the little industrial centres of the region palatial wool churches appeared in the fifteenth century, just as they did in those parts of the Cotswolds and Wessex which supported a booming trade in cloth. A great surge of church building in Devon during the fifteenth century

St Govan's chapel at Bosherston, Dyfed, on the south coast of Wales, is steeped in myth and legend and could easily be mistaken for the chapel of a Dark Age saint or hermit. In fact it was probably built sometime in the thirteenth century and demonstrates the problems of dating the more modest churches of the Celtic countries, which were deprived of any tell-tale ornamentation.

removed the greater part of the legacy of older churches. The same was true in Cornwall, where more of the Norman legacy, though very little from the earlier centuries, survives. In parts of rural Wales there were no such surges of prosperity, so that once a modest church had been provided in the earlier medieval centuries there might not be the funds available for any lavish rebuilding. Cumbrian communities which failed to obtain a church in the Norman building era often had to wait until the seventeenth or eighteenth century, while vast tracts of the Scottish Highlands were churchless until quite recent times.

The exploration of medieval churches is fraught with pitfalls. It is all too easy to do as the architects have done and see the evolving church as a search for answers to the structural problems of engineering. It is equally easy to follow the art historians and see it as a fruit drop of masonry and decoration, to be sucked and then savoured or discarded according to the merits of the work. Yet churches were there to serve congregations – and it is unlikely that the average fellow at the back of the nave cared two groats about the role of squinch arches or the geometry of bar tracery. For him the church was a magnificent experience, an omnipotent master and an onerous burden. Whether or not he realized it, he did not need a vast purpose-built church. (The old monastic communities and early dissenters showed that devotion and piety were not to be measured in masonry and painted glass.) But he did need supernatural help to protect his crops against flood and drought, to keep the demons away from the milk cow and to save the flocks from disease. This was the responsibility of the Church. Most of the time it met it quite well. It also offered to save one's soul from eternal damnation – but it charged a heavy price.

The age of the minster was followed by the era of the proprietorial, 'field' or parish church. This was usually provided by the lord of the local estate. Thereafter a heavy burden of taxes for the upkeep of the building, the priest and the ecclesiastical establishment fell upon the congregation. Parishes began to form within the network of pre-existing boundaries in late Saxon times, and new ones continued to be created during the Middle Ages. One tenth of the produce accruing from the parish lands was taken as a tithe to support the church, the old system being regularized in the twelfth century. Eventually the convention was established that the rector, who administered the tithes, would have responsibility for maintaining the chancel, while the upkeep of the nave devolved upon the parishioners (although landed patrons normally sponsored the greater rebuildings, and bequests helped with maintenance and minor additions). The tithes apart, a system of feudal fines and 'mortuaries' ensured that between them the lords of the manors and the Church managed to fleece members of their flock of most of their remaining wealth. The responsibility for the furnishing of the church could not be taken lightly, and in the thirteenth century an Archbishop of Canterbury decreed that parishioners should provide the church with bells and ropes, a locking font, images, a bier, a vessel for the holy water, a candelabrum for the Easter candle, a banner for Rogation Days and various other costly items. At a feast day, or when kinsfolk were buried, communicant members of the congregation were likely to be charged altarage, and some priests were adept at discovering occasions when such charges might be imposed. Funerals were dreaded for a variety of reasons, not least because the lord of the manor would surely seize the deceased's best beast and because the rector was likely to step in and take a mortuary of the second beast. This was done on the assumption – probably correct – that the dead man had evaded tithes during his lifetime.

It is not easy today to imagine the wealth which was invested in parish churches; forgetting the cathedrals and abbeys and the costs of building parish churches, let us look at the situation in 1291, as recorded in a survey produced for Pope Nicholas. England and Wales then contained 8085 churches, and 5374 of these churches had annual incomes of more than ten marks – the minimum sum needed to support a priest properly being estimated at five marks.

The priests themselves varied enormously in their piety, learning and conduct. Some were devout, caring and erudite, others were lazy, licentious and virtually illiterate. Some rectors took the church revenues, disappeared to lead a comfortable and lazy life at court or university, and hired a substitute or vicar to handle the parish. Some vicars struggled hard on the church land or glebe to live at the level of the average peasant. While the parishioners were generally fairly devout if somewhat mystified worshippers (being illiterate and quite unable to translate the Latin services, which were not always explained in the 'vulgar tongue'), the worst churchmen were treated with a healthy disrespect. For reasons unknown the rector of Easton was besieged in his church for four days in 1293 and then attacked by his flock when he emerged. The vicar of St Mary Church in Devon cannot have been much better, for in 1301 the parishioners reported: 'the . . . vicar keeps all manner of his beasts in the churchyard, by which

it is badly trampled and vilely fouled. . . . The same vicar also has his malt prepared in the church and keeps his corn and other things therein, by reason of which his servants, going in and out, leave the door open, and the wind getting into the church in bad weather is wont to unroof it.'

In return for burdensome taxes and the possibility of a wastrel as rector, the community received quite a lot. If the rector was more conscientious than normal then one third of his income would be given in alms and hospitality to the poor, according to the established traditions. The churchyard was used for sports, rowdy gatherings, gossip and flirtation – irrespective of how determinedly the bishop sought to protect its sanctity. Little business deals were set up in the church porch, while anyone deeply in trouble could make a dash for sanctuary in the church. With a measure of luck they might then live to experience banishment. The church also served a secular function, providing a community centre which might be used for quite beery and boisterous celebrations. It also served two more important roles. On the psychological and spiritual planes it not only dispensed the only tolerated form of religion and promise of escape for a superstitious congregation hardened by uncomfortable lives of repetitive drudgery, but it also existed as a world of space, colour and mysterious ritual, open to people who mainly spent their lives in dark, smoky, flea-ridden hovels. Secondly, it bore the burden of responsibility for protecting the farmland against natural disasters and the forces of evil.

To appreciate the medieval church we must try to see it through medieval eyes. It was not just a large building among many, visited on Sundays by a small minority of the population. It was the universal temple of a jealous and sometimes ruthless God, a pillar of the established order, a tax office, a school and a storehouse, fun palace and community centre, the headquarters of the social services, a sanctuary, sports ground and meeting place. It was close to being all things to all men.

8
Cathedrals

The sorrow and distress of the sons of the church were so great that no one can conceive, tell or write them; but to relieve their miseries they fixed the altar, such as it was, in the nave of the church, where they howled, rather than sang, matins and vespers.

Gervase, a Canterbury monk, writing about the burning of the eastern section of Canterbury Cathedral in 1174.

Ely, one of the monastic churches which also served as a cathedral.

FAR RIGHT *The medieval bishop was a man of great influence and power who would often initiate magnificent programmes of cathedral development. This is the tomb of Bishop Anselm, Bishop of St David's 1230–48.*

RIGHT *The cathedral at Canterbury has a history which goes back to Augustine's arrival in 597, although, as at York, building continued into the fifteenth century, and the famous Bell Harry tower was not completed until the latter part of this century. The adjacent cathedral school in the foreground of the photograph has a history extending back to 631.*

The communities of monks who established and nurtured Christianity in the stark, moist environments of the north and west led lives of simplicity and self denial. Doubtless they hoped that these ascetic virtues would be preserved as the religion passed from strength to strength. Had one of these monks been able to visit England some six hundred or eight hundred years after the establishment of Christian communities, then he would surely have been bemused and concerned to see so much of the wealth of the kingdom being channelled into the construction of majestic buildings which were somewhat incidental or even superfluous to the biblical requirements: buildings which, in reality, did as much – or more – to glorify the magnificence of bishops and the Church establishment as they did to proclaim the glory of God. Today we can stand apart from the discomforts of ethical arguments. It now matters very little whether the resources invested in the great medieval cathedrals should more justly have been spent to alleviate the hardship and suffering of the poor and the sick or to provide chapels in the remote corners of the uplands, where churches were still few. Instead, we can enjoy the wonder and splendour of buildings of a kind which our own society is quite incapable of producing. For if there are any man-made things in Britain to equal the beauty of unspoilt countryside, mountains and coast then they are to be found at the ecclesiastical hearts of dioceses such as York, Lincoln, Canterbury or Salisbury.

The word 'cathedral' has for long been synonymous with a building which is stunningly large, exceptionally beautiful and lavishly embellished with the finest carving in wood and stone,

W. H. Auden's 'Luxury liners laden with souls'. Technically, however, a cathedral is just a church which differs from other churches by virtue of the fact that it contains the throne of a bishop. The splendour of the medieval cathedrals originated in the decisions of bishops and their supporters rather than in the demands of theology. Cathedrals were not the only vast and exquisite churches to be found in the medieval realm. There were a few remarkable town churches and a quite spectacular collection of monastic churches. Where the monastic churches were also cathedrals, as at Ely, they survived the destruction of the Reformation. Otherwise we experience the cathedrals as living buildings which preserve much of their medieval appearance, while the abbey and priory churches are seen as stark, haunting ruins.

The tendency towards the aggrandizement of cathedral churches became apparent during the Saxon era, although disasters and rebuilding have rendered this heritage virtually invisible. Winchester Old Minster must have seemed a wondrous place when seen through the rustic eyes of the tenth century; an account of the rebuilding work, which continued throughout most of the second half of the century, tells how: '... whoever walks within these courts with unfamiliar tread, cannot tell whence he comes or whither to return, since open doors are seen on every hand, nor does any certain path of a way appear.' This building, which grew in at least seven stages between about 648 and 994, would in some ways seem as puzzling to modern eyes, for excavations close to the living cathedral have revealed its peculiar layout. It was an elongated building with an apsidal chancel, and with lateral apses protruding like transepts flanking the high altar. Ranges of rectangular porticus providing accommodation for a further sixteen subsidiary altars also projected from the sides of the building.

Warwick Rodwell and James Bentley have suggested that the Old Minster may have had more than thirty and, perhaps, more than forty altars. Such altars were numerous in all the greater churches of the time and were often associated with fashionable religious cults and saints and with local martyrs. While Winchester Old Minster seems to have embodied many of the peculiar fancies of the Saxon Church, the pre-Conquest cathedral at Canterbury will have seemed more forward-looking. Here the raised apsidal chancel seems to have stood above a crypt, the nave was flanked by aisles and a pair of towers rose from the middle of its sides. Crypts, often holding the relics of saints, were an important feature of the greater Saxon churches, and the crypt of the late seventh-century cathedral at Hexham in Northumberland survives beneath the nave of the priory church.

To see a Saxon cathedral as a ruin rather than as an excavation one must travel to North Elmham in Norfolk, and even here there are problems. The partly surviving walls of flint and conglomerate trace out the plan of an unusual church with a long nave without aisles and with transept-like porticus, which endow the building with a layout like a Greek 'tau' cross. It is still not known whether this building *was* Elmham Cathedral, a church built here when the see was moved to Thetford in 1075 above the real timber cathedral, or whether South Elmham, with the ruins of a minster church, was the original diocesan centre.

The Saxon cathedral, with its irregular layout, multitude of altars, its crypts and its preoccupation with holy relics and obscure saints, and with porticus bursting from its sides like buds from a twig, accentuated the 'eccentricities' of the Saxon Church. The effects of the Norman Conquest were more immediate in the case of the cathedrals than in that of most parish churches. They involved both wholesale rebuilding and the reorganization of the diocesan system. This latter change, underlining closer ties between the Church and the State, began with Archbishop Lanfranc's demand that semi-rural sees should move to new locations in major towns. In East Anglia the shift was from Elmham to Norwich, via a twenty-year spell when the diocese was centred on the important old Saxon town of Thetford. In the same year the Lichfield see in the Midlands embarked on a prolonged circular tour, eventually returning after sojourns in Chester and Coventry

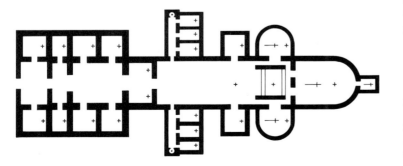

LEFT *Plan of Winchester Old Minster.*

RIGHT *The Norman nave at Norwich was completed in the first half of the twelfth century, while the beautiful lierne vault above was added in 1470.*

(which existed as a co-cathedral with Lichfield), Selsey (West Sussex) moved to Chichester, Wells to Bath (with the existence of Bath and Wells as co-cathedrals bringing a new twist to this long story of rivalry) and the Dorchester see (Oxfordshire) was involved in a long-distance transfer to Lincoln. But perhaps the most interesting shift was that which moved a Wessex diocesan centre from Sherborne (Dorset) to a new town and castle setting at Old Sarum in Wiltshire, a dry and windy situation ringed by the ramparts of the ancient hillfort. The choice was a poor one in terms of the environment and was also a social disaster, since the clerics and garrison were close but discordant neighbours. In 1219 the see slipped downslope with the construction of a new cathedral at Salisbury nearby. New sees were also

created at Ely in 1109 and Carlisle in 1133. At the end of the reign of Henry I the pattern had stabilized, and it is interesting that of the seventeen English dioceses then existing, eight still had roots which went back directly to the seventh century.

Wales did not escape reorganization. At least four dioceses there had probably existed since the sixth century: St David's and diocese, for example, equating to the kingdoms of Glamorgan, Gwynedd and Powys. In the Norman period new sees were established at St Asaph (Clwyd), Bangor (Gwynedd) and Llandaff (South Glamorgan). At this time Wales

The Norman nave arcade at St David's.

lacked fully-fledged Welsh towns and both Bangor and St David's were defended by earthworks, while Llandaff and St Asaph were linked to new castle towns. In Scotland the situation was rather different. The province lacked a metropolitan, and although archbishops of York had claimed to act as metropolitan of the Scottish dioceses, in 1192 the Scottish Church was granted the unusual status of a 'special daughter' of the Papacy. Thus the existing sees of Dunblane, St Andrews, Aberdeen and Moray, Caithness and Ross, Glasgow, and Brechin and Dunkeld, were regarded as equals under the direct authority of Rome – there were no archbishoprics until the fifteenth century. Several of the Scottish dioceses were not named, according to the English fashion, after the place where the bishop had his see, but after ancient political provinces, earldoms and other secular lordships, while many of the cathedrals, such as Elgin (Grampian), Fortrose (Highland) and Kirkwall (Orkney), were built close to the castle of a particular lay lord.

In England the Normans also brought changes in the internal organization of the cathedrals. The monastic cathedral was unique to Britain, and there were several examples in the South, Midlands and East Anglia, such as Peterborough, Winchester and Worcester. Otherwise the secular cathedrals were staffed by a small number of secular canons. The Normans accepted the concept of monastic cathedrals and Canterbury Cathedral was reorganized under the Benedictines, as were Durham and Rochester and the new cathedrals at Ely and Norwich. The Wells see was transferred to the Benedictine priory at Bath and the new cathedral at Carlisle was staffed with Augustinian canons. The monastic cathedrals were ruled by priors, while the bishops were regarded as titular abbots – although the respective roles and powers of the two important churchmen were often a source of disagreement. The secular cathedrals, of which York was the most important, meanwhile acquired a more elaborate organization, with the chapters of canons being led by deans and a group of specialized dignitaries, now needed as ritual, organization and administration became more complex. Only one bishop, Wulfstan at Worcester, survived the Norman episcopal purge, and he is said to have wept as the old church was demolished to make way for a new cathedral. The purge was gradual in most cases, but when English bishops died they were replaced by foreigners.

Following the Norman Conquest a very heavy programme of cathedral-building works was begun. Although the finest examples of architecture in the Early English style are to be found in cathedrals, abbeys and priories, the greatest intensity of building took place during the currencies of the Norman and Decorated styles. Each medieval cathedral experienced several major campaigns of enlargement and rebuilding. A survey published by Richard Morris and based on a sample of 85 cathedrals and abbeys shows that between 1070 and 1530 there were about 360 important episodes of building – an average of 4.2 per church. At some cathedrals, like York Minster, the different building works were in progress for most of the medieval period.

Not only did the Normans reshape the diocesan structure and organization, their period also witnessed a remarkably energetic cathedral-building campaign. It is calculated that during the closing decades of the eleventh century about thirty cathedrals and large monastic churches were begun, and this at a time when the conquerors were also engaged in a gigantic contemporary exercise in castle building. No mason will have looked far for work. Perhaps the sheer scale of the programme may help to explain why so much of the building seems crudely monumental and was sometimes inclined to collapse. A reliance on unskilled and impressed labour, rapid building techniques involving walls and piers with poorly-bonded rubble cores, and the shortage of the time and skills needed to execute fluent carving may have been the price which was sometimes paid for all the diffuse endeavour. The building campaign is all the more amazing when one realizes that it took place against a background of local and even regional revolts against Norman rule, at a time when the genocidal reaction to dissent had led to the devastation of much of the north of England and when estates throughout what had been a very prosperous Saxon kingdom were often disrupted and severely devalued by the Conquest and its aftermath.

At a few cathedral sites the funds for wholesale rebuilding may not have been immediately available, but whenever possible the Normans undertook a programme of demolition which has deprived us of a legacy of greater Saxon churches. They were a conquering power, intent upon stamping both their authority and the close integration of Church and State upon the landscape and, presumably, on obliterating much of the indigenous building heritage. Their outlooks contrasted with those of the English in the way that those of the modern development corporation clash with conservationist attitudes, for the English had been loath to destroy old buildings, preferring to integrate them in organically developing structures. Unlike the more insular Norman parish churches, which mainly appeared rather later in the era, the new cathedrals borrowed

The Norman cathedral at Rochester. The church was founded by St Augustine in 604, destroyed by Danish raids, rebuilt after the Conquest in 1080 and damaged by fire in the twelfth century. The fourteenth-century rebuilding was partly financed by donations made by pilgrims at the shrine of the (not officially canonized) St William of Perth. However, St William was not sufficiently popular as to allow the rebuilding to be completed.

RIGHT *At York Minster building work was in progress throughout most of the medieval period, culminating in 1485. This is the largest of the English cathedrals.*

architectural designs directly from the continent, although English influences were soon asserted. The important cathedral-building works of the eleventh century included Westminster, completed under strong Norman influences before the Conquest, Ely, Chester, Carlisle, Winchester, Worcester, St Albans, Canterbury, Lincoln, York and Chichester. The construction of Norman cathedrals at St Asaph, St David's, Bangor and Llandaff began in the first half of the following century.

Most Norman cathedrals developed as buildings which were more elongated than most comparable structures on the continent, although no broader. York was unusual in being an aisle-less building, though in other cases the aisles, with their various side chapels, either terminated at the apse or continued around it in the form of an ambulatory. Most building work was influenced by the considerations of contemporary ritual, and the monk Gervase, when describing new building work at Canterbury, mentioned the difficulties of incorporating the chapels and crypts of St Anselm and St Andrew: 'The

designer, therefore, not willing to lose [them], but not able to remove them entirely . . . yet preserving as much as possible the breadth of that passage which is without the Choir [this was the ambulatory] on account of the processions which were frequently to be made there, narrowed his work with a general obliquity, so as neatly to contract it over against the altar. . . .' Durham made a major contribution to the development of the later Gothic architecture. Pointed arches in the nave vaulting were an important innovation in this building, and concealed flying buttresses carried the thrusts down to the aisle buttresses.

The twelfth century witnessed the beginning of work on the new Welsh cathedrals and also the gradual completion of cathedral works begun during the reigns of the three Norman kings. No sooner had the projects been completed than the Norman structures created often became either the subjects for considerable enlargement, or for piecemeal demolition and reconstruction according to the new fashions. In fact, when the elements of the Gothic style had been effectively assembled even the relatively recent Norman buildings were rendered outmoded, and churchmen everywhere sought the lighter, brighter interiors and the increased range of building possibilities. In many respects the cathedrals, now rooted in the hearts of the bustling and expanding cities, were better placed to command attention and influence than were the rural abbeys and priories. Buildings embodying the new Early English style would have been more numerous had not John's kingdom been placed under papal interdict in 1208, causing a suspension of ecclesiastical construction. But by the second quarter of the thirteenth century the momentum of building had recovered, and as the masons became fluent in the design and decoration of Gothic buildings they produced work of the highest possible quality. By the start of the thirteenth century the cult of the Virgin was enjoying enormous support and most cathedrals acquired a lady chapel in the course of this and following centuries. Sometimes it was the most beautiful feature of the church, as at St Albans, and even at glorious Ely the lady chapel almost rivals the wonders of the famous octagon tower.

As the Early English style matured into the Decorated there was another astonishing surge of build-

LEFT *The south transept at St Albans Cathedral; Saxon columns saved from the earlier church were incorporated in the triforium.*

RIGHT *Gothic arches at Lincoln, pointing skywards like arrows packed in a quiver.*

The cult of the Virgin Mary had become very powerful by the thirteenth century and several cathedrals obtained Lady Chapels. The beautiful Lady Chapel at St Albans dates from the early fourteenth century.

ing, which was sustained even at a time when so much in the way of skills and resources was being consumed by the Edwardian programme of castle building in Wales, and when the masons engaged in ecclesiastical work ran the risk of conscription to the king's works. But the frantic pace of cathedral rebuilding could not continue forever. The most prosperous centres had already acquired cathedrals of great magnificence, and in the fourteenth century a daunting array of problems concerned with land exhaustion, climatic deterioration, overpopulation and economic decline combined in the grim prologue to the national catastrophe of the Great Pestilence. Although the rebuilding of parish churches in the Perpendicular style of the fifteenth century exerted a staggering effect on the village landscape, no new Perpendicular cathedrals were built and the main impact of the style at this level was confined to additions to the cathedrals of the West Midlands. Bath Cathedral, however, was built as the priory church in 1501–39, its absolute completion being overtaken by the Dissolution of the Monasteries. When Wren began work on new St Paul's in 1675 the architectural fashions had changed, although the Perpendicular continued to linger in the building of parish churches, where it has never really been extinguished.

The redirection of building efforts towards the parish churches had social as well as economic dimensions. The aristocracy of the earlier medieval centuries managed to combine a quite deep, if 'establishment', form of piety with manners of living which were frequently in discord with the ethics of the New Testament – and sometimes with those of the Old as well. However, it was generally accepted that one's chances of salvation could be dramatically improved as a result of gifts of land and other donations to the Church. For some time such endowments were of a relatively impersonal nature and were directed mainly towards the leading churches and abbeys. Before the Tudor period, however, the donors had begun to seek more personalized manifestations of their generosity towards the Church, and so the endowments tended to gravitate towards parish churches and, particularly, family chapels. New chapels, towers, porches or entire new churches helped to advertise the piety and status of the family making the endowment: they gave the benefactors more to show for their money.

After centuries of spectacular wealth, magnificent building and, quite often, the lavish and colourful lifestyles led by its clergy at all levels, the Church had also developed what we today would call an 'image problem'. Leading churchmen were sometimes held in open contempt, although public-

spirited people often retained a large measure of respect and admiration for the friars. These monks worked as priests and instructors amongst the laity and survived by begging, being forbidden to own buildings or lands, which were held in trust for the friars by corporations of citizens. By the fourteenth century the friars too had sometimes earned an image problem as begging became organized under efficient professional 'procurators', or was leased to 'limitors'. Fierce and unseemly rivalries over begging territories resulted. However, the Franciscan and Dominican friars had established about seventy convents in England by the middle of the thirteenth century and a hundred by an early stage in the fourteenth. At the height of their popularity the friars received a donation in almost every important will. And since they based themselves in towns they, like the town and country parish churches, attracted a substantial share of endowments which would otherwise have gone to cathedrals.

This discussion on the relative decline of cathedral building in the years at the close of our period and beyond brings us back to the question of how the prodigious building works of the eleventh, twelfth and thirteenth centuries were financed. The great churches consumed an almost incredible amount of investment, and although the available income was remarkable, building was almost always constrained by the astronomical costs of buying, dressing, importing and shaping stone, purchasing timber, moving the bulky materials to the building site and paying armies of masons, carpenters, glaziers, tilers and unskilled labourers. In consequence, building tended to be done a bit at a time, as funds allowed – and as a result of this step-by-step approach our cathedrals almost always display something of three or four distinctive medieval styles. As Richard Morris has pointed out, a cash-flow problem at Westminster in the 1270s resulted in a delay of over a century in the completion of the nave, while the building of a cathedral usually took more than four decades and sometimes well over half a century – by which time plans for additions and improvements in a new architectural style would doubtless have materialized.

During the early medieval centuries the Church had received or inherited spectacularly generous endowments of land, and these estates and urban landholdings yielded a continuous torrent of rent, tolls, leases and services which could be directed into the physical fabric of the Church. In addition there were individual donations and endowments, and profits accruing from the sale of indulgences and the performance of special masses. Offerings were made at the shrines of the saints, so that the possession of important relics – genuine or quite blatantly fraudulent – was a crucial component of some ecclesiastical balance sheets. Lichfield had a special chapel devoted to the popular cult of St Chad, Canterbury boasted the shrine of Thomas Becket, Hereford had shrines to Thomas Cantilupe and St Ethelbert, St Albans flourished on the long-established cult of its semi-mythical martyr, St David's on that of the patron saint of Wales, while Winchester had a virtual boneyard of saintly relics. Such relics were big business and sometimes the authorities used all their influence to press for the canonization of a promising set of bones, while Glastonbury Abbey compounded its fraudulent claim to have the body of St Dunstan by 'discovering'

bones in the monks' cemetery which were brazenly attributed to King Arthur and Guinevere.

Gifts from the Crown enhanced the ecclesiastical coffers and there were also special donations of building materials or transport given by royal or other wealthy benefactors. Tithes could also help to swell the funds and an early teaching of the Church held that a quarter of the tithes from a parish church should be offered to the bishop if he required it. In Scotland the appropriation of parish churches and their tithes or 'teinds' by more powerful religious

The aisles of the medieval cathedral were lined with tombs, side chapels and subsidiary altars; something of the atmosphere of medieval devotion is captured in this interior at Wells.

The central tower at Hereford was paid for by the offerings of pilgrims made at the shrine of St Thomas Cantilupe, Bishop of Hereford, who died in 1282. The western towers, weakened by Cromwellian shelling and neglect, collapsed in the eighteenth century, destroying the west front. This was rebuilt in a Gothic style by Wyatt in 1788.

institutions led to the impoverishment of many parishes, and goes some way to explain the relative paucity of medieval parish-church architecture there. As cathedral chapters were instituted the rural parishes supported the majority of the canons, a practice which began in the diocese of Glasgow in the middle of the twelfth century and spread to most other territories in the following century. Although Scotland and Wales were not particularly wealthy countries during the medieval centuries, England was one of the most prosperous kingdoms in Christendom with much of the affluence underpinned by the wool and textile industry, important before the Conquest and supreme in the national economy thereafter.

All the wealth in the world would have counted for nought had there not been the ability to convert dreams and ambitions into buildings of stone, timber, glass and lead. While pre-Conquest England had been uniquely endowed with illustrators and carpenters, in the decades immediately following the Conquest there was a partial reliance on a top flight of masons attracted from France and other parts of the continent. Even some stone was imported, coming across the English Channel from Caen to works in the south of England in the period before the opening up of some of the best English quarries. Long before the Norman period had run its course, however, Eng-

Arguably the finest exhibit in the British heritage of medieval architecture is the chapter house at Wells, the roof supported by a central pillar which cascades into the vaulting like a glorious petrified fountain. The building dates from the second half of the thirteenth century.

land was producing master masons as skilled as any. The execution of a building was entrusted by its patrons to one of these men, who was simultaneously a craftsman, architect and overseer. All the medieval churches were designed by craftsmen whose roots were in the quarrying and building trades; architects as such did not exist. Beneath the master mason were the skilled carvers, dressers and layers of stone as well as the glaziers, metal-workers, carpenters, tilers and scaffolders of the ancillary trades, all supported by an army of lesser artisans and unskilled labour.

Many masons came from the main quarrying districts and learned the rudiments of their skills as youngsters working in the local quarry, so that districts such as Corfe in Dorset, Barnack near Peterborough, Ketton in Leicestershire or Weldon in Northamptonshire would always be well represented on any important building site. Even the leading

This superb flight of steps leads to the chapter house at Wells Cathedral.

masons were peripatetic workers and any great building project would recruit craftsmen from a nation-wide catchment area. Craftsmen departing after the completion of building at a new cathedral might next find employment at a parish church, so that the latest ideas about construction and decoration would diffuse down the ecclesiastical building hierarchy. Despite the mystique, perhaps created by the mumbo-jumbo of freemasonry, the masons were not particularly well-paid or privileged workers and, being peripatetic, they lacked the ability to become 'big fish in small ponds' which was enjoyed by other craftsmen who were permanently associated with particular urban guilds. Their work was often dangerous, they lived under the risk of being impressed to the king's works whenever an important new castle or palace project was in the offing, and they always faced the stoneworker's threat of death from silicosis.

While stone was often cut to size and dressed in the quarry to minimize the burden on the weak and groaning transport system (stone was often carried by water, but it would have to be hauled to a suitable landing point), the final stages of the work were accomplished on the building site, either in the open or in permanent or temporary lodges. The essential tools of the mason's trade have scarcely changed since medieval times, although windlass-like treadmills were sometimes used in the lifting of stone. At Salisbury Cathedral the forest of internal scaffolding used in building the amazing spire is still *in situ* within the soaring structure.

Until the drive to build and rebuild began to lose momentum in the fourteenth century, the cathedral was more an evolving idea than a completed masterpiece, each one embodying work of several different ages and styles. However, some, though embellished with additions and enlargements of other periods, are particularly expressive of a particular building style. Norman work is superbly represented at Durham, Norwich, St David's, and Peterborough; Salisbury celebrates the Early English style, Wells has superb carving in the Decorated manner, while the Perpendicular style graces the choir, east window and north transept at Gloucester.

Medieval piety, craftsmanship and ecclesiastical wealth and power created such a glittering heritage of building that any attempt to select a 'best' example

The new cathedral at Salisbury, begun in 1220 and completed about 1270, formed the centre-piece of a planned town which enjoyed more elbow room than had been available on the cramped and windswept hilltop at Old Sarum, nearby.

is pure folly, although each enthusiast will have his or her favourites. Perhaps it is regional bias that makes me think that York Minster is unsurpassed, although those who arrive before the milling throngs and wander round Canterbury in the early morning light may be able to conceive of nothing more lovely. Yet York and Canterbury are rather hemmed in, so that they cannot present panoramic views to equal the serenity of Salisbury, or the unique view of Ely as it erupts from the flat Fenland. Lincoln too is a magnificent landmark and the charms of St David's, so often overlooked, and Lichfield, battered by the Reformation and subject to so much restoration, should not be forgotten. And so the discussion could go on, but of one thing we can be certain: whatever the injustices and ills of medieval society it provided an architectural legacy which dwarfs the best that our own civilization can create. Crushingly.

LEFT *Canterbury has preserved its cathedral close, with medieval gateways providing portholes on the bustling world outside.*

ABOVE *The breathtaking Norman nave at Durham.*

9
The Monastery

I am tormented and oppressed by the length of the vigils, I often succumb to the manual labour. The food cleaves to my mouth, more bitter than wormwood. The rough clothing cuts through my skin. . . .

> A monk complains to St Ailred, Abbot of Rievaulx 1147–66.

A cleric's duty is to serve Christ and leave carting and labouring to ignorant serfs. And no one should take Holy Orders unless he comes from a family of freemen. . . . Serfs and beggars' children should toil with their hands, while men of noble birth should serve God and their fellow men as befits their rank. . . .

> Langland, *The Vision of Piers Plowman* (*c.* 1362).

The abbey church at Rievaulx, North Yorkshire, one of the greatest of the Cistercian monasteries.

In modern Britain monasticism has such a low profile that it is difficult for us to imagine the power and vitality of the movement during the earlier medieval centuries. Even on the eve of the Reformation, at the end of a prolonged phase of monastic decline, the movement was said to control about half the wealth of the Church in Britain and it supported some 825 religious houses, large and small. We have become accustomed to change in our world of transient institutions and technological revolutions, and so it may also be hard to appreciate the durability of the monastic movement. Some monastic houses, such as those at Abingdon (Oxfordshire) and Glastonbury, had existed for more than six centuries by the time of the Dissolution of the Monasteries under Henry VIII (1509–47). Although the monastic ideal had proved so durable, the story of the movement was not one of torpor and stability, but a recurrent saga of periods of laxity and decline followed by a resurgence of idealism and spectacular growth.

At the end of the sixth century, with Celtic monasticism firmly established in Ireland and parts of Scotland, the pagan majority in England might have felt crushed in the grip of a great pincer movement, with the Benedictines under Augustine arriving at Canterbury and Aidan and his supporters in the Celtic Church making converts in the north. The first generations of Benedictine establishments in England crumbled under the Danish onslaughts, but in the 960s and 970s King Edgar struggled vigorously

RIGHT *Crowland, Lincolnshire, was one of the many eastern abbeys destroyed by Danish raiders. Following its foundation in 716 it had a singularly unfortunate history, being burnt by Danes c. 930 and burnt again in 1091, shaken by an earthquake in 1117 and burnt in 1146. Much of the surviving fabric dates from the late twelfth century and a remodelling in 1281.*

BELOW *St Aidan founded a monastery at Lindisfarne, Northumberland, in 635, but it was destroyed by Viking raiders in 793 and again destroyed in the following century. The surviving buildings were erected following a recolonization of the site by Benedictines from Durham in the eleventh century.*

to revive the monasteries and to replace the secular clergy with monks, while St Dunstan and his colleagues provided the ecclesiastical inspiration and momentum for the renaissance. Thereafter, monasticism experienced a sequence of important shocks and stimuli which regularly renewed and revitalized the movement.

The Norman Conquest was followed by a surge of new Benedictine foundations, and houses were established at, for example, Battle (East Sussex), Colchester, and Selby (North Yorkshire), while Cluniacs were eventually persuaded to establish members of their order at sites such as Lewes (East Sussex), Bermondsey (Greater London), Thetford and Castle Acre (Norfolk). A great European reforming movement in the twelfth century introduced vigorous new orders to Britain, the Cistercians and Premonstratensians. In the next century, when these seekers after solitude were sampling the material fruits which accrued from their spectacular success, the currents of monasticism were again revitalized by the arrival of the new orders of friars – men determined to shun the materialism and isolation of their predecessors, living in humble establishments and working amongst the people. By the close of our period, however, the fires of monasticism were burning less brightly. Although the Carthusians arrived in the fourteenth century and the Crown encouraged the establishment of the Franciscan Observants and Brigettines in the fifteenth century, there were relatively few new foundations. Many of the older houses, their communities severely depleted by the Great Pestilence and their buildings sometimes standing as virtually empty shells, were finding it difficult to attract new recruits in numbers sufficient to do much more than keep the institutions alive. It is notable that the various orders were continental phenomena, reflecting the great strengthening of European links which resulted from the Norman Conquest. Only the order of the Gilbertine canons, with ten double houses of nuns and canons and two other monasteries, actually originated in Britain. By the time of the Dissolution in the 1530s some great monasteries were supporting communities just a third or even a quarter the size of those which had existed in the High Middle Ages. Had there been no Reformation one can only wonder whether monasticism would have discovered a new dynamic, or whether the abbeys and priories would have sunk slowly and peacefully into oblivion.

Despite propagandist claims to the contrary, English monasticism was quite healthy and energetic on the eve of the Norman Conquest. What might have appeared to outsiders as faults were no more than the relaxed and insular qualities associated with English life in general. Benedictine monasteries here were almost as old as Augustine's landing, while England had always been a place of strong regional and insular identities. As a result, an array of local customs had developed within the broad limits of the rule of St Benedict. At the same time, the monasteries had relatively recently experienced a vigorous revival and modest reform. About 970, King Edgar met his bishops, abbots and abbesses at Winchester, and the meeting produced the *Regularis Concordia* which provided new guidelines for monastic life. They emphasized the unity of the monastic community, the pre-eminence of liturgy and ritual and the

The Cluniac priory church at Castle Acre, Norfolk, with its façade of blind arcading (left), and, to the right, the prior's quarters, later converted into a farmhouse.

importance of prayer for the souls of benefactors, all within the essential framework of the monastic ideal. Although these rules were influenced by ideas current in reformed abbeys in Flanders and Lorraine, much of the insular flavour of monastic life remained. For example, in cathedrals such as Worcester and Winchester, where the Church was served by a convent of monks rather than a chapter of secular canons, lay folk were allowed to attend Sunday Mass in the monastic church, and there was an enthusiasm for feast-day processions.

The impact of the Norman Conquest on English monasticism was not as traumatic as it might have been, thanks in part to the Norman veneration of the saintly English king, Edward the Confessor. A noted Italian theologian, Abbot Lanfranc, was installed as Archbishop of Canterbury, and new reforms were introduced which emphasized the close partnership of the Roman Church and the Norman State – at the expense of English customs, cults, saints, language

and office-holders. While English monasticism had been organized within the Benedictine order, new orders were emerging on the continent which would soon extend their influence to Britain. The Norman establishment had a particular enthusiasm for the ideals of the monks of Cluny in Burgundy, who, since 910, had been directly responsible only to the Pope. The Cluniacs, emerging as a distinct order in the eleventh century, were noted for the single-minded emphasis given to liturgy and ceremonial, influences which had coloured the *Regularis Concordia* and had come to England via the sympathetic communities at Fleury and Ghent. A request from William I to St Hugh of Cluny for the establishment of Cluniac organizations in England was turned down, and strangely it was in the reign of his perverted and scarcely God-fearing son, William Rufus (1087–1100), that the Cluniacs enjoyed even greater royal favour. Although thirty-six Cluniac priories were established in England during the century which fol-

The strange Augustinian church at Wymondham, Norfolk.

lowed the Conquest, most were small foundations; three houses were established in Scotland, including Crossraguel Abbey, Strathclyde, founded in the early thirteenth century. But the enthusiasm for the Cluniacs did not last, partly because some houses milked the kingdom for revenues that were sent to sister foundations on the continent and offered little in return. By the close of the Norman period benefactors generally must have become bored with the Cluniacs, whose obsessive praying and ceremonial seemed to consume all their energies.

The impact of the Cistercians was to prove much more profound. The order was founded in 1097 at Cistercium or Cîteaux in Burgundy by zealous monks seeking to recreate the asceticism which had distinguished the earliest Benedictine foundations. The Cistercians arrived at Waverley in Surrey in 1128, but they were preceded in England by the followers of an older order, the Canons of St Augustine, the Austin or Black Canons, who became established at St Botolph's Priory in Colchester about 1103. This movement was rooted in efforts to impose a stricter, if less than monastic, rule on chapters of canons, such as those associated with the minster churches, who had sometimes become lax and acquisitive. Less remote and unworldly than the Cluniac monks, the Austin Canons had a broad commitment to prayer and to preaching, which they sought to reinforce by the example of pious living. They enjoyed both popular support and royal patronage, acquiring almost 150 houses during the twelfth century, with more than 200 establishments by the time of the Plague. Most of these were small priories or churches whose patronage they had obtained and there were only 13 establishments of abbey rank. Individual canons were appointed to serve as vicars when a priory obtained the patronage or 'advowson' of neighbouring parish churches. Austin churches were sometimes shared with parishioners, and at Wymondham in Norfolk there is the strange sight of a massive church with two towers. Double use of the church by the abbey and parishioners created rivalries still expressed by the two massive towers. The larger of the Augustinian houses which still display impressive remains include Bristol, which became a cathedral after the Dissolution, Guisborough Priory in Cleveland, Carlisle Cathedral Priory and Lanercost Priory in Cumbria, Thornton Abbey in Humberside, St Augustine's Abbey in Canterbury, Walsingham Priory in Norfolk, Bolton Priory and Kirkham Priory

in North Yorkshire, Christ Church Cathedral in Oxford, Haughmond Abbey in Shropshire, Jedburgh Abbey in the Borders, Inchcolm Abbey in the Firth of Forth off the coast of Fife, Llanthony Priory in Gwent and Penmon Priory (NT) on Anglesey.

While the Augustinians followed their vocations amidst the currents of day-to-day life, the Cistercians or White Monks sought seclusion from the affairs of the sinful world. In spite of this the order attracted remarkable support in Europe, controlling some 750 abbeys by the close of the Middle Ages. The order enjoyed phenomenal popularity during the twelfth century, and influential people were clearly impressed by the Cistercian desire for peace, solitude and poverty under an egalitarian rule, by their refusal to accept the feudal perks or indulge in ecclesiastical profiteering, and by their desire for grants of barren land in isolated places rather than for prosperous and well-ordered manors. Although the order came initially to Surrey, it was the wastelands of the North which beckoned. There the Normans had created good Cistercian country as a result of the evil Harrying; the landscape had still not recovered and the ravaged and overgrown environments were ripe for recolonization.

Although the Cistercians were presumed to blend

ABOVE *The Augustinian priory of Penmon (NT) on Anglesey, Gwynedd.*

RIGHT *The monks at Fountains (NT), North Yorkshire, thoroughly exploited the adjacent stream which, amongst other things, helped to cleanse a virtual fleet of lavatories.*

compassion with their more spartan virtues, their arrival and expansion in the North were marked by the ruthless destruction of communities of peasants who were similarly engaged in the rehabilitation of the countryside. Thirty White Monks arrived at Rievaulx (North Yorkshire) in 1132, settling on lands in the Rye valley donated by Walter l'Espec, Lord of Helmsley. By 1216 the magnificent abbey supported a community of 140 monks and almost 600 lay brothers. (As an indication of the general decline of the monasteries, on the eve of the Dissolution Rievaulx harboured only 32 monks and 122 servants, although this represented a recovery from the situation in 1380, following the onslaughts of the Pestilence, when the community comprised only 15 monks and 3 lay brothers.)

If any single abbey encapsulates the story of the Cistercians, it must be Fountains (NT) – now probably the most impressive and beautiful of all abbey

ruins. Like the order itself, Fountains originated in a disenchantment with Benedictine organization, for in 1132 a group of thirteen Benedictine monks at the Abbey of St Mary's in York approached the archbishop with the request that they be placed under a stricter rule. The unpopular defectors were settled on barren lands in Skeldale near Ripon – and there they might have perished had they not been admitted to the Cistercian order and provided with an instructor. A period of hardship and victimization was followed by a century of spectacular building and the acquisition of an empire of landholdings which stretched beyond the Pennines and into Cumbria.

The very success of the White Monks' seemingly idealistic code resulted in the transformation of the order. Esteem and popularity in the twelfth and thirteenth centuries brought endowments amounting to an embarrassment of riches; the desire to be insulated from the evils of the day-to-day world produced inhumane evictions when estates were obtained which supported substantial peasant communities, and the fruits of Cistercian zeal and diligence were vast tracts of productive land turned over to great and highly lucrative flocks of sheep. The most important factor in this saga of material success was the use made of *conversi* or lay brothers, existing as large 'worker bee' colonies attached to each abbey. The lay brothers were kept illiterate and worshipped at the start and end of the working day, otherwise their time was devoted to building, farming and generally supporting the smaller community of monks. As the monastic estate expanded, so the lay brothers were settled in dispersed farmsteads or 'granges', some of them built on the sites of depopulated peasant villages, and some, like Ramsgill in Nidderdale (North Yorkshire), destined to become villages during and after the demise of the monastic system. The earthly success contained the seeds of corruption, and eventually the Cistercians were no more scrupulous than the Benedictine landlords in squeezing the maximum of feudal revenue from their holdings. These came to include peasant communities and assets which increased in number as the system of operating granges by lay brothers was superseded by one of leases and tenancies.

All the Cistercian houses in Britain were descended from the parent foundation at Cîteaux, many via a branch formed by the influential Abbey of Clairvaux. In Britain the new houses were prolific, spawning daughter foundations throughout the

The late twelfth-century abbey church at Abbey Dore, Hereford and Worcester.

island, with Fountains and Rievaulx together producing 30 offshoots. By the end of the twelfth century there were more than 100 Cistercian houses in England and Wales, and further expansion in Wales, Scotland and Ireland continued into the thirteenth century. The Cistercian houses which still display impressive ruins include Furness and Calder in Cumbria, Hailes (NT) in Gloucestershire, Beaulieu and Netley in Hampshire, Abbey Dore in Hereford and Worcester, Sawley and Whalley in Lancashire, Byland, Fountains, Jervaulx and Rievaulx in North Yorkshire, Buildwas in Shropshire, Cleeve in Somerset, Roche in South Yorkshire, Croxden in Staffordshire, Kirkstall in West Yorkshire, Melrose in the Borders, Dundrennan, Glenluce and Sweetheart in Dumfries and Galloway, Valle Crucis and Basingwerk in Clwyd, Strata Florida in Dyfed, Tintern in Gwent and Cymmer in Gwynedd.

Another defection from the Benedictine order was that of the Tironensian monks. This order was founded in 1109 at Tiron Abbey in France around the principle of austerity, and one of its characteristics was that the practice of handicrafts in the cloister was an important activity. The Tironensians attracted the support of David I of Scotland (1124–53), so that although the order remained insignificant in England it achieved several important establishments north of the border, including Kelso (Borders), Lindores (Fife) and Arbroath (Tayside). St Dogmael's Abbey in Dyfed was the only abbey of the order in Wales, although there were priories at Pill and Caldy in the same county.

An order which was partly modelled on the Cistercians and which was therefore rather overshadowed by their spectacular success was that of the Premonstratensian Canons, which had its nucleus at Prémontré near Laon. This order sought to stiffen the backbone of other orders of canons and stood to the Augustinians rather as the Cistercians did to the Benedictines. Canons of this order also sought foundations in desolate places, but they did not arrive in England until 1143, by which time the Cistercians had collared the most promising sites and the pick of the endowments. The 31 abbeys and 3 nunneries of the Premonstratensians tended to be rather impoverished, but they did include Bayham in East Sussex, sometimes described as the 'Fountains of the South'. Impressive remains of their houses can also be seen at Shap in Cumbria, Egglestone in Co. Durham, Titchfield in Hampshire, Easby in North Yorkshire, Dryburgh in Borders and Talley in Dyfed.

If the Premonstratensians were strict, the stern aspect of monastic life was carried to its extremes by

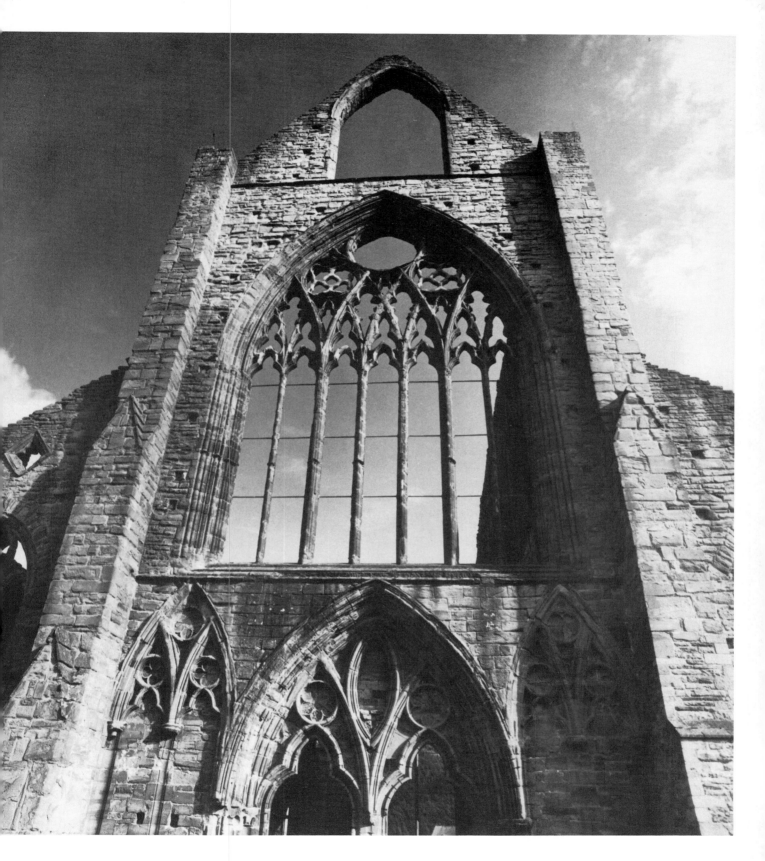

LEFT *The roofless ruins at Tintern Abbey, Gwent, allow one to appreciate how Gothic buildings were constructed in a way which concentrated the thrusts on piers and buttresses.*

Superb Decorated tracery at Tintern Abbey. The abbey was founded in 1131, but extensively rebuilt during the thirteenth and fourteenth centuries.

the Carthusians, born in 1084 of an attempt to recreate the eremetical lifestyles of early Christian Egypt – but initially in mountainous areas near Grenoble, where it was somewhat colder. The Carthusians lived in small priories accommodating no more than 12 monks and 18 lay brothers. The latter did most of the physical work of the community, while the monks spent long hours in solitude in their private cells, praying, reading and writing and emerging thrice daily for services in the priory church. This severe lifestyle was made harsher by the spartan vegetarian diet (consisting only of bread and water on three days of the week), and by wearing meagre garments of the coarsest cloth. And so it is not too surprising that the 'Charterhouses' of the Carthusians were not overwhelmed by throngs of hopeful recruits. The first was established at Witham in Selwood in Somerset as a part of the penance of Henry II for his unfortunate role in the Becket affair. Few new foundations followed, the most notable being Mount Grace Priory (NT) in North Yorkshire.

If the twelfth century belonged to the Cistercians, it was the friars who captured the popular imagination in the thirteenth. To some extent a need for the friars was created by a partial disillusionment with the existing orders, which had moved quite rapidly from conditions of poverty and austerity to prosperity and power. This need was most intense in the bustling towns which were shunned by the seekers after solitude. The Dominican or Black Friars, founded by Dominic of Osma, an Austin Canon, originated in an attempt to create an order of learned and erudite preachers who could counter the spread of heresies on the continent. The Franciscans or Grey Friars, one of the most appealing and democratic of the medieval orders, developed from amongst the disciples of Francis of Assisi, who had led a Christ-like life of poverty and devotion. Not being bound to any convent, the friars exploded on the British scene at the start of the thirteenth century and the two orders became established in thirty English towns. They were welcomed by bishops and townsfolk and patronized by royalty, though they were often unwelcome in the vicinity of great established abbeys, where their humility and zeal was sometimes chastening and unsettling. In due course other orders of friars, the Carmelites or White Friars, the Austin Friars, the Friars of the Holy Cross and more obscure orders – such as the Friars of the Penitential Sack – arrived to found several more institutions.

The enduring legacy of buildings inherited from the friars is quite disproportionate to their influence in England, and consists only of fragmentary relics. This reflects their repudiation of worldly comforts and possessions, which sometimes led friars to live in cellars and hovels. It is also a result of the fact that they entrusted their buildings to corporations of citizens, and of the urban setting of their work, which has resulted in churches and conventual buildings being obliterated by urban redevelopment rather than being left to decay quietly in isolated rural settings. No English priory of theirs has survived complete and the only intact friars' church is St Andrew's Hall in Norwich. 'Black Friars' in Newcastle upon Tyne has been restored in recent years. The church is reduced to foundations, but the cloister remains – albeit somewhat altered by the guilds who were granted it after the Dissolution.

Finally, there were the military orders, the Hospitallers and Templars, who were born of the Crusades. Both orders were charged with the succour and protection of pilgrims and enjoyed a flood of endowments generated by the climate of popular sentiment inspired by the Crusades. Each order had its convent in the Holy Land and a priory headquarters in London, and these priories were supported by a dispersed empire of estates, known as 'commanderies' or 'preceptories'. By the end of the thirteenth century the prosperous means which the Templars controlled seem to have distracted the order from its prime crusading goals, and the order was suppressed by the papacy in 1312, amid a welter of colourful and bizarre accusations. The Hospitallers, now centred on the crusading stronghold of Rhodes, emerged as the main beneficiaries of the Templars' forfeit properties. The surviving relics of the military orders include circular churches such as the ones at Little Maplestead in Essex and at Cambridge, modelled on the Church of the Holy Sepulchre in Jerusalem, and estate buildings such as the thirteenth-century wheat and barley barns at Cressing Temple in Essex. Otherwise most but not all of the many 'Temple' placenames in England help to identify the commanderies.

These then were the main orders of monks, canons and friars that were active in Britain. Lionel Butler and C. Given-Wilson have estimated that in the thirteenth century England supported almost 8000 monks, including 4000 Benedictines and 3000 Cistercians; around 5000 canons, including 3000 Augustinians; about 7000 nuns and 500 Hospitallers and Templars. To this total of around 20,000 monks, nuns and canons should be added a substantial if uncertain number of friars, but it still does not represent the full conventual population. This figure would have included several thousand lay brothers, whose numbers were to dwindle substantially as monastic holdings were sublet, and a good number of novices. The same authors suggest that there may have been some 40,000 people employed as monastic servants of one kind or another. Significantly, the number of monks, nuns and canons had declined to only around 10,500 by the Reformation. Since we do not know the actual population of England in the thirteenth century, it is not possible to estimate the exact demographic significance of the conventual populations, but one might guess that about one person in fifty was either a member of a monastic community or employed directly by one. It will therefore have been extremely common for a family to have had at least one member in a religious house, in one capacity or another.

The Church, through its various institutions, was also the largest landholder in the kingdom; Lewes Priory alone had land in 223 different parishes. On the eve of the Reformation it was alleged that clergy held one third of the nation's wealth and at that time Westminster Abbey had an astronomical yearly income of £3470, and several other abbeys had incomes of more than £2000. To put these figures into some sort of perspective, the total annual Crown revenue available to James IV of Scotland (1488–1513) at the start of the sixteenth century was about £11,000. When the English monasteries were dissolved, their lands, with an annual value of £90,000, were sold for £780,000.

Much of the wealth which had been yielded by the rents, profits, and tolls of several centuries was

Bar tracery made its English debut at Binham Priory in Norfolk. Inside there is a magnificent late medieval seven-sacrament font.

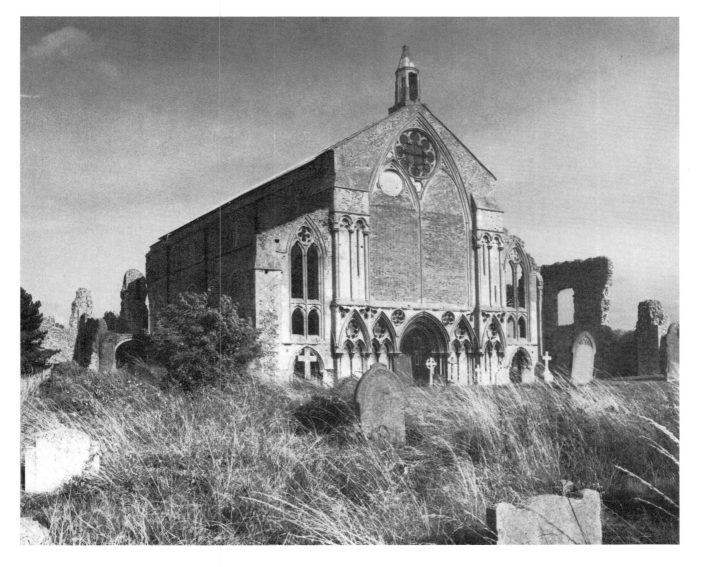

embodied in the fabric of the monastic buildings. These were now unroofed, demolished or pillaged for stone, or else incorporated in the Tudor and Elizabethan mansions of those who had purchased the abbey lands. (At Titchfield in Hampshire the changes were remarkable, for the nave walls were absorbed into a battlemented gate-house.)

The main phases of abbey and priory building coincided with those of the cathedrals. There was a lively rate of building during most of the currency of the Early English style and phenomenal activity during the Norman and Decorated phases. In contrast, relatively little was accomplished in the Perpendicular style, which arrived when the monastic high summer had declined into autumn. Some new building, however, was undertaken right up to the Dissolution, most notably the magnificent Perpendicular tower built by Abbot Marmaduke Huby in 1494–1526 at Fountains, while the splendid Abbot's parlour at Muchelney in Somerset dates from 1508.

In several cases the abbey builders acted as innovators, and the features which they introduced greatly influenced the contemporary architectural scene. A good example is Binham Priory in Norfolk, which, together with Westminster Abbey, was one of the first two English buildings to employ elegant bar tracery, adopting the new fenestration from France in the 1240s. Another, much later, exercise in monastic trend-setting was the progressive use of brick, largely neglected since Roman times, which

was combined with stone in the late fourteenth-century gate-house at Thornton in Humberside, while brickwork at the late twelfth-century abbey at Little Coggeshall in Essex is sometimes regarded as the earliest medieval use of brick. When closely inspected the surviving buildings may tell one the story of the evolution of architecture. At Castle Acre or at Ely one can see Norman shafts and mouldings embellishing the first pointed windows, heralding the arrival of the Early English style. Similarly at Melrose the transition from Decorated to Perpendicular tracery is enshrined in the abbey church, while at Rievaulx the second row of windows in the north transept announces the arrival of the Gothic style. Much of the architecture and decoration displayed in surviving monastic buildings is unsurpassed – the forest of piers and vaulting in the cellarium at Fountains, the Decorated tracery in the east windows at Dorchester Abbey church, the uniquely elongated eastern range at Furness, with its

PREVIOUS PAGE *The remarkable late twelfth-century cellarium at Fountains Abbey (NT), North Yorkshire, is more than 90 metres (c. 300 ft) in length; the northern end contained cellarage and the southern end served as the lay brothers' frater.*

BELOW *Dorchester in Oxfordshire was a Saxon cathedral centre and the Augustinian abbey was founded in 1140. Like several other Augustinian churches its dual role as a parish church enabled it to survive the Dissolution.*

superb Norman arches, and the stern Norman nave at Dunfermline Abbey in Fife are among the many exceptional features which could form part of a very long list.

For most visitors, however, the stroll round a ruined abbey site is something of a magical mystery tour, with spectacular pageants of standing masonry alternating with the rectilinear patterns formed by excavated footings, and with different components identified by strange labels like 'frater' or 'slype'. Consequently, the different ranges seem to form a maze and it is difficult to imagine them combined in a coherent entity. While the monasteries were not built to a stereotyped plan, there were many common features in the arrangement of the buildings. Worship and ritual occupied a central place in the life and routine of any monastic community, so that the focus of the building complex was the abbey or priory church, and within this church the choir was the scene of the repetitive activity of the seven services. Beside the church, and linked to it via a passage and staircase leading to the south transept, was the monks' dormitory or 'dorter', initially at least a vast, barracks-like chamber, placed here to reduce the discomforts of night services. While the church was the spiritual focus of the religious community, the exclusive rectangle of the cloister was the hub of the monastic site. It was normally set in the angle formed by the south transept and at its centre was a square garth, where herbs and vegetables could be grown. The monks sat around the northern side of the cloister in alcoves, working and studying in silence. Conversation was permitted in the 'slype', a broad corridor running between the chapter house and south transept and connecting the cloister with the monks' cemetery. The chapter house, a room or building reserved for formal meetings of the monastic body, for hearing confessions and resolving disciplinary problems, was commonly set on the eastern side of the cloister, with the dormitories often placed above and beyond it. The refectory or 'frater' and its associated kitchen, built above cellars, occupied the space to the south of the cloister, so that the main functions and activities of monastic life – prayer, study, eating and sleeping – were organized around the cloister garth. The lodgings of the head of the house and guest rooms often closed the western side of the cloister.

In many cases the ranges round the cloister were insufficient to accommodate all the functions of monastic life. The infirmary, with its own chapel and refectory, stood apart from the other ranges and was used not only for the sick but also for aged members of the community who were unequal to the rigours

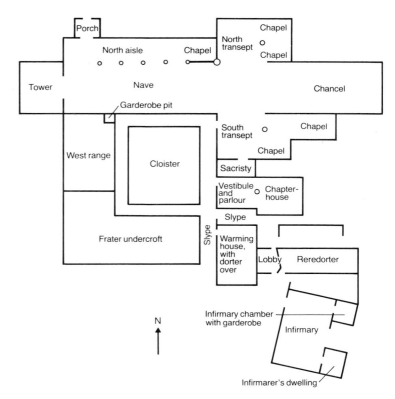

Shap Abbey, Cumbria, showing a fairly typical abbey layout.

of conventional monastic life. Accommodation for novices, the abbot's kitchen and, where the nature of the water supply advised it, the 'reredorter' or lavatory could also exist as separate ranges. There could also be storage buildings and more specialized structures – like the dovecote at Penmon. Occasionally, as at Crossraguel, one may see the remains of the dwellings of 'corrodians'. These were lay folk who had purchased an individual or family annuity from the monastery, guaranteeing support and shelter in old age, and sometimes allowing the aged to take holy orders and be buried in the monks' cemetery. Such arrangements proved costly to the monastery when the corrodian lived to a ripe old age, and at times of financial hardship a community might engage in the injudicial sale of corrodies.

Although this brief outline plan would allow the modern visitor to pick a path around many monastic sites, the arrangements were fairly flexible and some layouts departed considerably from this model. Different facets of monastic life have survived in different places. At Gloucester the alcoves in which the monks sat at desks or 'carrels' around the cloister still remain; at Glastonbury there is a fine abbot's kitchen; at Fountains and Lilleshall (Shropshire) one

can see the recesses in the stonework which served as book cupboards, and a well-preserved infirmary chapel endures at Furness (Cumbria). Even so, with the monastic buildings now either serving as secular cathedrals, fragmentary components of later mansions, like Anglesey Abbey (NT) in Cambridgeshire, or as gaunt ruins, it is not easy to see them as what they were, functional structures serving a large and active community of monks, lay brothers and servants. The monasteries were the contemporary equivalents of top-class hotels, universities, estate offices, typing pools, halls of residence, old folks' homes and counting houses all combined. Even if the buildings had survived the ravages of the Reformation untouched, a visit to a silent monastery would be rather like a trip to Lords or Headingley cricket grounds in the depths of winter. To picture the abbey or priory as a living entity one must imagine the patter of cold feet along candlelit corridors followed by the haunting sounds of plainsong, seeping into the night through the towering black walls of the choir. Similarly, there would have been a clatter of locker doors around the cloister as books were sought between services, and a flurry of chores and an atmosphere of excited anticipation preceding the return of the abbot from important meetings in distant places – and all the other sounds, emotions, colours and smells of life in a large, complex and highly organized institution. But now it is the serenity of the ruins which impress rather than the more human qualities of regimented bustle and devotion.

In any exploration of medieval monasteries it is always interesting to look for the architectural clues which still announce the identity of the different orders. The Cluniac commitment to liturgy and glorious ceremonial is still apparent in ruins such as Castle Acre, with its magnificent display of blind arcading in the west facade of the church and the use of chequerboard patterns of red and white stone in the piers of the aisle. The Cistercians, in contrast, embodied their quest for austerity in their churches, which were uncluttered with ornament though spacious, stylish and serene. There were other differences in the Cistercian buildings which reflected the particular priorities of the order. In most abbey churches the nave was set apart for use by lay folk, but the exclusiveness of the Cistercian life resulted in the naves of their churches being reserved for the large congregation of lay brothers. The most individual adaptations of the monastic layout to the requirements of a particular order were found in the Charterhouses of the Carthusian monks. At Mount Grace Priory (NT) the architecture is characteristically modest and austere, and one can still see the diamond-shaped great cloister and monks' cemetery surrounded by the relics of the small individual cells and their attached gardens – essential features of an order which placed so much emphasis on a severe, hermit-like existence.

Entry into monastic orders was a privilege that was not open to all. The conditions of life which were then experienced depended very much upon the date concerned, the particular order and its relative piety or laxity. More often than not the successful novice embarked on a life which was testing, punctuated with long hours of boredom and discomfort and demanding of a high degree of self discipline. And yet, for all these hardships and restrictions, it is not easy to resist the thought that, were one to be flung out of a 'time machine' and marooned in the Middle Ages, then membership of an order might well seem the most attractive goal. There one would not freeze or starve, one would be relatively safe from marauding lords and common thugs, the company would be civilized if rather silent, the music good and the conditions of cleanliness far superior to anything existing in the world outside. Of course, there are quite a few people today who will point out that all these selfish considerations are insignificant and that the monasteries provided unique opportunities for piety and devotion. In the twelfth and thirteenth centuries there were thousands who would have agreed.

The vaulted undercroft of the Augustinian priory of St Olave's near Great Yarmouth, Norfolk, is excellently preserved, though other remains of the priory are modest.

10
Town and Country in Medieval Britain

The bond-tenants aforesaid, on account of certain grievances which they were told the abbot made them suffer, went to complain to the king aforesaid, carrying with them their iron ploughshares; and the king said to them: 'As villeins you have come, and as villeins you shall return.'

The tenants of the Abbot of Vale Royal take their grievances to King Edward III in 1336.

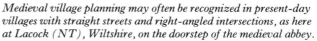

Medieval village planning may often be recognized in present-day villages with straight streets and right-angled intersections, as here at Lacock (NT), Wiltshire, on the doorstep of the medieval abbey.

The medieval period is sometimes regarded as an age of torpor, a time when change was slight and slow-moving. The field archaeologist will take a different view, seeing the centuries leading up to the grim events of 1348 as a period of active recolonization and transformation. It was a time which witnessed the recovery of the farmlands which were surrendered during the disasters and confusion of the early Dark Age centuries, the foundation of thousands of new villages and the reinstatement of the town as an important facet of the British scene. Also, whereas the schoolroom version of the Middle Ages often highlights the supposedly disorganized and hap-hazard nature of medieval development, the archaeologist is impressed by the high degree of planning which is so frequently evident in the settlements of the age.

The Romans had been able to capitalize on the remarkable successes of Iron Age farming and had superimposed coherent patterns of urbanization and communications on the essential bedrock of agricultural prosperity. In the centuries following the Norman Conquest the Roman levels of population were equalled and then perhaps surpassed. Yet although the countryfolk of medieval England often trod the same roads as their Romanized forebears, their countryside, with its villages and strip fields, was frequently quite different from that of Roman times. By the fourteenth century the tide of success was again turning. The pressures of sustained population growth had caused the exhaustion of many of the poorer lands, the climate was deteriorating, villages and hamlets were being abandoned and the stage was set for a new disaster epic in which Nature and the landlords would wage war on the rural communities.

Living on the Land

After about 800 the signs of recovery and change were apparent in some British countrysides. By the time of the Norman Conquest England was a relatively prosperous kingdom, and although the defeat at Hastings was followed by years of unrest and by the gruesome massacres in the north, in the twelfth and thirteenth centuries the population appears to have grown at an exceptionally rapid rate. If, as has been said, there were more people living in late Bronze Age Britain than were present at the time of the Norman Conquest, it may also be true that there were more people here in the reign of Edward I than ever before – and more than lived here in the reign of Elizabeth I. We will never again see landscapes as crowded with real countryfolk. There are many villages which are known to have doubled in size

between the time of Domesday Book and the arrival of the Great Pestilence, and at a guess Britain supported a population of around or over six million at the start of the fourteenth century. The overwhelming majority of these people were peasant farmers of various kinds. Such heavy rural populations could only be supported because lands which had become desolate early in the Dark Ages were being brought back into production, along with the reclamation of some fenland, salt marsh and moorland, while new methods of communal farming – like the open field system – were being adopted and extended.

In Chapter 3 open field farming was mentioned, with the promise of a more detailed description here. This was a complicated and variable method of communal farming. It involved remarkably detailed arrangements for the synchronization of cooperative efforts, with oxen being swapped around the village to form the plough teams, and intricate regulations being enforced to protect the boundaries of the frag-mented tenancies, keep the horn away from the corn and implement the plans for cropping and fallowing. Further complications resulted from particular local customs which were ingrained in the working relationships of each manor. But for all this, in the areas where the system was adopted it enjoyed a useful life of up to a thousand years and, despite the claims of its detractors, it was by no means a primitive and inefficient method of farming, although it could only operate in a highly disciplined society.

During the later Saxon and the early medieval centuries, open field farming was adopted in thousands of cell-like areas, which one can only presume were old estates. Each of these units tended to encompass a range of different types of land. The deeper and better drained soils were designated as ploughland, the low-lying and damper places became hay meadows. Small paddocks around the settlements and other areas on the slopes beyond the ploughlands were pastures, while the 'waste' of woodland and common occupied the poorer and more outlying portions of the estate. Each of the different types of farm-land made an invaluable contribution to the semi-sufficiency of peasant life. Geese might be grazed on the green, milk cows or vegetables could be supported on the compact 'closes' or ribbon-like 'tofts' which contained the house plots. The ploughlands yielded grain and legumes and provided open grazing during their regular fallow phases. The hay meadows provided winter fodder, essential when the grass ceased to grow on the closely cropped pastures and commons, while the waste produced vital supplies of constructional timber, fuel, bedding and woodland 'pannage', or fodder, for herds of swine. The typical

Medieval woods often resembled this managed woodland in the RSPB reserve of Wolves Wood in Suffolk, with tall standards growing above the coppiced underwood.

wood stood inside ditched wood banks and was divided into different sections which were felled according to various rotations to yield timbers of different sizes and qualities. Some trees, destined to provide studs, posts and beams for dwellings and barns, stood tall above the coppiced underwood, which was cleared every six years or so to yield light timber for fuel, wattle, hurdles and poles. In many other places livestock grazed amongst the mighty pollarded trees, which produced a crop of poles from the crown of the pollarded trunk well above the reach of browsers.

The use of each and every resource in the agricultural mosaic was governed by detailed customs and regulations, and the arrangements were most complicated on the ploughlands of the open fields. Villages developed as the foci of the local farming empires, sucking in the populations of scattered hamlets, and each village in open field country was at the hub of a set of two, three or more gigantic fields. Striping each field were the 'riggs' or plough ridges,

giving the bare winter ploughland the texture of a patchwork made from brown corduroy patches. These ridges were long ribbons of land, domed in cross section, that were deliberately created with the use of a mould board plough which turned the sod inwards towards the spine of the ridge. The creation of a corrugated surface of ridges and intervening furrows must have assisted the drainage of the heavier soils, and ridging may not have been practised on some lighter lands. Adjacent ridges were combined in groups of two or several to form strips or 'selions', and a moderately well-endowed peasant family might tenant around thirty such strips, averaging about 1 acre (*c*. half a hectare) each in area and scattered around the different open fields. Strips, all with the same orientation, were combined as blocks in furlongs or

LEFT *Low winter sunlight illuminates the corduroy patterns of ridge and furrow ploughland underlying an old Northamptonshire pasture.*

BELOW LEFT *Flights of medieval strip lynchets traverse the middle slopes in this Wharfedale tributary valley and appear to cut an older pattern of vertical lynchets.*

'shotts'. These were the major divisions of the open fields and, depending on time and custom, crop rotations could be operated on each furlong rather than on each larger open field. In some places it is possible that the furlongs equated to pre-existing fields which had been absorbed into the new open field arrangements.

The origins of this system of farming are still obscure and hotly debated, but it must have begun to spread by a process of imitation around the difficult period of the Danish invasions. Its adoption may have been connected with the fact that population pressure was beginning to be felt in some places. Since open field farming allows ploughland to be more intensively used, this would have released other areas, which had formerly been ploughed periodically, to serve as permanent pasture or meadow. At one level the new system can only have spread with the agreement and active support of the various aristocratic estate owners, while at another it must have involved peasant farmers coming together to live in larger, more compact settlements and develop a more integrated and cooperative system of working the land. Some elements of the system may already have been present, and recent work in the north of England has suggested that ridged ploughland probably existed in late Iron Age times. Excavation and

field walking in locations in Yorkshire and the Midlands have also revealed the existence, in late Saxon times, of remarkably elongated field strips and furlongs. But we still do not understand the process which brought the various elements of the system together. Neither is it really known why it was thought practical for tenants to have their strip holdings scattered around the open fields, for one cannot see how this contributed to the efficiency of farming. In the most elaborate cases an arrangement now known as 'solskift' operated, in which each village peasant had the same strip-holding neighbours in the open fields as he or she had at home in the village. It is strange to think that while the system, in essence, worked successfully in some places until around the time of the Crimean War (1854–6), we have still to discover how it was created. Currently there is some reason to believe that most open-field systems were the products of detailed and comprehensive local planning, and ultimately it is likely that this particular puzzle will be solved.

In some places open field farming had begun to disappear well before the close of the Middle Ages. Often this resulted from a process of 'enclosure by agreement', with the various tenants and yeomen agreeing to the exchange of strips of ploughland and meadow so as to obtain consolidated fields. The evictions and clearances of the Tudor and later centuries, described below, also helped to eradicate local systems of peasant farming, yet a great many of them survived into the eighteenth and nineteenth centuries, when, with very few exceptions, the field strips and the former commons were obliterated by the multitude of Acts of Parliamentary Enclosure.

Until quite recently one could commonly see the precise outlines of medieval plough ridges, headlands and furlongs plainly outlined in pasture. Such features were preserved as earthworks when medieval ploughlands were converted into permanent pasture or when areas of old farmland were engulfed by parks. Since the outbreak of World War II, however, this facet of the historical heritage has been severely eroded by ploughing and reseeding, practices which have gained momentum as a result of the astronomical EEC subsidies available to crop producers. In parts of northern and western England and the Midlands, where old pasture still survives, one can still see the corrugations of the old plough ridges. Walking round the fields, one can piece together the medieval agricultural jigsaw, seeing the raised headlands where the ox plough turned; the attenuated riggs, usually shaped like a stretched C or a backwards S, curving as the plough was swung to commence its turn; the changes in the orientation of the riggs at the junction of two furlongs, or the hollows of field tracks and entrances. Such fascinating relics are now rarely seen surviving amongst the prairie fields in the battered landscapes of the east, though at the time of writing one half of Wimpole Park (NT) in Cambridgeshire

still contains a particularly important set of medieval agricultural earthworks.

In a handful of places in England living strip fields escaped the various assaults of progress and survive in forms that have been modified by the gradual processes of evolution and amalgamation. The most celebrated strip network is at Laxton in Nottinghamshire, a fascinating village which has preserved the feudal institutions of farming and which, incidentally, has good motte-and-bailey earthworks. Strip holdings can be seen around Soham in Cambridgeshire, while others, of a rather different form, pattern the slopes behind the cliffs at Forrabury, Boscastle, Cornwall. A much more extensive network

formed the Great Field at Braunton in Devon. The Great Field, one of the village's two main open fields, covered some 350 acres (*c.* 145 hectares) and was divided into a pattern of small strips, each about $\frac{1}{4}$ acre (*c.* $\frac{1}{10}$ hectare) in area. Subsequent amalgamations had produced strips of over twenty times this size by recent times. Each furlong here had its name and some, like 'Longlands' and 'Pitlands', are known to have existed since they were recorded in 1324. To the north of the Great Field there are both squarish and strip-shaped fields that were once part of the open field and which have the curving hedgerows that are characteristic of early enclosure by agreement. The field was further reduced in 1811 when

the adjacent Braunton Marsh was enclosed.

Most children learn something about medieval open field farming at school, and usually the myth that this was the only or the typical form of farming practised is perpetuated. But even in its heartland in the Midlands the system was not stereotyped. In the Chilterns, for example, Tom Williamson and Liz Bellamy have described how the patterns of medieval farming contrasted, with the more characteristic Midlands situation prevailing below in the Vale of Aylesbury, while in the hills the villages were much smaller and the land was also worked from many dispersed farmsteads and hamlets. There were more extensive areas of wood and common on the higher ground, and also more small, hedged fields or closes which were individually owned and tenanted. There were not many extensive tracts of good ploughland, so instead of there being vast open fields, the communal ploughland existed in many smaller pockets, with many farmers tenanting strips only in the fields lying closest to their farmsteads. Rather than possessing two or three open fields as was normal in the Vale, some Chilterns parishes had many; Great Gaddesden in Hertfordshire, for example, had twenty small open fields. Other counties in the English lowlands, such as Essex and Kent, included many areas where small, individually owned or tenanted hedged fields were more common than the large, communally worked ones.

In the north and far west the situation was different again. Here the land tended to be of lower quality and the climate more severe. Although the 'conventional' two or three field systems could operate well in equable farming areas like the Vale of York, in most places the most favourable pocket of land was normally designated as permanent ploughland and existed as an 'in-field', receiving generous doses of farmyard muck to sustain its fertility. Around the infield were the pastures and hay meadows of the 'outfield', with the extensive waste, common or moor beyond. Patches of out-field land were periodically ploughed, cropped to exhaustion, and then left to recover as pasture for several years. A fine small infield, now enclosed, can be admired by visitors to Wast Water at Wasdale Head in Cumbria.

Each locality in Britain had its own position on the spectrum between the fat villages of the Midlands open field country and the small scattered hamlet patterns of the north and west. Thus, in the northern

The old in-field at Wasdale Head near Wast Water, Cumbria; note the enclosure walls and the scatter of clearance cairns holding stones picked from the ploughland.

uplands the townships were federations of small hamlets, contrasting with the parishes of the Midlands counties, which might, by the High Middle Ages, contain just one compact village with dozens of packed peasant dwellings. In the Celtic countries open field farming of the Midlands type was very rarely found, and then only in parts of the east of Ireland, Pembrokeshire, the Welsh borders and Cornish lowlands where powerful Norman feudal influences had wrought far-reaching transformations. Otherwise this was hamlet or *clachan* country, where regional variations of the in-field, out-field, or 'one field' system were operated.

In a few quite marginal environments, like the moors of the southwest, and often under some form of feudal sponsorship, pioneering farmsteads were periodically established as attempts to colonize areas of rough moorland grazing. Many were abandoned as the tides of reclamation turned. Another facet which was evident on upland estates which had passed into Cistercian hands was the monastic grange. All these forms of settlement and field system were likely to change as time passed by and as the emphasis on the estates shifted from communal tillage and pasturing to individual tenancies. While a few hamlets and granges might blossom into villages, many more would collapse into solitary farmsteads or disappear completely.

Change was not confined to the upland provinces. In England one can still recognize the evidence of medieval developments wherever the modern fashion for prairie farming has not yet devastated the historical landscape. Hedged fields with curving margins often commemorate the agreements by which tenants enclosed former open-field strips. Other little hedged enclosures further from the old ploughland may be recognized as 'assarts', hacked from the woods which had engulfed Roman farmland during the depths of the Dark Ages. Such clearings were not readily surrendered, and it was only the intense pressure on the land that resulted from the dramatic surge in population growth, and the periodic impecunity of the mighty, which prompted the sale of licences to assart the cherished and productive woodland. Occasionally assarting took place on quite a grand scale. Thus when Henry II charged 4d per acre for assarting in the Drax area of Yorkshire there must have been quite an influx of hopeful pioneers.

Other consequences of the increase in medieval population can be glimpsed in traditional grazing areas like the Yorkshire Dales, where the faint corrugations of ridge and furrow may just be detected on slopes which can have offered scant encouragement to the ploughman. Far more dramatic are the great flights of terrace-like strip lynchets engraved into steep hill-slopes by contour ploughing. Although similar lynchets dating from much earlier times have recently been recognized in the far north of England, most must represent the desperate attempts of peasant ploughmen to obtain a little more grain in the crowded decades before 1348. Fine flights of lynchets can still be seen in several places: near Malham, Linton and Littondale in the Yorkshire Dales, and in Wessex, near Abbotsbury, Winterbourne Abbas, and Worth Matravers in Dorset, and Coombe Bissett in Wiltshire.

Although some royal hunting forests and deer parks had existed before the Norman Conquest, in the centuries which followed vast areas of countryside were subjected to the despised forest laws (which were codified in 1184), while private deer parks proliferated in most parts of the country. Although royal hunting forests were found in the remote corners of the realm, the heaviest concentrations were in the populous countrysides of the south and Midlands, which were most accessible to the capital. In a pentagon-shaped area with its points at the Thames estuary, the Wash, Shrewsbury, the Bristol Channel and the Hampshire Basin almost half the countryside was under the forest law. This does not mean that these areas were blanketed in woodland, for while the shrinking acres of wood which blotched and stippled the countryside were the refuges of deer and boar, the huntsmen rode across common, meadow and growing crops alike in the pursuit of their unfortunate quarry. In addition to the eighty-six substantial royal forests of the Norman kingdom there were around sixty private 'chases', where the leading aristocrats and churchmen could vent their bloodlust. By the end of the twelfth century the forests and chases had reached their maximum extent and the growing pressure on farmland led to the gradual reduction and conversion of forest land.

The heyday of the deer park arrived rather later, and in the fourteenth century England contained over two thousand of them. The parks were popular and increased in number until the time of the Pestilence, after which many were neglected and abandoned. They were compact hunting areas, often closely associated with a noble manor or lodge, and provided a reliable source of fresh venison when the lord arrived with his retinue of guests. Unlike the great forests and chases, the parks were defined by strong palings, banks and ditches, and their perimeters were breached at intervals by scarp-like deer leaps, which allowed the deer to enter the parks but prevented them from escaping over the steep-faced bank. In places the park boundaries survive as earthworks, while a very small proportion of them still contain deer today, such as those at Bradgate in Charnwood Forest, Leicestershire, or Ripley in North Yorkshire.

This then was the medieval countryside. In all its different moods it was surely a magical place, and today we must go to the richest of small nature reserves to experience the exquisite qualities of meadows spangled with fritillaries or orchids, or to see carefully managed, deciduous woodland. Even a grain field with red, white and blue confetti patterns of poppies, marguerites and cornflowers is now a rare sight – and before very long a thick and properly-tended hedgerow will be an unexpected treat for the rambler. Only in a few specially protected places can we begin to imagine the vibrant beauty of the old countrysides. Most of the roads and lanes which wove their dusty ways across the landscape had been inherited from prehistoric and Roman times. The commons – rather uncommon places today – carpeted the horizons, offering the hope of survival to the poorest peasant family which could claim commoners' rights to pasture a few cows or sheep, dig peat or gather sticks, herbs and bracken. Woods, hay meadows, hedged pastures and the ploughlands blended their hues in the colourful countryside mosaic, and a land which knew no herbicides, pesticides, reseeded pastures or monoculture sparkled with flowers and bubbled with bird song. It was an unjust and often merciless place, but it also offered

invaluable compensations, assets which we today have so easily surrendered.

What remains of the medieval countryside? In some senses the sweat and drudgery of the peasants is still fossilized in lovely churches, magnificent cathedrals and monstrous castles, all paid for by the fruits of servile rural toil. Other glimpses of the past are provided by living hedgerows or by the over-grown earthworks of lynchets, plough ridges, headlands and wood banks. There are other relics too from the agricultural past. Fish-ponds made a vital contribution to the manorial economy, yielding reliable supplies of protein for the lord's table and fresh carp for the Friday meals. They came in various forms, but commonly a shallow rectangular main pond, formed by low earthen banks, was served by several smaller 'stew ponds' in which young fish were raised. In other cases the ponds existed as broad scoops in the ground and most ponds were filled and regulated by streams or canals and systems of small sluices. Examples can be seen as earthworks at several monastic houses, including Fountains Abbey and Bolton Priory in North Yorkshire, or at deserted medieval village sites, like Cublington in Buckinghamshire and Clopton in Cambridgeshire, while a sophisticated complex of fish-ponds can be recog-

The fish-pond of the deserted village of Cublington in Buckinghamshire, with the motte of the Norman castle beyond.

nized as troughs in the lawns at Anglesey Abbey (NT) in Cambridgeshire. Another interesting survival of the important fish-farming economy of the Middle Ages is the late medieval Fish House of the Abbot of Glastonbury at Meare in Somerset. Meare Pool, about 5 kilometres (c. 3 miles) from the abbey, provided about five thousand eel each year, and the rectangular dwelling-cum-storehouse of the abbot's fisherman was built nearby.

Deer parks and fish-ponds both reflected the aristocratic desire for fresh meat in times when there was no refrigeration and when the palate would tire of smoked, salted and decaying provisions. Humbler folk might aspire to keep a pig and so obtain a meagre family ration of bacon (calculated by the local historian Philip Brooks as $3\frac{1}{2}$ ounces (c. 99 grammes) per family per day). Pigs were released to forage on the varied resources of the woodland floor – but often not until their owners had purchased the right to such pannage. Thus in 1292 the men of Bentley in Hampshire, having no common rights to pannage in woods at Luxegrove and Dudingeham, paid the reeve 2d per pig and 1d per piglet.

The right to keep doves, however, was jealously guarded by the landowning classes, whose birds doubtless gorged themselves on peasant corn. This they carried back for the squabs in the dovecote, which were usually eaten before they had mastered the art of flight. A few medieval dovecotes survive, several of them associated with monastic houses. Two of the best surviving examples can be seen at

The (post-Reformation) dovecote at Penmon Priory (NT) on Anglesey.

Penmon (NT) on Anglesey (a post-Reformation structure) and near Bruton in Somerset. The finest of all dovecotes, built just after the close of the Middle Ages by Sir John Gostwick, Cardinal Wolsey's Master of the Horse, from materials pillaged during his involvement in the dissolution of monastic houses, is excellently preserved by the National Trust at Willington in Bedfordshire.

Thousands of small mills were needed to grind the medieval harvest. Particularly in the upland areas where the grain harvest was modest, milling was often accomplished by small 'click mills' with horizontal water-wheels. More substantial water mills existed since at least Roman times and Domesday Book records no less than 157 examples in Sussex alone, with a national total of over 5600. Although the medieval mills have decayed or experienced several rebuildings, many millponds are of a medieval vintage. At the deserted medieval village of Wharram Percy the pond, with a history going right back to a Saxon mill dam, has recently been excavated and restored. An eighth-century water-mill site was excavated at Tamworth in Staffordshire in 1971, and some fragments of a well-constructed timber structure were recovered; reconstructions of Saxon water-wheels are kept in the Science Museum, South Kensington, London. Windmills are said to have been introduced by returning crusaders. The earliest recorded example was at Weedley in east Yorkshire, which was mentioned in 1185. Most medieval windmills will have been very small and flimsy structures of the post-mill type, with a body that revolved upon a central post which was anchored in a mound by cross trees. Although such medieval mills perished long ago their earthen mounds frequently survive, and can be mistaken for small mottes or round barrows.

The most delightful and imposing of all agricultural relics must be the great barns, the cathedrals of medieval agriculture. Some served individual farms or manors, but many of the survivors were built as tithe barns, where the rector's, bishop's or abbot's dues were assembled. Where these magnificent structures have endured they tend to have experienced less modification than domestic buildings, and the quality of their timber-framing is equal to any which will be seen in the dwellings of the time. Several fine examples survive in Wessex, most of them having been linked to monastic houses. The longest is the fifteenth-century example at Abbotsbury in Dorset, which extends more than 82 metres (c. 270 feet), but this is less capacious than the one at Place Farm, Tisbury in Wiltshire, the largest such barn in England. The excellently preserved

Superb medieval timber-framing in a Hertfordshire barn.

fourteenth-century abbey barn at Glastonbury is now at the core of a delightful Rural Life Museum, and another superb example, also open to the public, is the fourteenth–century barn at Barton Farm on the outskirts of Bradford-on-Avon, where some of the produce of the lands of Shaftesbury Abbey was stored. Other fine examples in stone include the abbey barns at Lacock in Wiltshire (NT), the barn at St Leonard's Grange near Beaulieu and the tithe barns at Cerne Abbas (Dorset) and West Dean (Wiltshire). One of the oldest surviving abbey barns is at Great Coxwell in Oxfordshire (NT). Thought by some to be the finest example in England, the barn was built in the thirteenth century for the monks of Beaulieu. It is 46 metres (152 feet) long by 13.5 metres (44 feet) wide and stands 14.5 metres (48 feet) high.

Medieval agriculture was not solely concerned with food production, and by far the most commercial cash crop and export commodity was wool. The most numerous monuments to the industry are the earthworks of villages which were swept away in order to create extensive sheep ranges, while the most imposing relics are the ruins of the Cistercian abbeys and the wool churches, wrought in stone but bought in wool. One of the most interesting legacies of the industry, however, is the fine fourteenth-century timber-framed Court House at Long Crendon in Buckinghamshire, now maintained by The National Trust. The upper floor of the building was the 'staple hall', where local wool was stored before its despatch to market.

Village Life and Landscape

Throughout much of England, though not in the Celtic lands, the village became a prominent feature of the medieval countryside. For the first time in a very long history of occupation it was the most important form of settlement in many areas. Village

The superb abbey barn at Glastonbury, the roof supported by cruck blades which rise from the walls.

England in its infancy has been described in Chapter 3, and in the following centuries thousands of established villages grew and sucked in the populations of nearby hamlets, while many new villages were created. Eventually all the more attractive settings were colonized and small villages were established in areas with meagre resources. By the fourteenth century the expansion had been stemmed and desertion rather than colonization became the dominant theme in the countryside. The trickle of abandonment became a flood in the period following the Great Pestilence, when marginal settlements were depopulated or deserted, tenancies lay vacant on the plusher farmlands and hundreds of viable farming communities were cruelly evicted to make way for sheep.

Although there had been some movement towards the creation of substantial and compact 'nucleated' rural settlements in Roman times, the new village foundations of the late Saxon and early medieval centuries achieved a far more comprehensive trans-formation of the countryside in most parts of the English lowlands. This was the greatest period of village vitality, when the young and coltish settlements grew, shifted and changed their forms. By the close of the medieval period this youthful exuberance was outgrown, so that the first village plans which were drawn at this time generally showed villages which were settling down into the layouts which often survive to this day. Consequently the best information about the livelier periods of village development comes from the study of the earthworks of villages which were deserted during the Middle Ages and from excavations at deserted village sites.

In the past writers tended to emphasize the spontaneity of village foundation and growth, conjuring images of lusty pioneers who would band together and hack out the elbow room for a new settlement in the supposed wildwood. Yet when the character of medieval villages is properly studied it is not the haphazard or 'organic' features which impress. Rather, it is clear that village planning was a very common practice. The process of village creation was masterminded by the owners of estates, and frequently this masterminding would extend to the precise determination of the size of a village, the number and exact dimensions of its house plots and all the details of its form and function. Such planning could mould new settlements completely and could be evident in the neat extensions which were often grafted on to existing villages. Although the concept of planning might seem to affront traditional ideas about the disorganized nature of medieval life, it is quite reasonable to imagine that in the autocratic and strictly regulated feudal world the masters of the countryside would be influential in shaping the contents of their estates.

The medieval repertoire of village plans was not great, but the layouts often proved so durable as to be recognizable at a glance on the map of the modern village. The basic component was the row or package of house plots, with each dwelling placed at the street end of a long, narrow plot or 'toft', and with the tofts, equal in size, running back from the street to terminate at a back lane. Such packages could occupy just one side of the street or through road, line both sides of the road, or could be arranged to define a triangular green, as at Nun Monkton in North Yorkshire.

Planned villages with these layouts can be recognized in most areas of England and appeared in the parts of Scotland, Wales and Ireland which were most strongly affected by Norman feudalism. The greatest concentration is in the north of England, particularly the Vale of York – the areas devastated by the dreadful Harrying of the North. Having exterminated a large proportion of their potentially valuable peasant assets, the Norman masters must have realized that empty estates yielded no wealth, and the rehabilitation of the ravaged areas was accomplished partly by the Cistercians, operating from their new abbeys, and partly by landlords who provided new villages to attract settlers and accommodate the surviving communities. An inspection of existing villages in the Vale has shown that about half of them show fairly obvious signs of medieval planning, while there are others which preserve fainter traces. It is now quite generally accepted that this wholesale reorganization of the countryside took place in the aftermath of the Harrying, while meticulous work by June Shepherd has revealed that the planning involved was detailed and comprehensive. The new settlements seem to have been laid out using

a measuring rod, and units of 18 or 20 feet (c. 5.5 or 6 metres) are still often preserved in the dimensions of the villages. It also seems that the dimensions could be chosen according to the guidelines that were used to assess tax for Domesday Book, with two perches of village frontage being provided per 'bovate' of assessment. (The bovate was a land-unit holding favoured in the north and consisting of 8 to 15 acres (c. 3 to 6 hectares) of arable, 1 to 2 acres (less than a hectare) of meadow, and common grazing rights.) More recent work by Mary Harvey has shown that planning could also extend to the surrounding fields, as at Fangfoss near Pocklington (Humberside), where a survey made in 1363 shows that the strips in the various furlongs had been placed in the same relative positions, with the Dean of York always having strips at one end of the furlong, while at Wressle near Goole (Humberside) twenty-five other strips always separated each glebe strip. Such detailed organization of the field patterns might have been accomplished at the time when the planned villages were founded, as would seem likely, though there is still a possibility that it could have pre-dated the Conquest. Also, since the English were perfectly capable of planning substantial towns, like Hamwith (Southampton), there is no reason to deny the possibility that some planned villages also existed in Saxon times.

Once established a planned village might lead a rather sleepy existence, so that although the individual dwellings might experience around twenty different rebuildings, the basic pattern of house plots, boundaries and streets or lanes will survive to this day. One of the most perfect examples, and one which is almost always quoted, is the rigidly planned village of Appleton-le-Moors near Pickering (North Yorkshire). Rather more interesting is the charming little village of Old Byland near Helmsley (North Yorkshire). The village was provided in the 1140s to house a community evicted from their homes by the monks of a convent at Hood who were establishing an abbey. The monks moved on to found Byland Abbey after complaints about their disturbing proximity to the monastery of Rievaulx, less than 2 kilometres (c. 1 mile) away. But Old Byland village survived the changes, and today the layout of dwellings and church round a rectangular green is probably very little different from the one which the Norman monks created. This is one of many genuinely charming little places which very few tourists have discovered.

More commonly, a village would undergo several important changes in the course of the medieval period. A high proportion of villages were of a type

ABOVE LEFT *Old Byland village, North Yorkshire, still preserves the outlines of the planned settlement created by the monks of Byland.*

ABOVE *The cottages in the picturesque Cotswolds village of Lower Slaughter have encroached upon a medieval green.*

LEFT *The long rectangular green in the planned North Yorkshire village of Arncliffe.*

which has been called polyfocal. Such villages often grew from the merging of hamlets or smaller villages, reinforcing the belief that village England was preceded by a land full of hamlets. Polyfocal villages often lack coherent layouts and the identities of their different cores may still be preserved in the fabric of the settlement. At Great Shelford in Cambridgeshire the original hamlet and manor-house groupings, one of them including the parish church, were about 0.8 kilometre (half a mile) apart, and the union was only gradually achieved.

In other places the expansion of a village could be a much more sudden and deliberate affair, with whole new streets being attached to an existing settlement. This must have happened at the picture-book village of Okeford Fitzpaine in Dorset, which gained a substantial extension complete with a large green in the twelfth or thirteenth century. As the village continued to develop, the green was engulfed by new buildings. Another much admired village is Cerne Abbas in the same county, and here the market area and flanking streets were remodelled about the same time.

Although the village green is at the heart of most olde worlde romance, much is still to be learned about greens, but it is clear that in many cases the green was not an original village feature. The green could be the centre-piece of a planned layout, as at Arncliffe in North Yorkshire and so many other northern villages, or it could be an additional component, inserted on the orders of the local magnate – who was doubtless eager to establish a market and to profit from its tolls. Folkingham in Lincolnshire, described by Christopher Taylor, is dominated by its long market square, perhaps inserted by Henry de Beaumont in the early twelfth century, although the original village seems to have huddled round the church in what is now a backwater above the square. Normally the market was guarded by its cross. Occasionally the medieval cross will survive intact, although more commonly the base and a stump of the shaft may be all that has survived the vandalism of the Reformation and the subsequent assaults on such symbols.

The growth of one part of a village could be paralleled by the contraction or abandonment of another. This might result from the reorganization of the settlement around a new green and market area, or it could occur when a reorientation of the local trading and transport system caused the original high street to become a cul de sac or side street while other lanes attracted the bustle and growth. In these ways a village could change its entire alignment. In extreme cases the whole village could migrate to a new market site which was cunningly developed beside a promising highway, leaving the old houses to decay. Often the hopes and prospects of the market would prove to be highly inflated, so that eventually dwellings would colonize the designated market area, though sometimes a green and a base of a cross will remain as reminders of the medieval aspirations.

Changes such as these ensured that the facets of the village scene were always in a state of flux. Until the closing years of the thirteenth century the emphasis was firmly on the theme of growth, but then retreat and decay added their touches to the scene as settlements often contracted or vanished completely. Perhaps the most surprising thing of all is the fact that, despite many generations of change and rebuilding, so many clues to the history of village development have survived fossilized in the landscape. The examples which have been quoted are only 'special' in the sense that somebody has studied these villages and worked out their history. In general, it is quite common for a village to reveal traces of early planning, a polyfocal layout, an inserted green or market square, or a reorientation of the high street. It would be a rather rare and dull village which had survived through the medieval period without experiencing any interesting changes and developments.

The methods of the archaeologist and field worker have opened our eyes to the form and growth of the medieval village, but we must turn to historical sources to discover the villagers themselves. The medieval peasant is usually regarded as a hardworking and cruelly exploited figure. In many ways this impression is correct, but underlying this simple image the reality was complex. People were exceedingly conscious of the subtleties of social status: these were not only concerned with the touchy issue of one's standing in the local community, but also affected one's position under the law and were of major importance in determining the outline and details of the working life. We still live in a class society, but now the divisions are more blurred and uncertain, and at least we enjoy the notion of equality under the law. It is hard to imagine that a slander case would result were one to brand a middle-class neighbour as being 'working class', but in the medieval village the chap who described a freeman as a villein was very likely to suffer the attentions of the contemporary equivalents of m'learned friends. The freeman might have less land and an even tattier abode than some villein neighbours, but there were occasions when his free status could be a priceless asset. Status was decided by complex and sometimes conflicting sets of regulations, but it was regarded as a matter of great consequence by all concerned, so that inquiries to establish the standing of an individual in the village pecking order were quite common.

The most important social division was between freedom and bondage. The main class of bondmen in the village were usually the villeins. This name was not liked, even by those who were quite plainly villeins; it was a French name introduced by the Normans to apply to their English tenants. After the Conquest royal lawyers had sought to rationalize the complicated social and legal realities by introducing the Roman concept that men were either free or serfs – and if they were serfs they could be regarded as villeins. This legal simplification rested uncomfortably on the complex social and legal realities of the realm, where true serfs or slaves had almost disappeared and where much depended on the peculiar customs of particular manors. Another layer of complexity was added by the fact that the divisions did not only relate to the personal positions of people, but also to the tenure of land. Some pieces of land were held by free tenure and, to make things even more tricky, this tenure might be by military service, special services, the giving of alms, or by 'socage'. This was the tenure of the lesser freeholders and was governed by local customs and not subject to feudal wardship and marriage rights. The freedoms associated with status and tenure did not always coincide, so that a villein might hold some free land. Lands held in villeinage were subject to the court of the manor in which they lay rather than the royal courts. The villein held his lands at the will of the lord and he could be sold along with the lands concerned, while his possessions were – at least in theory – also the property of the lord. Local custom could be as strong as, or stronger than, the letter of the law, so that while the lord or lady had the notional right to adjust rents and services due from the villeins, in most cases these were fixed by custom. Free tenants, meanwhile, had their rents and services fixed by law.

In practical terms, the freeholders tended to render money rents to their lords, while the work services which they performed were usually light or nonexistent. Villeins, on the other hand, tended to perform heavy work services while also paying some rent. Yet a class of villeins emerged mainly paying a money rent, or 'mol', for their holdings, and they were known as 'molmen'. Sometimes a villein could buy his freedom – at a hefty price – and thereafter pay 'head money' or 'chevage' of a few pence a year for the privilege of being free. He might also become free by marriage to a free woman, by entering the church or by living undiscovered for a year and a day in a royally chartered town or on the royal demesne. The bottom layer in the broad class of bondmen was largely composed of cottars or cottagers, who held a cottage and very small holdings of land but enjoyed access to the village commons. They performed fewer services than did the villeins, who had more substantial and sometimes quite large holdings. Sometimes the cottars were known as 'Mondaymen', since they worked for the lord on just one day of the week rather than on several days. Although the cottars always had the meanest dwellings and holdings, it was possible, according to the complicated social order, to be both a cottar and free.

Complex as it may seem, this description of medieval society is only a simplified sketch of a more intricate situation. The conditions of village life varied from region to region and from manor to manor. They also changed through time, and as the medieval period progressed, so the distinctions between freemen and bondmen weakened. The payments of rents increased in importance over the rendering of services and the employment of hired farmhands correspondingly increased in importance. In the thirteenth century most village communities would have recognized the existence of three main classes: 'franklins', the freemen; 'husbonds' or 'neats', the villeins; and the impoverished cottars. By this time the bordars of pre-Conquest England had more or less disappeared as a distinct class, having merged into the ranks of the cottars. The peasant classes took their English names from the type of dwelling which they occupied. All were flimsy hovels, but a house was less vile than a 'cote' or cottage, or a bordel.

The husbonds tenanted strips which were scattered throughout the village open fields, sometimes in a regular pattern as has been described. Taken together these strips would amount to between 10 and 40 acres (c. 4 and 16 hectares). In the north a holding of 2 bovates or 'oxgangs' was common, while in the south husbonds tended to hold 'yardlands' or 'virgates' averaging around 30 acres (c. 12 hectares), and so they were sometimes referred to as 'yardlings', or else they would hold half-yardlands. Many cottars squeezed a living from holdings of 5 acres (c. 2 hectares) or less, with the saddest cases being the 'coterells', who might not hold their lands from the lord but sub-tenant morsels of land on the holdings of the greater husbonds. Also present, in numbers which increased as the period advanced, were landless farm labourers or 'undersettles', who might be employed by the lord or by his tenants.

The various members of the village community were squeezed by their lord or lords for whatever rents and services might be wrung from them, while the Church was always waiting to grab a share of anything that remained. Famine and disease would arrive from time to time to take a toll of the peasant population, but otherwise there were limits to what the community was expected to bear. After all, the peasants were valuable assets, by far the most important creators of wealth. One did not want to have them too starved or broken to work and dying on one's doorstep. So the masters of the countryside were always likely to weigh in with a measure of alms and charity when times were really tough.

Originally the lord of the manor had a major share in the scattered agricultural resources of the vill, though as the medieval period progressed the lords were often able to pull their lands together to create a compact demesne. Normally a number of enclosed paddocks, including such assets as a dovecote, or-

In the twelfth and thirteenth centuries, and particularly in East Anglia, the prosperous landowners of less than castle-owning rank frequently built their houses on land surrounded by a status-giving homestead moat. Many of these moats survive complete or in part and many still contain later dwellings.

chards and fish-ponds, would surround the site of the manor house, while many lords also kept coneys (the term 'rabbit' being used only for young coneys). The coneys were originally kept in enclosures and it was only later that warrens, now sometimes represented in the landscape by low 'pillow mounds', were introduced.

Unless they became molmen, the tenants were obliged to devote a considerable amount of time to working on the demesne strips and meadows. The size of this obligation was normally proportional to the extent of the tenant's holding in the estate, so that a yardling or virgater would have very onerous duties and would hope to sire a number of lusty sons in order to work both his own substantial holding and meet his obligations to the lord. Such a yardling would be an obvious candidate for the important office of reeve, although he might look askance at service in the more menial roles of swineherd, shepherd or ploughman, duties which would generally devolve on the lesser lights of village society. In many places particular tenants or small communities

had specialized obligations, such as the delivery of a specified quantity of eggs, fish or ale on a particular day, or the feeding or exercising of the lord's hunting dogs. Duties did not end with the performance of the prescribed services and the payment of a rent in money, kind or both. Just when a peasant had fulfilled his obligations and was looking forward to a few days of uninterrupted work on his own holding the lord was likely to demand extra labour in the form of 'boonwork' – and there are plenty of records to show that such 'favours' to the lord were often grudgingly given by peasants who did as little as they could get away with.

Then, at times of celebration or bereavement the lord was likely to exact other payments. When a daughter married – and particularly if she married outside the vill – the lord would demand a 'merchet' of money or a valuable beast. The death of a tenant became a cause of even greater anguish to the family when the lord demanded a 'heriot', often consisting of a very important animal. Then as the heir succeeded to the family holding the lord would take payment of an 'entry fine'. In 1296 the lord of Amberley in West Sussex did rather well from the family of Mabel of Middleton. When Mabel, who had a villein holding, died the lord took a heriot of a mare. Her heir, Richard, then paid his entry fine and gave the usual pledges and fealty and in addition gave the lord a further 12d for licence to marry. Perhaps he had been waiting to inherit before marrying, but his married life will certainly have begun in reduced circumstances. The bishop who had estates near Farnham did not have things as easy as the lord of Amberley. Some pigs were shared between tenants, and his heriot sometimes consisted of half a pig, so that a sale or the purchase of the pig's other half then had to follow!

All that has been said underlines the complexity of the social and economic life of the village. The court leet, at which the reeve presided, and the manor court together provided the intricate regulations and discipline needed to make the system work, and certain bodies within village society – particularly the husbonds – functioned as virtual 'estates', with important mutual obligations and responsibilities. Sometimes the husbonds would be penalized as a body when one of their number defaulted on a prescribed task. Yet the villagers themselves were neither so burdened down by their feudal obligations that they lost all identity, nor so enmeshed in common tasks that they functioned like some kind of communistic cooperative. The bonds were not tight enough to control a lively community of little entrepreneurs. Each person was ever eager to cobble together some

The medieval peasant – here suffering from toothache – portrayed on a capital at Wells Cathedral.

little deal or pursue an opportunity. The lack of any real meritocracy ensured that the village contained the most astute individuals as well as the dullards and wasters. From time to time successful wheeling and dealing would allow an enterprising soul to burst through the feudal bonds and, as Professor W. G. Hoskins described in his fascinating study of the Midlands peasant, the family might then flourish or sink: rags to rags in two generations. Anyone who bought or clawed a way up into the ranks of the franklins could then have his dynasty rise to a position of great wealth and power in the later medieval centuries – and the old communal ties were easily forgotten. Some of the most cunning lawyers and the cruellest evictors of peasants were families such as the Spencers from Wormleighton in Warwickshire, who rose from the yeoman classes at the expense of their former neighbours.

Village society was not as parochial as has been imagined. The study of old records shows that peasants could be quite worldly wise, and it was very common for them to marry outside their native village community. Neither was peasant society an absolute haven of male chauvinism. Many tenants were women and several 'lords' were ladies. When a widow was unable to manage her holding it was common for her heirs to arrange an agreement which would ensure her support through old age. The conditions for the housewife in her poky, smoke-wreathed hovel were scarcely more comfortable than those experienced by the menfolk in the muddy fields, yet to the credit of these women – and the chagrin of modern archaeologists – excavations at some deserted village sites show that house floors were regularly swept clean of domestic debris. Even so, the village itself was an unhealthy and filthy place, with heaps of dung encroaching upon the streets and contaminating the stream or pond which supplied households and stock alike with their water.

The most lively introductions to medieval village life are found in the manor-court records which describe the many fines imposed for misdemeanours. The impression which emerges is one of communities which were comprehensively exploited, which were capable of remarkable feats of cooperation and which could sometimes show compassion to their members – but which were also permeated with petty

feuds, cruel gossip and slander and which contained their fair share of louts. Monotonous and uncomfortable days of drudgery in the fields formed the background to drunkenness and hooliganism, and violent fights and assaults were not uncommon. Many offences were extremely silly, if only in the sense that their perpetrators had not the faintest hope of escaping retribution. Others must have been committed by men who were so disgruntled by the imposition of onerous duties that they had ceased to care very much whether they were fined or not. Others still, like the shirking of boonwork and petty poaching, seem to reflect the village consensus that the only crime was that of being caught.

Robert, son of Christine of Illey in Worcestershire (now West Midlands), quoted by G.C. Homans, must have been a daft fellow, for three weeks after settling with his neighbour, Thomas, for slander he was brought to court and fined for calling his neighbours 'villeins'. Rowland Parker has described the many misdemeanours of the villagers of the Foxton locality in Cambridgeshire, which produced a steady

Hawkshead court house (NT). Dating from the thirteenth and fifteenth centuries, this is the only surviving relic of the manorial buildings on a Cumbrian estate owned by the monks of Furness Abbey.

trickle of fines to the manor court: Matilda Nutrex fined 6d for selling ale without possessing a gallon measure; the village tenants collectively fined 3s 4d for refusing to fetch the Lady's straw; William Cock fined for saying the tenants did not know that they were supposed to mow in a swamp; John Rose fined 3d for breaking into the pound to remove a cow impounded for trespass; John Hille fined 4d for poaching fish; Henry Atthill fined 2d for ploughing six inches off a public way, and John Dikeman and fourteen others distrained for lodging outside workers ('foreigners') at harvest time. Such fines not only helped to keep the local miscreants in check, but over the course of time they produced a quite considerable amount of manorial revenue. On many manors the pattern of fines for silly, harmless or petty 'crimes' and peasant pig-headedness continued to be apparent to the close of and well beyond the Middle Ages. Thus, at Wrington in Somerset (now Avon) in the 1520s, Joan Shipster was fined 6d for failing to mend her outhouse roofs; she took no notice and was fined 11d two months later. Three more months passed and the work was still not done, while Joan's funds may have been so reduced by the fines that this time she was fined only 4d. One can quite imagine the mood of the court shifting from retribution to resignation.

*   *   *

We can meet the medieval villagers via the old manorial records, but it is less easy to picture their villages. We have seen that modern village maps often reveal a plan which preserves many medieval features, yet the scene that is viewed as we stroll along the High Street will look nothing like the one which was seen by villagers of the twelfth or thirteenth century. The hovels have become large and permanent houses, the rutted street is now smoothly surfaced and the filth and stench are no more; mains drainage and piped water have come to stay. Today there are no villages which are remotely medieval in appearance, and the old patterns are best seen at the sites of villages which were deserted during the Middle Ages.

These desertions had various causes. In the earlier medieval centuries the accent was on growth and colonization. Scores of English settlements must have perished in the Harrying of the North and it may be that the new planned villages were built directly upon their scorched remains. A few dozen more villages were extinguished by the Cistercian quest for splendid isolation, while quite a few will have been burned in the interminable Anglo-Scottish raids. In these latter cases, however, the villagers would normally return from their refuges in the woods and begin rebuilding while the ashes of their homes were still warm.

Far more insidious and destructive were the changes wrought by climatic deterioration and soil exhaustion. The rapid post-Conquest surges in population soon caused communities to be pushed into places which could only sustain village life under the most favourable circumstances. Continuing growth increased the pressures on the land and the intensification of farming could often lead to a disastrous reduction in the period of fallow and the use of fertilizers. At first the climate was generous. It seems to have improved quite steadily as the Dark Ages progressed, reaching an optimum around 1200. Then it worsened during the remainder of the medieval period, and continued to deteriorate for a couple of centuries more. In general the changes were in the direction of cooler, cloudier conditions, but after the middle of the thirteenth century the broader tendencies were overlain by a series of rapid fluctuations. Recent researches based on estate accounts have allowed H. E. Hallam to provide a more detailed picture of the conditions experienced in eastern England in the century 1250–1350. The general drift into wetter conditions was accompanied by a high incidence of summer droughts, so that between 1297 and 1307 only two years seem to have escaped the phenomenon and harvests were mediocre or poor. A succession of very poor harvests could have catastrophic effects, with the exhaustion of food stocks and the likelihood that starving peasants would be tempted to eat their seed corn. Heavy rain fell throughout 1315, launching a famine which was perpetuated by dreadful harvests for the next six years. By the fourteenth century fearsome coastal storms were being reported from all parts of Britain. A few coastal settlements disappeared in quite dramatic circumstances, along with the sections of the shore on which they stood, but more extensive desertions occurred inland, where villages slowly bled to death.

Communities scratching a living from thin, sandy, upland soils were probably already experiencing soil exhaustion, the consequence of overcropping and overgrazing, but now they discovered that the growing season was too short to allow crops to ripen and be harvested during the cloudy summers. On the upland plateaus black carpets of acid peat again advanced upon the fields and pastures. Meanwhile, on the heavier clay soils of the lowlands the drift to cooler, wetter conditions meant that the ploughlands were cold and waterlogged during the spring, and excavations at deserted village sites such as Goltho in Lincolnshire suggest that on the clay lands there was a shift in emphasis from arable cultivation to livestock.

These environmental problems were combined with an ailing economy, all the difficulties bearing down on an overworked and overpopulated countryside. Bad enough, one might imagine, but such problems will have seemed modest in comparison with the arrival of the Great Pestilence in 1348. In the plague years which followed, the foul epidemic probably exterminated between one third and one half of the population, devastating town and country, English, Irish, Scots and Welsh alike.

Babies born into a land of crowded fields might survive to live in half-empty countrysides before they were old enough to walk. The problems of land pressure and overpopulation were solved at a stroke, but the way was paved for a form of farming, already established and proven in some places, which would see thousands of communities ejected from their homes as the land was converted into sheep pasture. Usually the communities departed without a murmur and most must have been so enervated by the Plague and the environmental problems that they lacked the resolve to put up a struggle. The best hope for a threatened village was that it would have more than one manor and that not all the lords would opt for eviction. Villages which were completely and permanently extinguished by the Pestilence were far fewer than is generally imagined. More usually the portions of the community which survived were too weakened and demoralized to resist the assaults of the new sheep barons, such as the Spencers or the Knightleys. And whenever a community had begun to rebuild, the Plague was always likely to return and continue its ghastly work, as it did at quite frequent intervals until the middle of the seventeenth century.

Thousands of deserted village sites are now known, but many display nothing of obvious interest since their earthworks have been obliterated by ploughing. Many others are still interesting, but lie in the domains of unwelcoming farmers. There are a number, however, which are both fascinating and accessible to the public. Pride of place must go to Wharram Percy on a valley slope of the Yorkshire Wolds near Wharram-le-Street. Not only is this an enchanting and unspoiled corner in a landscape which is again being farmed to death, but it would be regarded by many archaeologists as the most important medieval excavation site in Britain. For more than thirty seasons the devoted enthusiasts of the Medieval Village Research Group have systematically been excavating the evidence which has transformed our understanding of medieval rural settlement, revealing its complexity and the ways in which features of the prehistoric and Roman landscape influenced the medieval patterns of farming, settlement and overlordship. Visitors approaching the site along the approved trackway during the late afternoon will see the low shafts of sunlight outlining the earthworks of dwellings, tracks and boundaries on the facing grassy slope, while the path then runs past the earthworks of the former dwellings and down to the ruined church and the pond and dam.

Ruined churches form dramatically symbolic features at only a minority of deserted village sites. The church could survive if it remained in use after the

FAR LEFT *Sheep were the cause of much village destruction in the latter centuries of the medieval period. These are carved on the bench ends at Altarnun church in Cornwall, and one can see that they were allowed to keep their tails.*

ABOVE *The excavated pond at the beautiful deserted village site of Wharram Percy in North Yorkshire.*

abandonment of its settlement, as at Wharram, or when the stone was worthless flint or conglomerate, as at several Norfolk sites. Otherwise the building was swiftly demolished for its materials and vanished from the scene. One of the most striking church ruins stands amongst earthworks at Egmere in Norfolk. In 1581 Sir Thomas Gresham was said to be in control of 'decayed tenements' here; in the 1550s the parson had complained that his predecessor had robbed the church of its lead and exported the bell, and about 1602 the building was converted into a barn. The exact story of the demise of a medieval village seldom survives and normally it must be pieced together from fragments of information such as these. Often the first hint of desertion is found when a village disappears from the taxation lists.

Hound Tor on Dartmoor in Devon, almost in the shadow of the famous rocks of this name, boasts no church, but is unusual in that it displays the excavated footings of several stone dwellings. In prehistoric times communities colonized or abandoned the moor according to climatic conditions, and a recolonization occurred in Saxon times. Near the vanished huts of Saxon herdsmen and amongst the stone litter of Bronze Age huts and compounds a medieval village of turf-walled huts developed. In the middle of the thirteenth century the hopeful villagers built stone long-houses, but as the climate deteriorated the village withered in the centuries which followed.

Documents rather than excavations allow us to discover the story of Cublington in Buckinghamshire,

which lies – or lay – in damp pasture just below the surviving ridge-top village. Here a declining population living on a soggy and ill-chosen site was extinguished by the Pestilence. As so often happened, new colonists returned to the village lands a few years later, but this time they chose to build on the better ground where the modern village stands. The original church has vanished, but one need be no expert in the identification of earthworks to recognize the dome of the Norman motte, the trough-like holloway of the old high street, the still partly-filled fish-pond and the banks of the property boundaries.

Such sites, especially when excavated, are our most potent and rewarding links with our medieval forebears, the peasant masses. Sadly, our inheritors will find it hard to understand why the powers in the land

ABOVE *The stone wall-bases of excavated dwellings at the deserted medieval village of Hound Tor on Dartmoor.*

TOP *The ruins of a massive church serve as a reminder of the former glories of the largely deserted village of Covehithe on the East Anglian coast.*

LEFT *The landscape of village desertion at Egmere in Norfolk.*

229

have provided such meagre sums for excavation work and have allowed vital archaeological sites to be ploughed up for crop land or reseeded pasture. They will also be unable to imagine why we sometimes spend hundreds of thousands of pounds to keep paintings by foreign masters within our shores and yet allow treasuries of information about our history to be ploughed into oblivion. Personally I doubt whether one archaeologist in ten would deny that one Wharram Percy is worth a dozen Windsor Castles, even though such sentiments are plainly not shared by the touring public. Half a dozen of the places mentioned in this book probably receive more visitors than all the rest together, and this is unfortunate, because Britain contains hundreds of really fascinating sites and monuments which tend to be unknown and overlooked during the treks between the 'big name' places. The potential interest and appeal of the deserted-village sites is immense, and the annual upkeep budget of one of the larger stately houses would finance the excavation and *reconstruction* of a medieval village. How schoolchildren would enjoy and profit from a visit to such a place, and how surprising that such a place has not yet been created!

The Medieval Town

Britain has witnessed three great surges in urbanization, but only the one which accompanied the Industrial Revolution succeeded in tipping the population balance from the rural to the urban side. The Roman experience in town creation was far past its peak and many towns were in decay by the time that the Romans departed. The Saxon and medieval urbanization proceeded at a steadier pace and with much less élan, but it achieved new or rehabilitated centres which were more firmly rooted than the Roman towns had been. Even so, at the end of the Middle Ages townsfolk were still only a very small if disproportionately influential minority in Britain.

In order to keep the situation in perspective we should realize that even at the end of the Middle Ages London will have been about as populous as a medium-sized modern town like Harrogate (North Yorkshire), while the leading provincial centres were much smaller, sometimes comparable to small modern towns such as Huntingdon, St Ives, or Ely in East Anglia. The run-of-the-mill town at the end of the medieval period could be smaller than many successful modern commuter villages. Consequently, in those towns which boast a medieval pedigree, the old core will only occupy a tiny proportion of the modern urbanized area, unless the town has since stagnated, like Thaxted (Essex), declined,

like Broadway (Hereford and Worcester) or New Winchelsea (East Sussex), or decayed completely, like Caus in Shropshire or Torksey in Lincolnshire. In contrast to the situations which prevailed in several continental countries, such as Italy and France, medieval England and Wales had few sizable towns, but many townlets and a heavy stipple of villages. Wales had many fewer villages than England, while Scotland and Ireland were hamlet countries, with few substantial villages and hardly any towns of note. This does not mean, however, that the towns which did exist in Britain were insignificant. They exerted influences in politics, commerce and administration which were out of all proportion to the size of their populations.

Many of the Saxon *burhs* continued to flourish during the Middle Ages, when scores of new towns were created. These new towns were very much products of their feudal environments. Almost all were deliberate and calculated creations, though many developed from successful villages which had obtained the right to hold markets. Kings, nobles and bishops all realized that market villages established on their estates could be expected to produce a regular crop of feudal tolls. The Domesday records identify about fifty markets, though there must have been many other customary or traditional markets, not all of them in populous places. Between the start of the thirteenth century and the arrival of the Pestilence well over a thousand new markets were licensed by the king, many of them in poky little places where optimism and avarice were their only support. The acquisition of a market charter was not necessarily a sure passport to urban stardom. Market villages, whether newly created or the sites of old customary markets which had been regularized in the medieval era, were very much feudal creations. But once a market village began to enjoy some commercial success it soon developed an identity of its own. It then became the goal of the community to obtain a borough charter which would allow a measure of self-government and which would safeguard the townsfolk against interference from feudal overlords. Since there were frequent occasions when the monarch was pressed for funds, the sale of borough charters was a handy source of revenue. In the medieval world the town was a progressive and emancipating institution, and when royally chartered it could offer freedom to villeins who had supported themselves and escaped detection for the requisite period of time.

In Scotland towns were few, vestigial and mainly insignificant until the medieval period. Some were founded as Norman-influenced feudalism penetrated

The magnificent fifteenth-century guildhall overlooks the former market square at Thaxted in Essex.

the realm. 'Royal burghs', such as Aberdeen, Banff (Grampian) and Inverness (Highland), were the creations of the king and often existed as the 'caputs' or capitals of the new administrative counties or 'sheriffdoms' – thus they were the very nerve centres from which feudal influences permeated across the kingdom. Other towns, most of them still small today, were 'burghs of barony', created by Scottish barons and churchmen. Many of them failed to expand as a result of competition from neighbouring and more highly-privileged royal burghs, although there were a few exceptions, most notably Glasgow. In Wales most of the older medieval towns were the artificial creations of the Norman and English aristocratic invaders, though at the end of the period these armoured plantation towns began to experience keen commercial competition from other expanding Welsh settlements. In Ireland most of the Viking trading foundations developed their urban characteristics and other towns which appeared were feudal foundations confined to the eastern and southern areas where Norman and English feudalism was normally ascendant.

The notion that history is about dates has many ill effects. If the only date that lodges between the ears of many children is 1066 then they may tend to regard this as a universal historical watershed. Yet the people living in England in 1067 were more or less the same folk who lived there in 1065, with most of the same habits and hopes. Norman control did inject a little more vitality into commerce with the continent, and this will have encouraged growth in towns which were already expanding. As the years rolled by and the rivalry between the Crown and the barons became endemic, the kings realized that the townsfolk were their natural political allies. These townsfolk, sometimes already almost independent by the time of the Conquest, craved exemption from outside feudal controls, and the king was the person who could grant this freedom – at some pecuniary gain to himself.

The creation of the Saxon *burhs* had been the direct

result of royal policy. Similar policies, but now more economic and administrative than military in their inspiration, were resumed after the Conquest and pursued with vigour and few interruptions for almost two centuries. Professor M.W. Beresford has shown that between 1191 and 1230 some forty-nine new towns were established in this way in England. At first royal towns, often fortified administrative centres, amounted to about one in three of the new foundations, though after the Norman period the baronial proportion increased and, with the main administrative and defensive niches filled, the commercial role became even more important. The potential for new town creations was constrained by commercial factors, with each foundation hoping to monopolize its trading precincts and curtail the activities of 'forestallers' who would attempt to trade before reaching a licensed market. By the middle of the thirteenth century most of the gaps in the urban network had been plugged, competition was fierce, and hopeful new arrivals were likely to be overwhelmed in the commercial contests.

Darwinistic forces stalked the urban world, and one village market might vanquish its neighbouring competitors only to be submerged by the commerce of an upstart town. To survive in this competitive world a town needed good luck, a steady crop of home-grown entrepreneurs and some more good luck. So-called geographical advantages often seem to have been less important and some of the most competitive towns had very unfavourable sites. For each town which managed to prosper there were others which stagnated or collapsed into villages. This competition weeded out the less promising candidates, and by the start of the fourteenth century the great majority of towns which were prospering at the close of the medieval period had already begun to flourish.

Since towns were normally the products of royal or baronial patronage it is not surprising that there is a high degree of planning displayed in the medieval urban landscapes. In the cases of some older towns, such as Winchester and York, Dark Age street alignments were superimposed across the Roman grids. Most new medieval towns were as planned as the New Towns of today, and if anything the planning was more stereotyped. However, the town founder was not usually painting on an empty canvas and he would want to exploit and incorporate the highways which were already pulsing with fair and market commerce. The medieval fairs stood to markets as hypermarkets now stand to corner shops, so that normally a charter would specify a market on one or more days of the week and a fair or fairs only on notable days of the year. The fairs allowed the circulation of luxury goods imported from the continent and beyond, but much manufacturing was also accomplished by members of the urban craft guilds and in the larger towns the workshops and outlets of a particular trade could virtually commandeer a particular side street.

The heart, brain and pocket of the medieval town merged in its market place, the key component in any town plan. It could be created by a broadening of the through-road, so that the properties which lined the High Street or Broad Street had direct access to the trading area. Such medieval market places are often still plainly evident in the modern town plan, as at Chipping Campden in Gloucestershire, Cilgerran in Dyfed and scores of other places. At Thame the Oxford to Aylesbury road was diverted in 1219 to run through the vast market place of the Bishop of Lincoln's new town. Often, as the pressure for space for shops and residential properties increased, encroaching buildings would mask but not entirely obscure the outlines of the original trading area as at Ludlow, or at Chepstow. (The town of Chepstow was originally named 'Stroguil' after the castle and lordship, but became 'Cēapstow', meaning 'market place', by the fourteenth century.) Market founders would normally seek to attract tradesmen and artisans to their new creations by offering attractive tenures, while tradesmen would jostle for footholds around the market area. The associated planning produced characteristic layouts, with long, narrow house plots extending back in parallel lines from the narrow market frontages. Later growth has generally brought an infilling of such plots, as at Devizes in Wiltshire, but their outlines can be preserved as back streets, as in Skipton or between High Street and Bear Lane in Oxford. Such plots gave the villagers or the burgesses opportunities for horticulture, while cultivation of the associated town fields played an important role in the urban economy and lifestyle – albeit one which tended to decline in importance as the period advanced. In various places the concept of the broadened High Street type of market place was rejected in favour of a more compact and geometrical trading area, as with the triangular market places at Bampton (Devon) or Taunton (Somerset). In the larger towns distinct market trading areas could be designated for specific spheres of commerce, and such uses may survive in names such as Haymarket, Butcher Row, Horsemarket, and so on.

Particularly in the case of the castle towns and the plantation towns of Wales, feudal origins were underlined by the provision of a market place which was dominated by the castle, as at Ludlow or Warkworth (Northumberland), and as is still evident in the broad street below the castle at Appleby (Cumbria). At Montgomery, where the castle represents a shift in 1223 from the congested but spartan motte-and-bailey site (which has recently been excavated) at Hen Domen c. 2½ kilometres (1½ miles) to the northwest, the terrain of the castle-bearing outcrop prevented the close juxtaposition of castle and market. The market place, one of the best surviving examples of medieval planning, was built on the lower slopes, below the new castle.

Often planning would end with the demarcation of the market place and the associated burgage plots. In other cases efforts were made to delimit a rather Roman-like grid of streets which outlined rectangular *insulae* or development blocks. Such planning is most clearly seen in the failed borough of New Winchelsea, founded by Edward I but never growing to fill up the designated chequerboard, where the traces of the street grid are detectable in the rural areas beyond the existing blocks of houses. Other towns with surviving grid-like street patterns include Salisbury, Castleton in Derbyshire and Newport in Dyfed. Growth could be accomplished by the addition of a planned extension, as at Clun in Shropshire, but in other cases it could lead to the accretion of a chaotic jumble of suburbs. At Lincoln the ancient Roman defences remained in use and the sprawling suburbs beyond were protected by new earthworks and gates. Areas of congested and winding back streets could result from the constrictions on the urban area imposed by the girdle of surrounding walls. Such walls had obvious defensive advantages in the plantation towns and frontier zones and they could also prove useful in the more settled areas during the hurly-burly of medieval warfare and sieges. Equally, they made it easier for the authorities to regulate access to market trading and to ensure that dues were collected. Less obviously, they were also important symbols of urban status – a fact not to be overlooked when we remember the sensitive independence and competitive nature of the medieval town.

In 1971 H. L. Turner was able to identify more than 130 towns in England and Wales which had medieval defences, and there are many others where future excavations may reveal the traces of walls. Defences could be continuous in the form of walls, or only involved defended gateways. In a few cases the defences were carried on the bridges which gave access to the town, examples of which can still be seen at Warkworth and Monmouth (Gwent). The main period for the construction of town walls appears to have been the thirteenth century, when a large number of 'murage grants' was issued. By the sixteenth century the concept of the walled town was largely redundant in Britain, although towns continued to be provided with massive defences on the continent. The walls then became a valuable source of building materials and would be quarried as a matter of policy or illegally robbed. Consequently it is exceptional for extensive circuits of wall to survive. The Edwardian plantation towns of Conwy and Caernarfon preserve most of their defences, as do Chester and Tenby (Dyfed), while York, Chepstow and the old core of Denbigh (Clwyd) still display most of their walls.

The prevalence of planning in the urban layout should not blind us to the limitations in the urban infrastructure. One suspects that the traveller would often smell a medieval town long before it came into sight. Sewage could be piled at the roadside for collection, townsfolk depended on wells and streams which were ideal for the dispersion of epidemics, while the use of timber and thatch in the closely packed dwellings ensured that comprehensive conflagrations were a frequent occurrence. This being said, the authorities often did what they could to minimize the squalor. Streets could be paved and cleaned by rota, and by the thirteenth century several of the larger towns had provided the equivalents of public conveniences or had organized a piped water supply. Cesspits and garderobes were becoming common in the fourteenth century, although the response to the arrival of the Great Pestilence apparently involved the exploration of ever more bizarre remedies and a neglect of practical sanitary arrangements. Edward III complained of the vile stench of York in 1332, and judged it to be '. . . more than in any other city of the realm from dung and other filth and dirt wherewith the streets and lanes are filled and obstructed'. He ordered a general clean-up.

In many cases the town street must have been a charming but malodorous conglomeration of cramped dwellings, workshops and stores, all of different heights and sizes, some perhaps with overhanging jetties darkening the street below. In others the buildings were grouped more neatly around squares or closes and, perhaps more surprisingly, there were also regular terraces, apparently built, as in the nineteenth century, as cottage rows by speculative builders. Such rows have been recognized at Coventry, and the Lower Brook Street excavations in Winchester in 1967 explored a terrace of four standardized thirteenth- or early fourteenth-century cottages. They were virtually identical single-celled units, each about 5 metres (c. 17 feet) square, with internal partitions subdividing the chamber into entrance passage, hall and bed cubicle.

Recognizable features of the medieval layout are common in the cores of many British towns, and space will only permit the description of a few outstanding examples. The Celtic countries have scarcely featured so far in this chapter, largely because of a shortage of evidence and the general persistence of older field and hamlet patterns – so perhaps the balance can be redressed with Welsh examples here. In 1093 the Norman Earl Roger of Shrewsbury made impressive conquests in Dyfed and his son, Arnulf de Montgomery, obtained the Pembroke area. Following the construction of a motte-and-bailey castle, a planted town was established at Pembroke and Monkton Priory was developed nearby, perhaps on the site of a Celtic foundation. The characteristic castle, town and church package was neatly tied up around 1200, when the centre was chartered, giving the new mayor, burgesses and freemen of the borough charge of its administration and commerce. The fortification of the site had been encouraged by the formidable ridge of limestone which was guarded to the north by the Pembroke River and to the south by a tribu-

tary stream. This topography conditioned the form of the town, which developed along the long street which ran from the castle eastwards along the spine of the ridge. At some uncertain date, perhaps early in the fourteenth century, the town was walled and gates were provided in the west and east, and at the mill and river crossing in the north. The attenuated form of the ridge curtailed any development of cross streets, so that essentially Main Street *was* the town. Pembroke had a Sunday market and two annual fairs; one market is represented by a broadening of the eastern end of Main Street, near St Michael's Church, and the second was held towards the western end of the street, near its junction with the lane that ran down to the river crossing.

The success of this plantation is marked by the fact that by 1324 some 220 burgage plots flanked Main Street. Much of the medieval layout survives, including the formidable castle that succeeded Arnulf's modest motte and the street pattern, while the medieval burgage plots are recognizable in the modern property boundaries. But only fragments of the town wall survive in the northeast.

Pembroke is still well preserved, though medieval success did not guarantee survival. By 1304 New Radnor in Powys, founded in the middle of the thirteenth century, supported slightly more burgesses than did Pembroke. By the end of the sixteenth century it was in decline and a century later the courts and market had been lost. Today the village lies amongst the relics of its former grandeur, with earthworks marking some of the lost streets and defences.

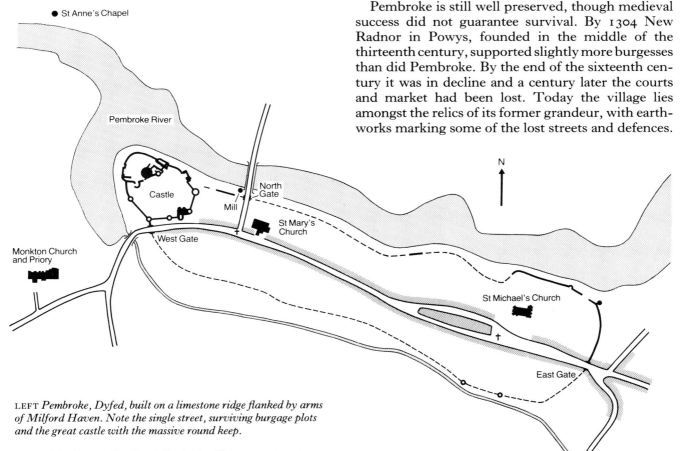

LEFT *Pembroke, Dyfed, built on a limestone ridge flanked by arms of Milford Haven. Note the single street, surviving burgage plots and the great castle with the massive round keep.*

ABOVE *The layout of medieval Pembroke. The two market places are shown by crosses.*

Denbigh, Clwyd, where the town migrated downhill from the inconvenient castle site.

Denbigh, like Pembroke, developed at a site chosen for its military attributes rather than its commercial advantages. The castle and walled town were planted by the Earl of Lincoln in the reign of Edward I and the earl granted the town its charter of privileges in 1285. The walled area around the castle proved far too restrictive, so that soon Denbigh consisted of a walled borough with an adjacent market town which had developed on more inviting terrain to the north and east of the walls. The market developed on the short, broad High Street, and beyond the rather formless area of the commercial core three long, parallel streets ran off to the northeast. The walls, medieval street pattern and the Burgess Gate which linked the borough and market town are all well preserved.

Though lacking the terrain problems of Denbigh or Pembroke, Grosmont and Skenfrith (Gwent) were two castle towns of the Welsh Marches which failed to live up to their founders' expectations. Grosmont may have been founded at the start of the thirteenth century and got off to quite a good start, with perhaps around 160 burgage plots by the middle of the century. However, the decay of the castle and devastation during the Glyndwr revolt at the start of the fifteenth century almost proved terminal. The town collapsed towards its High Street, so that only a village with a now withered triangular market place and a fine medieval church which is several sizes too large

for the present community remains. Skenfrith, a few kilometres away, now consists of the thirteenth-century castle (NT), the church and not a great deal more. The associated town grew up round the church, perhaps at a site which had supported a Roman settlement and then a Celtic religious community. The town does not seem to have been a particularly significant place and its collapse has proceeded even further than that of Grosmont.

Queenborough on the Isle of Sheppey in Kent was the last royal medieval town foundation, being founded by Edward III in 1368. Though built around the arc of its harbour the town had some physical resemblance to Pembroke, with a long High Street running down from the earthworks of Sheppey Castle. Bewdley in Hereford and Worcester was arguably the last medieval new town of all. Throughout the period it had a very modest existence, being mainly noted as a haven for fugitives as a result of its position astride the boundary of Shropshire and what was then Worcestershire. In 1539, the chronicler Leland remarked that Bewdley was a new town. It must have originated as a regular grid-planned town established after the construction of a bridge in 1447 enticed an earlier and unsuccessful market settlement to migrate to the site from its original situation on Wyre Hill, just under a kilometre (half a mile) to the west.

The exploration of Dark Age and medieval Britain is, at least for the moment, over for this author, but hopefully it may only be beginning for the reader. It is fitting that I should close with the story of the medieval town. For all the discomforts and perils of life in these places, and despite the numerous examples which failed to make their mark, this is a success story. We began with the collapse of the Roman province and the decay of its towns, but the urban developments of the later centuries were sustained and the new towns generally prospered. By the middle of the nineteenth century Britain had become a country in which townsfolk outnumbered their country cousins – a situation which would have seemed quite amazing to the medieval minds of the English, who were still essentially a nation of village, townlet and hamlet dwellers, and utterly fantastic to the peoples of the Celtic countries, where the agricultural hamlet was still the essential abode and workplace.

If we are to have any hope of understanding the past then we must try to see the world and the neighbourhood through the eyes of former communities. While the Dark Ages may have seemed dark to many people living at the time, for others things were much as before and new opportunities might be just around the corner. The term 'medieval' would be totally meaningless to the people of the Middle Ages. As far as they were concerned they were thoroughly modern, and they faced the future with much the same hopes and suspicions as we do today. It is unfortunate that these former communities and their works are often presented as being rather comical and primitive when it is the dogged tenacity, survival and ingenuity of the people which should impress us most. Without the advances achieved by the folk who lived during the period covered by this book, we might all be living early Dark Age lifestyles – which most of us would not enjoy very much. These folk, like ourselves, could be brutal as well as compassionate, selfish as well as idealistic. Their civilizations may have been a good many steps behind our own, but they still lacked the ability to destroy all life and beauty on this planet. Had there been nuclear or biological weapons in the British arsenals at the times of the Saxon, Danish or Norman landings or the Crusades then doubtless they would have been used. Yet history has shown that people have a remarkable ability to overcome catastrophes and to survive invasions. If we were able to identify our ancestors precisely we would find that our roots are buried deeply in prehistoric times. Invaders did not permanently transform the fabric of society – and any group conquering Britain did so at the ultimate price of submerging their identities in the evolving but indestructible characters of the islanders.

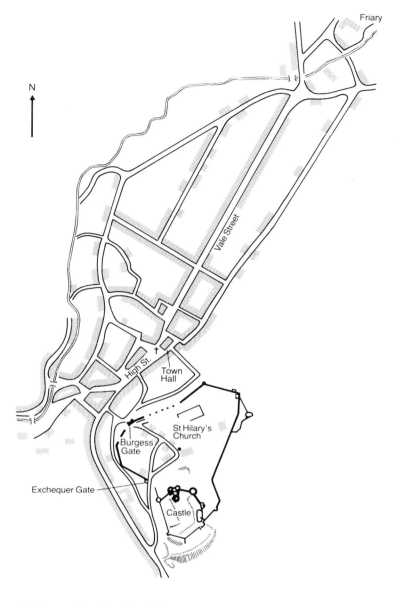

The layout of medieval Denbigh.

Gazetteer

The following gazetteer is a county listing of all those places shown on the maps:

1 Aspects of Dark Age Britain
2 Medieval castles
3 Saxon church architecture
4 Monastic sites
5 Town and country in medieval Britain: some places mentioned in Chapter 10.

NT The National Trust
NTS The National Trust for Scotland

England

Avon
Bath (1): Cathedral Priory (4)
Bristol Cathedral (4)
Hinton Priory (4)
Wansdyke, linear earthwork (1)

Bedfordshire
Bedford Castle (2)
Chicksands Priory (4)
Clapham (3)
Dunstable Priory (4)
Elstow Abbey (4)
Willington (5)

Berkshire
Donnington Castle (2)
Reading Abbey (4)
Windsor Castle (2)

Buckinghamshire
Burnham Abbey (4)
Cublington (5)
Long Crendon (5)
Wing (3)

Cambridgeshire
Anglesey Abbey (NT) (4, 5)
Barnack (3)
Cambridge: Castle (2); St Benet (3)
Denney Abbey (4)
Devil's Dyke, linear earthwork (1)
Ely (1, 5): Castle (2); Cathedral Priory (4)
Fleam Ditch, linear earthwork (1)
Foxton (5)
Great Paxton (3)
Great Shelford (5)
Heydon Ditch, linear earthwork (1)
Huntingdon (5)
Ickleton (3)
Isleham Priory (4)
Peterborough (3): Abbey (4)
Ramsey Abbey (4)
St Ives (5)
Soham (5)
Swavesey Priory (4)
Thorney Abbey (4)
Wimpole Park (NT) (5)
Wittering (3)

Cheshire
Beeston Castle (2)
Chester (1, 5): Castle (2); Cathedral (4)
Denbigh (5)
Norton Abbey (4)
Sandbach, free-standing cross (1)

Cleveland
Guisborough Priory (4)
Norton (3)

Cornwall
Bolster Bank, linear earthwork (1)
Boscastle (5)
Giant's Hedge, linear earthwork (1)
Launceston Castle (2)
Restormel Castle (2)
St Germans Priory (4)
St Michael's Mount Priory (NT) (4)
Tintagel: Castle (2); Celtic monastery (1)
Trematon Castle (2)

Cumbria
Addingham, free-standing cross (1)
Appleby (5): Castle (2)
Bewcastle, free-standing cross (1)
Brough Castle (2)
Brougham Castle (2)
Calder Abbey (4)
Carlisle (1): Castle (2); Cathedral Priory (4)
Cartmel Priory (4)
Cockermouth Castle (2)
Furness Abbey (4)
Gosforth, free-standing cross (1)
Heversham, free-standing cross (1)
Irton, free-standing cross (1)
Kendal, free-standing cross (1)
Lanercost Priory (4)
St Bees Priory (4)
Shap Abbey (4)
Wasdale Head (5)
Wetheral Priory (4)

Derbyshire
Bakewell, free-standing cross (1)
Beauchief Abbey (4)
Bradbourne, free-standing cross (1)
Castleton (5)
Dale Abbey (4)
Duffield Castle (NT) (2)
Eyam, free-standing cross (1)
Grey Ditch, linear earthwork (1)
Melbourne (3)
Peveril Castle (2)
Repton (3): Priory (4)
Wirksworth, free-standing cross (1)

Devon
Bampton (5)
Berry Pomeroy Castle (2)
Bickleigh Castle (2)
Braunton (5)
Buckfast Abbey (4)
Buckland Abbey (NT) (4)
Cornworthy Priory (4)
Dunkeswell Abbey (4)
Exeter: St Nicholas' Priory (4)
Frithelstock Priory (4)
Hartland Abbey (4)
Hound Tor (5)
Lydford Castle (2)
Marisco Castle (2)
Plympton Priory (4)
Tavistock Abbey (4)
Tiverton Castle (2)
Totnes Castle (2)

Dorset
Abbotsbury (5): Abbey (4)
Bokerley Ditch, linear earthwork (1)
Cerne Abbas (5): Abbey (4)
Christchurch Priory (4)
Combs Ditch, linear earthwork (1)
Corfe Castle (NT) (2)
Forde Abbey (4)
Milton Abbey (4)
Okeford Fitzpaine (5)
Shaftesbury Abbey (4)
Sherborne (3): Abbey (4); Castle (2); Cathedral (1)
Wareham: St Martin (3); St Mary (3)
Wimborne Minster (3)
Winterbourne Abbas (5)
Worth Matravers (5)

Durham
Barnard Castle (2)
Bishop Auckland, free-standing cross (1)
Bowes Castle (2)
Croft, free-standing cross (1)
Durham: Castle (2); Cathedral (1); Cathedral Priory (4)
Egglestone Abbey (4)
Escomb (3)
Finchale Priory (4)
Seaham (3)

East Sussex
Battle Abbey (4)
Bayham Abbey (4)
Bishopstone (3)
Bodiam Castle (NT) (2)
Hastings (5): Castle (2)
Lewes: Castle (2); Priory (4)
Pevensey Castle (2)
Robertsbridge Abbey (4)
Wilmington Priory (4)

Essex
Beeleigh Abbey (4)
Bradwell-on-Sea (3)
Coggeshall Abbey (4)
Colchester: Castle (2); St Botolph's Priory (4); St John's Abbey (4)
Greensted (3)
Hadleigh Castle (2)
Hadstock (3)
Hedingham Castle (2)
Little Dunmow (4)
Ongar Castle (2)
Pleshey Castle (2)
Prittlewell Priory (4)
Rayleigh Mount (NT) (2)
St Osyth's Priory (4)
Strethall (3)
Thaxted (5)
Tilty Abbey (4)

Gloucestershire
Berkeley Castle (2)
Chipping Campden (5)
Cirencester (3)
Coln Rogers (3)
Deerhurst: Odda's Chapel (3); Priory (4); St Mary (3)
Dymock (3)
Flaxley Abbey (4)
Gloucester: Llanthony Secunda Priory (4): St Oswald's Priory (3, 4); St Peter (3)
Hailes Abbey (NT) (4)
Leonard Stanley Priory (4)
Lydney Castle (2)
Lypiatt, free-standing cross (1)
Tewkesbury Abbey (4)

Hampshire
Beaulieu (5): Abbey (4)

Bokerley Ditch, linear
  earthwork (1)
Breamore (3)
Monk Sherborne Priory (4)
Mottisfont Priory (NT) (4)
Netley Abbey (4)
Odiham Castle (2)
Portchester Castle (2)
Romsey Abbey (4)
Southwick Priory (4)
Titchfield (3): Abbey (4)
Winchester (5): Castle (2);
  Castle Chapel (3);
  Cathedral (1); Cathedral
  Priory (4); Hyde Abbey
  (4); New Minster (3); Old
  Minster (3)

Hereford and Worcester
Abbey Dore Abbey (4)
Aconbury Priory (4)
Bewdley (5)
Broadway (5)
Evesham Abbey (4)
Goodrich Castle (2)
Great Malvern Priory (4)
Hereford Cathedral (1)
Leominster Priory (4)
Little Malvern Priory (4)
Longtown Castle (2)
Offa's Dyke, linear earthwork
  (1)
Pembridge Castle (2)
Pershore Priory (4)
Richard's Castle (2)
Rowe Ditch, linear earthwork
  (1)
Wigmore Abbey (4)
Worcester: Cathedral (1);
  Cathedral Priory (4)

Hertfordshire
Berkhamsted Castle (2)
Great Gaddesden (5)
Hertford Castle (2)
Royston Priory (4)
St Albans Abbey (4)
Waltham Abbey (4)

Humberside
Barton upon Humber (3)
Bridlington Priory (4)
Broughton (3)
Danes' Dyke, linear
  earthwork (1)
Ellerton Priory (4)
Skipsea Castle (2)
Swine Priory (4)
Thornton Abbey (4)
Watton Priory (4)

Isle of Wight
Carisbrooke Castle (2)

Kent
Allington Castle (2)
Canterbury: Cathedral (1); St
  Augustine (3);
  St Augustine's Abbey (4);
  St Martin (3); St Mary (3);
  St Pancras (3); SS Peter
  and Paul (3)
Chilham Castle (2)
Dover (3): Castle (2); St

Martin's Priory (4);
  St Radegund's Abbey (4)
Eynsford Castle (2)
Hever Castle (2)
Lyminge (3)
Lympne (3)
Maidstone Castle (2)
Minster (3)
Minster Priory (4)
Queenborough (5)
Reculver (3)
Rochester (3): Castle (2);
  Cathedral (1); Cathedral
  Abbey (4)
Saltwood Castle (2)
Sutton Valence Castle (2)
Tonbridge Castle (2)
Wigmore Castle (2)
Winchelsea (5)

Lancashire
Clitheroe Castle (2)
Heysham, free-standing cross
  (1); St Patrick (3)
Hornby, free-standing cross
  (1)
Lancaster: Castle (2); free-
  standing cross (1);
  St Mary's Priory (4)
Upholland Priory (4)
Whalley Abbey (4)

Leicestershire
Ashby da la Zouch Castle (2)
Bradgate (5)
Leicester Castle (2)
Owston Abbey (4)
Ulverscroft Priory (NT) (4)

Lincolnshire
Bardney Abbey (4)
Bolingbroke Castle (2)
Bourne Abbey (4)
Crowland Abbey (4)
Deeping St James' Priory
  Cells (4)
Edenham, free-standing cross
  (1)
Folkingham (5)
Kirkstead Abbey (4)
Lincoln (1, 5): Castle (2)
Stow (3)
Torksey (5)

London
All Hallows (3)
Barking Abbey (4)
London Cathedral (1)
Southwark Cathedral Priory
  (4)
Tower of London (2)
Westminster Abbey (4)

Greater Manchester
Nico Ditch, linear earthwork
  (1)

Merseyside
Birkenhead Priory (4)

Norfolk
Attleborough (3)
Bichamditch, linear earthwork
  (1)
Binham Priory (4)

Castle Acre: Castle (2); Priory
  (4)
Castle Rising (2)
Devil's Dyke, linear
  earthwork (1)
Dunham Magna (3)
Egmere (5)
Elmham Cathedral (1, 3);
  now North Elmham
Foss Ditch, linear earthwork
  (1)
Great Yarmouth Priory (4)
Hales (3)
Ingham Priory (4)
Launditch, linear earthwork
  (1)
Melton Constable (3)
Newton (3)
North Creake Abbey (4)
Norwich (1): Castle (2);
  Cathedral Priory (4):
  St John Timberhill (3)
Pentney Priory (4)
St Olave's Priory (4)
South Lopham (3)
Thetford (1): Castle (2);
  Priory (4)
Walsingham Abbey (4)
Weeting Castle (2)
West Acre Priory (4)
Wymondham Abbey (4)

Northamptonshire
Brigstock (3)
Brixworth (3)
Canons Ashby Priory (NT)
  (4)
Clopton (5)
Earls Barton (3)
Rockingham Castle (2)

Northumberland
Alnwick: Abbey (4); Castle
  (2)
Bamburgh: Castle (2); Priory
  (4)
Berwick upon Tweed Castle
  (2)
Blanchland Abbey (4)
Brinkburn Priory (4)
Bywell: St Peter (3)
Corbridge (3)
Dunstanburgh Castle (NT)
  (2)
Hexham (3): Priory (4)
Lindisfarne (1): Priory (4)
Mitford Castle (2)
Norham Castle (2)
Prudhoe Castle (2)
Rothbury, free-standing cross
  (1)
Stamfordham, free-standing
  cross (1)
Warkworth Castle (2)

North Yorkshire
Appleton-le-Moors (5)
Arncliffe (5)
Bolton Priory (4, 5)
Boroughbridge, free-standing
  cross (1)
Byland Abbey (4)
Coverham Abbey (4)

Drax (5)
Easby: free-standing cross
  (1); Abbey (4)
Fountains Abbey (NT) (4, 5)
Hacanos, free-standing cross
  (1)
Helmsley Castle (2)
Jervaulx Abbey (4)
Kirkdales (3)
Kirk Hammerton (3)
Kirkham Priory (4)
Knaresborough Castle (2)
Lastingham Abbey (4)
Linton (5)
Little Ouseburn (3)
Malham (5)
Masham, free-standing cross
  (1)
Middleham Castle (2)
Mt Grace Priory (NT) (4)
Northallerton, free-standing
  cross (1)
Nun Monkton (4, 5)
Old Byland (5)
Old Malton Priory (4)
Pickering Castle (2)
Pocklington (5)
Richmond: Castle (2); Priory
  (4)
Rievaulx Abbey (4)
Ripley (5)
Ripon (3)
Rosedale Priory (4)
Scarborough Castle (2)
Scot's Dyke, linear earthwork
  (1)
Selby Abbey (4)
Skipton (5): Castle (2)
Spofforth Castle (2)
Weaverthorpe (3)
Wharram-le-Street (3)
Wharram Percy (5)
Whitby Abbey (4)
Yedingham Priory (4)
York (5): Castle (2): Holy
  Trinity Priory (4); Minster
  (1); St Mary's Abbey (4)

Nottinghamshire
Blyth Priory (4)
Laxton (5)
Mattersey Priory (4)
Newark-on-Trent Castle (2)
Newstead Abbey (4)
Nottingham Castle (2)
Rufford Abbey (4)
Stapleford, free-standing
  cross (1)
Thurgarton Priory (4)
Welbeck Abbey (4)
Worksop Priory (4)

Oxfordshire
Abingdon Abbey (4)
Deddington Castle (2)
Dorchester: Abbey (4);
  Cathedral (1)
Great Coxwell (NT) (5)
Langford (3)
Oxford (5): Castle (2); St
  Frideswide's Cathedral (4)
Steventon Priory (4)
Thame (5): Abbey (4)

Littleferry Links, Pictish symbol stone (1)
Lynchurn, Pictish symbol stone (1)
Moil Castle (2)
Raasay, Pictish symbol stone (1)
Reay, Pictish symbol stone (1)
Strathpeffer, Pictish symbol stone (1)
Tobar na Maor, Pictish symbol stone (1)
Urquhart, Pictish symbol stone (1)

Lothian
Aberlady, free-standing cross (1)
Dirleton Castle (2)
Dunbar Castle (2)
Edinburgh, Pictish symbol stone (1)
Hailes Castle (2)
Morham, free-standing cross (1)
Tantallon Castle (2)

Orkney
Aikerness, Pictish symbol stone (1)
Birsay, Pictish symbol stone (1)
Garth, Pictish symbol stone (1)
Greens, Pictish symbol stone (1)
South Ronaldsay, Pictish symbol stone (1)

Shetland
Jarlshof, Pictish symbol stone (1)
Lerwick, Pictish symbol stone (1)
St Ninian's Isle, Pictish symbol stone (1)
Sandness, Pictish symbol stone (1)
Uyea, Pictish symbol stone (1)

Strathclyde
Bothwell Castle (2)
Crossraguel Abbey (4)
Duart Castle (2)
Dumbarton Castle (2)

Dunstaffenage Castle (2)
Iona Abbey (4)
Kilfinan, free-standing cross (1)
Kilmory Knap, free-standing cross (1)
Kilneave, free-standing cross (1)
Kilwinning Abbey (4)
Paisley Abbey (4)
Riskbuie, free-standing cross (1)
Rothesay Castle (2)
Saddell Abbey (4)
Sween Castle (2)

Tayside
Aberlemno, Pictish symbol stone (1)
Arbroath Abbey (4)
Blair Atholl Castle (2)
Collace, Pictish symbol stone (1)
Coupar Angus Abbey (4)
Edzell, free-standing cross (1)
Glamis Castle (2)
Kirriemuir, Pictish symbol stone (1)
Restenneth (3): Priory (4)
Strathmartine, Pictish symbol stone (1)
Struan, Pictish symbol stone (1)

Western Isles
Kiessimul Castle (2)

Wales

Clywd
Basingwerk Abbey (4)
Castell Dinas Bran (2)
Chirk Castle (NT) (2)
Denbigh Castle (2)
Ewloe Castle (2)
Flint Castle (2)
Hawarden Castle (2)
Holt Castle (2)
Hope Castle (2)
Offa's Dyke, linear earthwork (1)
Prestatyn Castle (2)
Rhuddlan Castle (2)

Ruthin Castle (2)
St Asaph Cathedral (1)
Valle Crucis Abbey (4)

Dyfed
Aberystwyth Castle (2)
Carew Castle (2)
Carmarthen Castle (2)
Cilgerran (5): Castle (NT) (2)
Dynevor Castle (2)
Haverfordwest Castle (2); Priory (4)
Kidwelly: Castle (2); Priory (4)
Llanddewi-Brefi, Celtic monastery (1)
Llanstephan Castle (2)
Llawhaden Castle (2)
Manorbier Castle (2)
Narberth Castle (2)
Nevern, Celtic monastery (1)
Newcastle Emlyn Castle (2)
Pembroke (5): Castle (2); Priory (4)
St David's Cathedral (1)
Strata Florida Abbey (4)
Talley Abbey (4)
Tenby (5): Castle (2)
Whitland Abbey (4)
Wiston Castle (2)

Gwent
Abergavenny: Castle (2); Priory (4)
Caerleon Castle (2)
Caldicot Castle (2)
Chepstow (5): Castle (2); Priory (4)
Grosmont (5): Castle (2)
Llanthony Priory (4)
Monmouth: Castle (2); Priory (4)
Newport Castle (2)
Offa's Dyke, linear earthwork (1)
Skenfrith (5): Castle (NT) (2)
Tintern Abbey (4)
Usk Priory (4)
White Castle (2)

Gwynedd
Bangor Cathedral (1)
Beaumaris Castle (2)
Beddgelert Priory (4)

Caernarfon (5): Castle (2)
Castell Carndochan (2)
Castell y Bere (2)
Conwy (5): Castle (2)
Criccieth Castle (2)
Cymmer Abbey (4)
Dolbadarn Castle (2)
Dolwyddelan Castle (2)
Harlech Castle (2)
Penmon (5): Priory (NT) (4)
Pennant Melangell, free-standing cross (1)

Mid Glamorgan
Caerphilly Castle (2)
Coity Castle (2)
Kenfig Castle (2)
Newcastle Castle (2)
Ogmore Castle (2)

Powys
Brecon: Castle (2); Priory (4)
Bronllys Castle (2)
Crickhowell Castle (2)
Dolforwyn Castle (2)
Double Dyche, linear earthwork (1)
Offa's Dyke, linear earthwork (1)
Montgomery (5): Castle (2)
New Radnor (5)
Painscastle Castle (2)
Powis Castle (NT) (2)
Short Ditch, linear earthwork (1)
Short Ditches, linear earthwork (1)
Tretower Castle (2)
Wanten Dyche, linear earthwork (1)

South Glamorgan
Cardiff Castle (2)
Castell Coch (2)
Llandaff Cathedral (1)
St Fagans Castle (2)

West Glamorgan
Loughor Castle (2)
Margam Abbey (4)
Neath Abbey (4)
Oxwich Castle (2)
Oystermouth Castle (2)
Pennard Castle (2)
Weobley Castle (2)

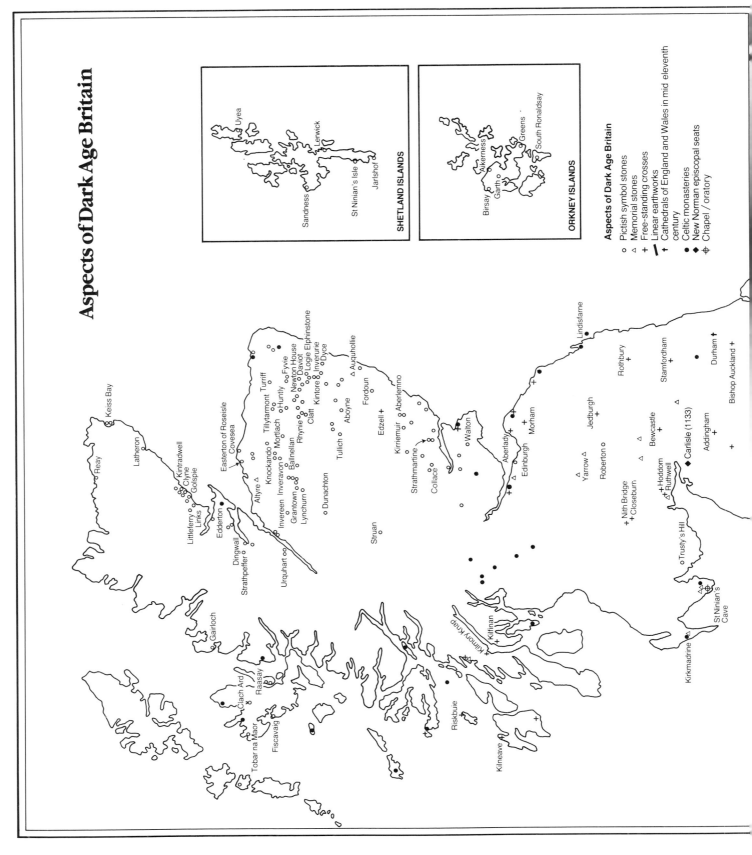

Aspects of Dark Age Britain

SHETLAND ISLANDS

Uyea
Sandness
Lerwick
St Ninian's Isle
Jarlshof

ORKNEY ISLANDS

Birsay
Garth
Aikerness
Greens
South Ronaldsay

Aspects of Dark Age Britain

- ○ Pictish symbol stones
- △ Memorial stones
- + Free-standing crosses
- \ Linear earthworks
- † Cathedrals of England and Wales in mid eleventh century
- ● Celtic monasteries
- ◆ New Norman episcopal seats
- ⊕ Chapel / oratory

Keiss Bay
Reay
Latheron
Kintradwell
Clyne
Golspie
Littleferry
Links
Edderton
Dingwall
Strathpeffer
Easterton of Roseisle
Covesea
Altyre
Knockando
Mortlach
Invereen
Inveravon
Grantown
Lynchurn
Urquhart
Ballnellan
Rhynie
Clatt
Kintore
Inverurie
Dyce
Newton House
Daviot
Logie Elphinstone
Fyvie
Turriff
Tillytarmont
Huntly
Dunachton
Tullich
Aboyne
Fordoun
Auquhollie
Struan
Edzell
Kirriemuir
Aberlemno
Strathmartine
Collace
Walton
Aberlady
Edinburgh
Morham
Lindisfarne
Rothbury
Stamfordham
Durham
Bishop Auckland
Jedburgh
Yarrow
Roberton
Bewcastle
Addingham
Carlisle (1133)
Nith Bridge
Closeburn
Hoddom
Ruthwell
Trusty's Hill
St Ninian's Cave
Kirkmadrine
Kilmory Knap
Kilfinan
Riskbuie
Kilneave
Gairloch
Clach Ard
Raasay
Tobar na Maor
Fiscavaig

Scot's
Dyke + Croft
+ Easby

Hacanos
+

+ Northallerton

Masham +

+ Boroughbridge

Danes'
Dyke

Ilkley + Collingham
Otley + York

Roman Rig
Dewsbury +

Becca Banks

Gosforth
+ Irton
Kendal
+

+ Heversham
+ Hornby
+ Lancaster

Heysham +

St
Asaph +

Bangor +

Nevern

St David's +

Chester (1075) ◆

+ Sandbach

Nico Ditch

Roman
Ridge

Grey Ditch + Eyam
+ Bakewell

Sheffield
+

+ Wirksworth
+ Bradbourne

+ Stapleford

+ Lincoln (1075) ◆

+ Edenham

+ Lichfield
+ Wolverhampton

Pennant
Melangell +

Wanten
Dyche
Double Dyche
Short Ditches Short Ditch

Llanddewi-
Brefi

Rowe Ditch

Otfa's Dyke

+ Hereford

Llandaff +

+ Coventry (1095)
+ Rugby

+ Worcester

+ Lypiatt

Wansdyke

+ Dorchester

+ Ramsbury

Bath (1088) ◆
+ Wells

Ponter's Ball

+ Sherborne

Sarum (1075) ◆
+ Winchester

Bokerley Ditch

Combs Ditch

Laundltch

Bichamditch

Foss Ditch

+ North
Elmham

Norwich (1097) ◆

Devil's Dyke

Ely (1109) ◆ Black Ditches Thetford (1075) ◆
Devil's Dyke

Fleam Ditch

Heydon Ditch

London +

Rochester +

Canterbury +

Selsey

Giant's
Hedge

Tintagel +

Bolster Bank

243

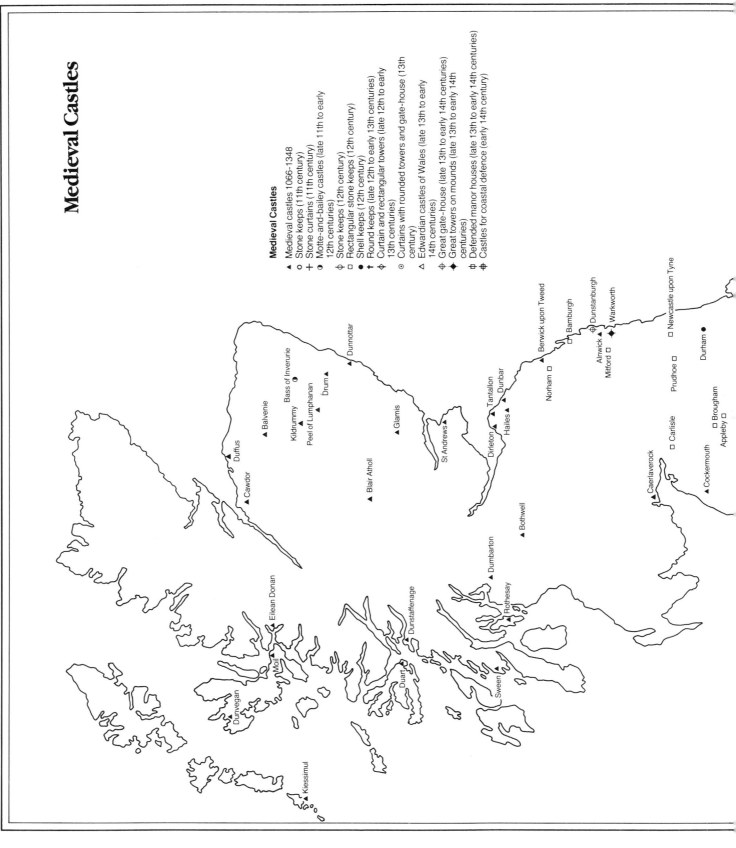

Medieval Castles

Medieval Castles

▲ Medieval castles 1066–1348
○ Stone keeps (11th century)
+ Stone curtains (11th century)
◔ Motte-and-bailey castles (late 11th to early 12th centuries)
φ Stone keeps (12th century)
□ Rectangular stone keeps (12th century)
● Shell keeps (12th century)
✝ Round keeps (late 12th to early 13th centuries)
◈ Curtain and rectangular towers (late 12th to early 13th centuries)
⊙ Curtains with rounded towers and gate-house (13th century)
△ Edwardian castles of Wales (late 13th to early 14th centuries)
⊕ Great gate-house (late 13th to early 14th centuries)
◆ Great towers on mounds (late 13th to early 14th centuries)
⊞ Defended manor houses (late 13th to early 14th centuries)
⊕ Castles for coastal defence (early 14th century)

Dunnottar ▲
Duffus □
Balvenie ▲
Kildrummy ◔ Bass of Inverurie
Peel of Lumphanan ▲ Drum ▲
Cawdor ▲
Glamis ▲
Blair Atholl ▲
St Andrews ▲
Dunvegan ▲
Eilean Donan
Moil ▲
Dirleton Tantallon ▲
Dunbar ▲
Hailes ▲
Bothwell ▲
Dumbarton ▲
Dunstaffenage ▲
Rothesay ●
Duart ▲
Sween ▲
Kiessimul ▲
Berwick upon Tweed
Bamburgh □
Dunstanburgh ⊕
Alnwick ▲ Warkworth ◆
Mitford □
Newcastle upon Tyne □
Norham □
Durham ●
Caerlaverock ▲
Carlisle □
Prudhoe □
Cockermouth ▲ Brougham □
Appleby □

244

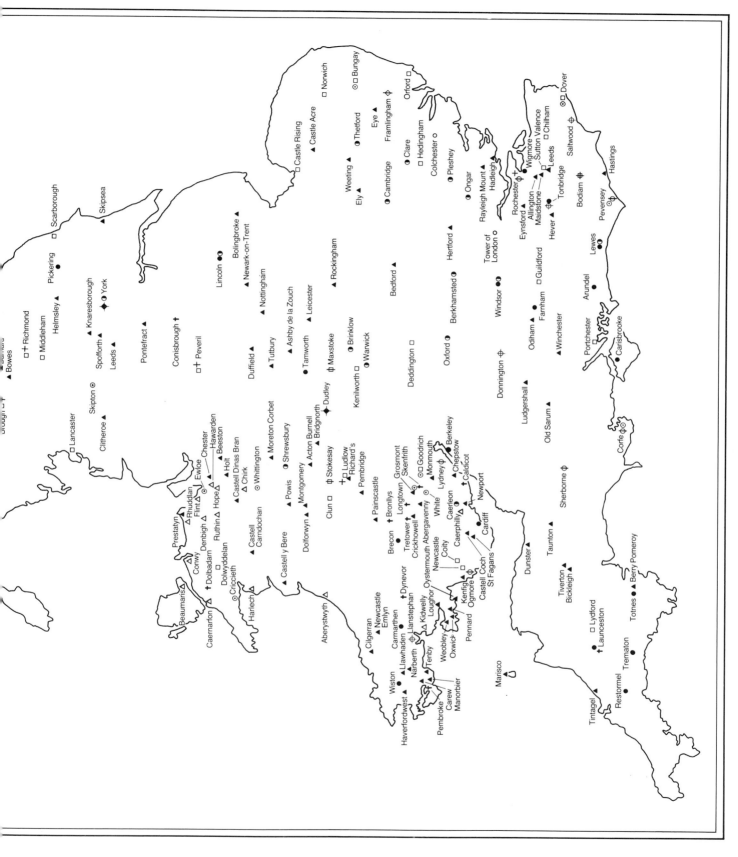

Bowes ▲
Richmond □✝
Middleham □
Helmsley ▲
Pickering ●
Scarborough □
Skipsea ▲

Lancaster □
Clitheroe ▲
Skipton ⊙
Spofforth ◆
Knaresborough ▲
Leeds ▲
York ✦⊙
Pontefract ▲
Conisbrough ✝
Peveril □✝

Lincoln ●●
Newark-on-Trent ▲
Bolingbroke ▲
Duffield □
Nottingham ◉
Tutbury ▲
Ashby de la Zouch ▲
Tamworth ▲
Leicester ▲
Rockingham ▲

Castle Rising □
Castle Acre ▲
Norwich □
Bungay ⊙□
Orford ⬡ □
Dover ⊙□

Weeting ▲
Thetford ⊙●
Eye ▲
Framlingham ⬡
Saltwood ⬡
Hastings ▲
Pevensey ⊞

Ely ●
Cambridge ▲
Clare ●
Hedingham ▲
Colchester ○
Pleshey ●
Ongar ▲
Rayleigh Mount ▲
Hadleigh ▲
Rochester ✝□
Wigmore ●
Allington ⬡
Sutton Valence □
Chilham □
Leeds ▲
Tonbridge ⬡
Bodiam ⊞
Hertford ▲
Tower of London ○
Eynsford ⊙
Maidstone ⬡
Hever ⬡
Lewes ⬡

Bedford ▲
Berkhamsted ◉
Windsor ●●
Odiham ▲
Guildford □
Arundel ▲
Portchester ▲
Carisbrooke ●

Oxford ◉
Deddington □
Donnington ⬡
Farnham ●
Winchester ▲
Old Sarum ▲
Ludgershall ▲
Corfe ⬡⊙

Dudley ◆
Kenilworth □
Brinklow ⊙
Warwick ▲
Maxstoke ⬡

Chester ▲
Hawarden ▲
Ewloe ▲
Beeston ▲
Holt △
Castell Dinas Bran △
Chirk ⊙
Whittington ▲
Moreton Corbet ▲
Shrewsbury ◉
Acton Burnell ▲
Bridgnorth ◆
Ludlow □✝
Richard's ✝
Pembridge ▲
Clun □
Stokesay ⬡

Prestatyn
Rhuddlan △
Flint □△
Denbigh ▲⊙
Ruthin △
Hope △
Powis ◉
Montgomery ▲
Dolforwyn ▲
Conwy ⬡
Dolbadarn ✝
Dolwyddelan ▲
Criccieth ⊙
Harlech △
Castell Carndochan ▲
Castell y Bere ▲
Aberystwyth △
Caernarfon △
Beaumaris △

Brecon ●
Tretower ✝
Crickhowell ✝
Newcastle □
Coity □
Oystermouth ▲
Abergavenny ⊙
White ✝
Caerleon △
Newport ▲
Caerphilly △
Cardiff ▲
Castell Coch ▲
St Fagans □
Kenfig ⬡
Ogmore □
Longtown ✝
Grosmont ✝
Skenfrith ⊙
Goodrich ●
Monmouth ▲
Lydney ⬡
Chepstow ▲
Caldicot ▲
Berkeley ●

Cilgerran ▲
Newcastle Emlyn △
Carmarthen ●
Dynevor ✝
Llawhaden ⬡
Llanstephan △
Kidwelly ▲
Loughor ▲
Narberth ▲
Tenby ▲
Weobley ▲
Oxwich ✝
Pennard ▲
Wiston ▲
Haverfordwest ▲
Pembroke ▲
Carew ▲
Manorbier ▲

Marisco ⬡

Taunton ▲
Dunster ▲
Tiverton ▲
Bickleigh ▲
Sherborne ⬡
Lydford □
Launceston ✝
Totnes ●
Berry Pomeroy ▲
Tintagel ▲
Restormel ●
Tremanton ●

245

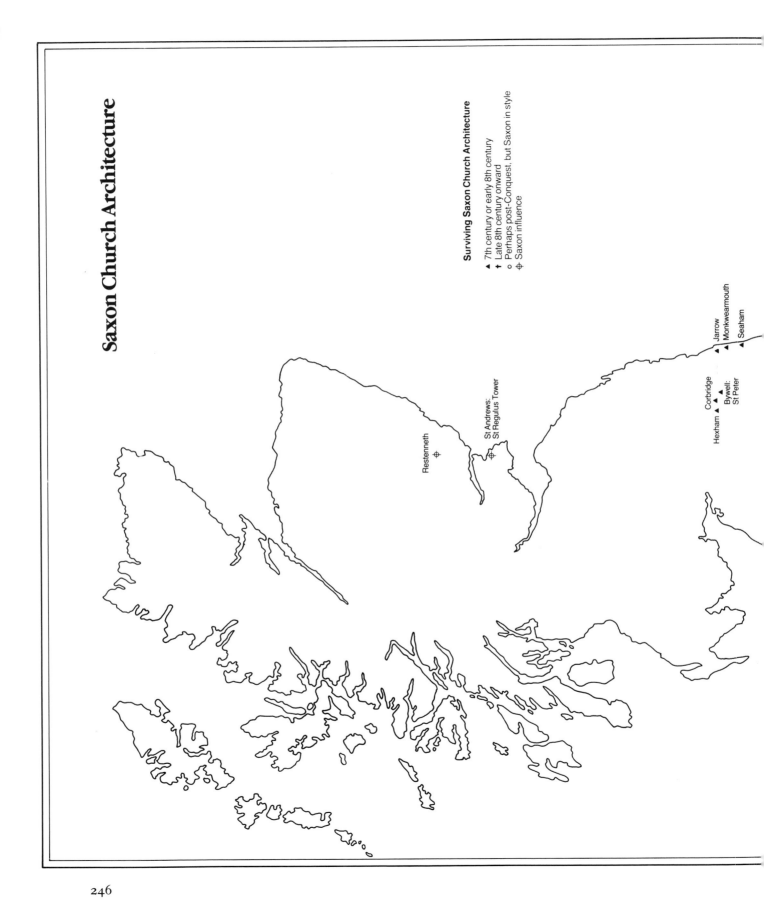

Saxon Church Architecture

Surviving Saxon Church Architecture

▲ 7th century or early 8th century
† Late 8th century onward
○ Perhaps post-Conquest, but Saxon in style
✛ Saxon influence

Restenneth ✛

St Andrews:
St Regulus Tower ✛

Hexham ▲ Corbridge ▲

Bywell:
St Peter ▲

Jarrow ▲
Monkwearmouth ▲
Seaham ▲

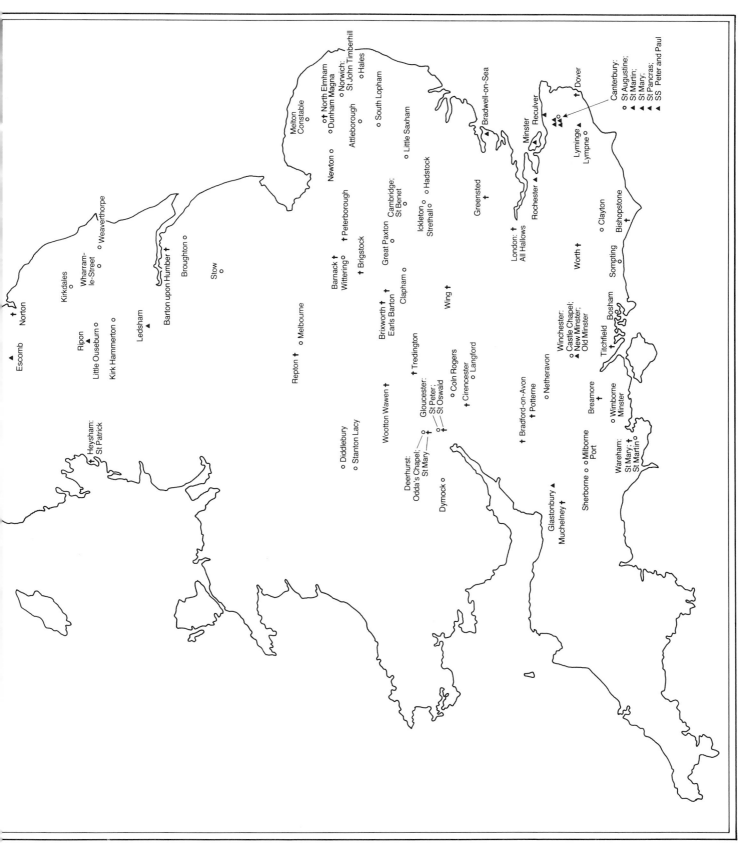

Escomb ▲

Heysham:
St Patrick ▲

Kirkdales
Wharram- ○ Weaverthorpe
le-Street
Ripon ▲
Little Ouseburn ○
Kirk Hammerton ○
Ledsham ▲
Barton upon Humber ✝
Broughton ○

Norton ✝

Melton
Constable ○
North Elmham ○✝
Dunham Magna ○
Norwich:
St John Timberhill ○
Attleborough ○
Hales ○
South Lopham ○
Little Saxham ○

Newton ○

Stow ○
Barnack ✝
Wittering ○
Peterborough ✝
Brigstock ✝
Brixworth ✝
Earls Barton ✝
Clapham ○
Wing ✝

Great Paxton ○
Cambridge;
St Benet ○
Ickleton ○
Strethall ○
Hadstock ○

Greensted ○

Bradwell-on-Sea ✝

Minster
Reculver ▲
Rochester ▲
Lyminge ▲
Lympne ○
Dover ○

Canterbury:
○ St Augustine;
▲ St Martin;
▲ St Mary;
▲ St Pancras;
▲ SS Peter and Paul

London: ✝
All Hallows

Clayton ○
Worth ✝
Bishopstone ○
Sompting ○

Melbourne ○

Repton ✝

Wootton Wawen ✝
Tredington ✝
Gloucester:
St Peter;
St Oswald
Deerhurst:
Odda's Chapel; ✝
St Mary
Dymock ○

Diddlebury ○
Stanton Lacy ○

Coln Rogers ○
Cirencester ✝
Langford ○

Bradford-on-Avon ✝
Potterne ✝
Netheravon ✝

Winchester:
Castle Chapel; ○
New Minster; ✝
Old Minster ○

Titchfield
Bosham ✝

Breamore ✝
Wimborne
Minster ○
Wareham:
St Mary; ○
St Martin ○

Sherborne ○
Milborne ○
Port

Glastonbury ✝
Muchelney ▲

247

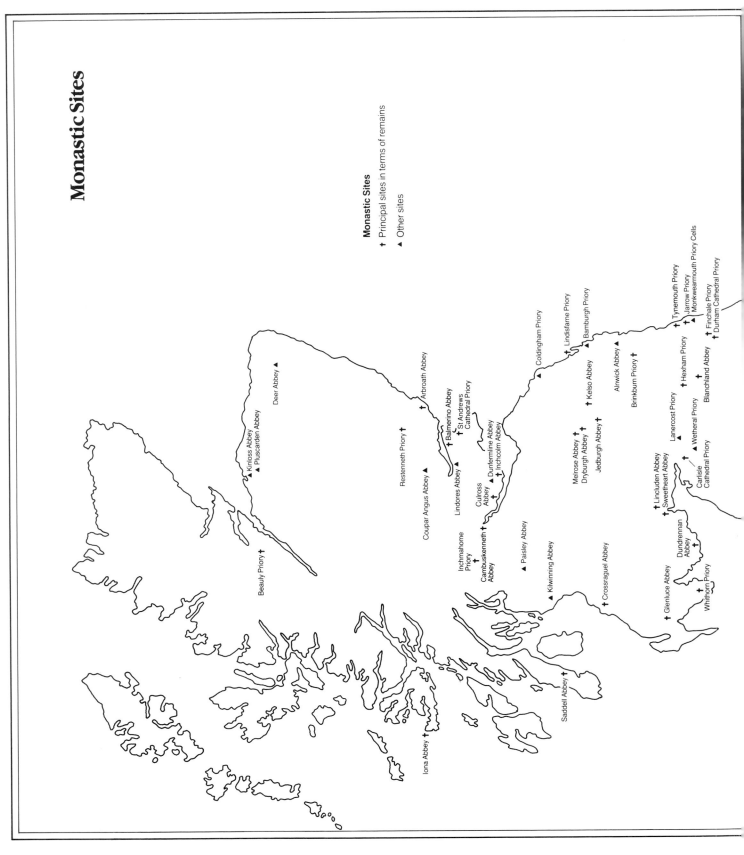

Monastic Sites

Monastic Sites

✝ Principal sites in terms of remains

▲ Other sites

Beauly Priory ✝

Kinloss Abbey ▲
Pluscarden Abbey ▲

Deer Abbey ▲

Restenneth Priory ✝

Arbroath Abbey ✝

Coupar Angus Abbey ▲

Balmerino Abbey ✝
St Andrews Cathedral Priory ✝

Lindores Abbey ▲

Culross Abbey ✝

Dunfermline Abbey ▲
Inchcolm Abbey ✝

Inchmahome Priory ✝

Cambuskenneth Abbey ✝

Paisley Abbey ▲

Kilwinning Abbey ▲

Crossraguel Abbey ✝

Iona Abbey ✝

Saddell Abbey ✝

Glenluce Abbey ✝

Dundrennan Abbey ▲

Whithorn Priory ✝

Lincluden Abbey ✝
Sweetheart Abbey ✝

Carlisle Cathedral Priory ✝

Melrose Abbey ✝
Dryburgh Abbey ✝

Jedburgh Abbey ✝

Lanercost Priory ▲
Wetheral Priory ✝

Kelso Abbey ✝

Alnwick Abbey ▲

Brinkburn Priory ✝

Hexham Priory ✝

Blanchland Abbey ▲

Coldingham Priory ✝

Lindisfarne Priory ▲

Bamburgh Priory ▲

Tynemouth Priory ✝
Jarrow Priory ▲
Monkwearmouth Priory Cells ▲

Finchale Priory ▲
Durham Cathedral Priory ✝

248

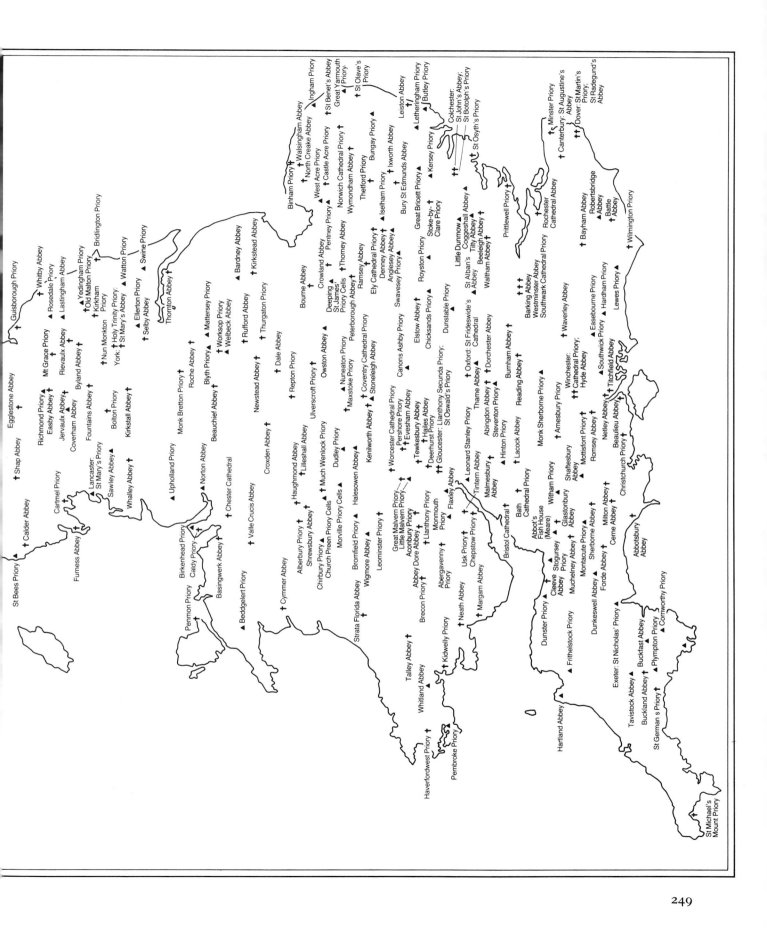

Guisborough Priory †
Whitby Abbey †
Rosedale Priory ▲
Lastingham Abbey ▲
Egglestone Abbey †
Mt Grace Priory †
Richmond Priory ▲
Easby Abbey †
Jervaulx Abbey ▲
Coverham Abbey †
Yedingham Priory ▲
Old Malton Priory ▲
Kirkham Priory †
Bridlington Priory †
Watton Priory ▲
Ellerton Priory ▲
Swine Priory ▲
Nun Monkton †
Holy Trinity Priory: †
York: St Mary's Abbey †
Selby Abbey †
Thornton Abbey †
Bardney Abbey ▲
Kirkstead Abbey ▲
Matterssey Priory ▲
Worksop Priory †
Welbeck Abbey ▲
Rufford Abbey †
Thurgaton Priory †
Shap Abbey †
Calder Abbey †
St Bees Priory †
Cartmel Priory †
Furness Abbey †
Lancaster: St Mary's Priory ▲
Sawley Abbey ▲
Whalley Abbey ▲
Bolton Priory †
Kirkstall Abbey †
Upholland Priory ▲
Monk Bretton Priory †
Roche Abbey †
Blyth Priory ▲
Beauchief Abbey ▲
Croxden Abbey †
Newstead Abbey †
Dale Abbey †
Repton Priory †
Ulverscroft Priory †
Owston Abbey †
Nuneaton Priory ▲
Maxstoke Priory ▲
Coventry Cathedral Priory †
Stoneleigh Abbey ▲
Canons Ashby Priory ▲
Peterborough Abbey †
Ramsey Abbey †
Deeping St James' Priory Cells †
Crowland Abbey †
Bourne Abbey †
Binham Priory †
Walsingham Abbey ▲
North Creake Abbey †
West Acre Priory ▲
Castle Acre Priory †
Penntey Priory †
Thorney Abbey †
Norwich Cathedral Priory †
Wymondham Abbey †
Thetford Priory ▲
Ingham Priory ▲
St Benet's Abbey ▲
Great Yarmouth Priory.
St Olave's Priory
Iselham Priory ▲
Denney Abbey ▲
Anglesey Abbey ▲
Swavesey Priory ▲
Ely Cathedral Priory †
Bungay Priory ▲
Ixworth Abbey ▲
Bury St Edmunds Abbey †
Great Bricett Priory ▲
Stoke-by-Clare Priory ▲
Royston Priory ▲
Elstow Abbey ▲
Chicksands Priory ▲
Dunstable Priory ▲
Leiston Abbey ▲
Letheringham Priory ▲
Butley Priory ▲
Kersey Priory ▲
Colchester: St John's Abbey; St Botolph's Priory ††
St Osyth's Priory †
Little Dunmow ▲
St Alban's Abbey †
Coggeshall Abbey ▲
Tilty Abbey ▲
Beeleigh Abbey ▲
Waltham Abbey †
Prittlewell Priory ▲
Barking Abbey †
Westminster Abbey ▲
Southwark Cathedral Priory ▲
Minster Priory ⌐
Canterbury: St Augustine's Abbey †
Rochester Cathedral Abbey †
Bayham Abbey ▲
Robertsbridge Abbey ▲
Battle Abbey ▲
Wilmington Priory ▲
Dover: St Martin's Priory; St Radegund's Abbey
Lewes Priory ▲
Hardham Priory ▲
Easebourne Priory ▲
Southwick Priory ▲
Titchfield Abbey ▲
Waverley Abbey †
Reading Abbey †
Burnham Abbey †
Thame Abbey †
Abingdon Abbey †
Steventon Priory †
Hinton Priory ▲
Lacock Abbey †
Dorchester Abbey †
Oxford: St Frideswide's Cathedral ▲
St Oswald's Priory ▲
Gloucester: Llanthony Secunda Priory; ††
Leonard Stanley Priory ▲
Tintern Abbey †
Flaxley Abbey ▲
Malmesbury Abbey ▲
Bath Cathedral Priory ▲
Witham Priory ▲
Monk Sherborne Priory ▲
Amesbury Priory ▲
Shaftesbury Abbey ▲
Glastonbury Abbey ▲
Abbot's Fish House (Meare) □
Mottisfont Priory †
Romsey Abbey ▲
Winchester: Cathedral Priory; Hyde Abbey ††
Netley Abbey ▲
Beaulieu Abbey †
Christchurch Priory †
Worcester Cathedral Priory †
Pershore Priory †
Evesham Abbey †
Tewkesbury Abbey †
Deerhurst Priory †
Hailes Abbey ▲
Great Malvern Priory; Little Malvern Priory; †
Haughmond Abbey †
Lilleshall Abbey †
Much Wenlock Priory ▲
Dudley Priory ▲
Kenilworth Abbey ▲
Halesowen Abbey ▲
Alberbury Priory †
Shrewsbury Abbey †
Church Preen Priory Cells †
Morville Priory Cells ▲
Bromfield Priory ▲
Wigmore Abbey ▲
Leominster Priory ▲
Chester Cathedral †
Norton Abbey ▲
Birkenhead Priory ▲
Caldy Priory ▲
Basingwerk Abbey ▲
Valle Crucis Abbey †
Cymmer Abbey †
Beddgelert Priory ▲
Penmon Priory †
Chirbury Priory †
Aconbury Priory ▲
Llanthony Priory ▲
Abbey Dore Abbey †
Abergavenny Priory †
Monmouth Priory ▲
Brecon Abbey †
Usk Priory ▲
Chepstow Priory ▲
Strata Florida Abbey †
Neath Abbey †
Margam Abbey †
Talley Abbey †
Kidwelly Priory †
Whitland Abbey †
Haverfordwest Priory †
Pembroke Priory †
St German's Priory †
Hartland Abbey ▲
Frithelstock Priory ▲
Dunster Priory ▲
Cleeve Abbey ▲
Stogursey Priory ▲
Muchelney Abbey ▲
Montacute Priory ▲
Dunkeswell Abbey ▲
Sherborne Abbey ▲
Forde Abbey ▲
Cerne Abbey ▲
Milton Abbey ▲
Abbotsbury Abbey ▲
Exeter: St Nicholas' Priory ▲
Tavistock Abbey ▲
Buckland Abbey ▲
Buckfast Abbey ▲
Plympton Priory †
Cornworthy Priory ▲
St Michael's Mount Priory ↑

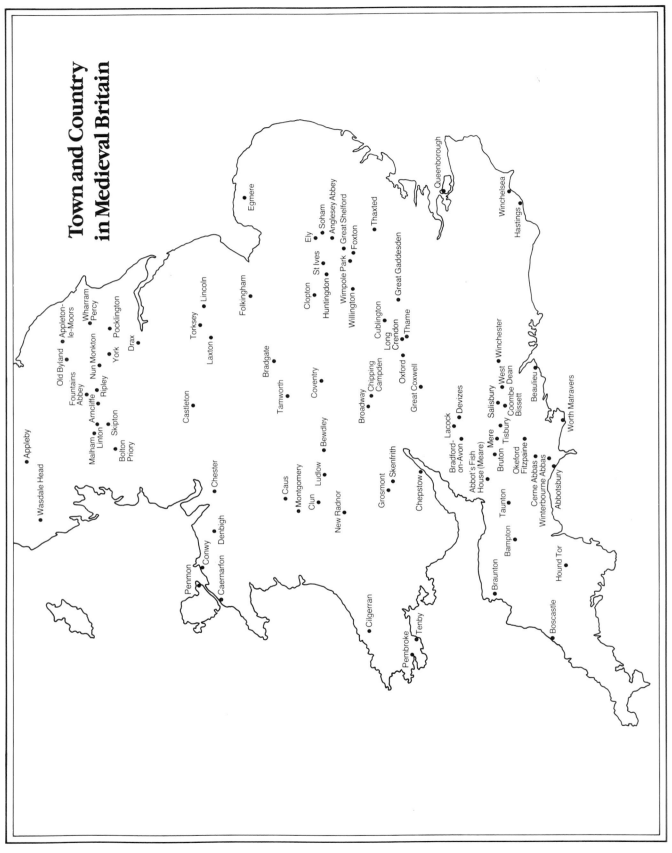

Town and Country in Medieval Britain

Further Reading

The list that follows is a selection from the wide range of literature available on Dark Age and medieval Britain.

ARNOLD, C.J., *Roman Britain to Saxon England*, Croom Helm, 1984.

BERESFORD, M.W. and ST JOSEPH, J.K., *Medieval England, An Aerial Survey*, CUP, 1979.

BROWN, R.ALLEN, *English Castles*, Chancellor Press, 1970.

CANTOR, LEONARD (ed), *The English Medieval Landscape*, Croom Helm, 1982.

FERNIE, ERIC, *The Architecture of the Anglo-Saxons*, Batsford, 1983.

FORDE-JOHNSTON, J., *Castles and Fortifications of Britain and Ireland*, Dent, 1979.

HOMANS, GEORGE C., *The English Villagers of the Thirteenth Century*, Norton Library, 1975.

LAING, LLOYD and JENNIFER, *A Guide to Dark Age Remains in Britain*, Constable, 1979.

MORRIS, RICHARD, *Cathedrals and Abbeys of England and Wales*, Dent, 1979.

MUIR, RICHARD, *Lost Villages of Britain*, Michael Joseph, 1982.

PLATT, COLIN, *The English Medieval Town*, Secker and Warburg, 1976.

REID, ALAN, *The Castles of Wales*, Letts Guides, 1973.

RODWELL, WARWICK, *The Archaeology of the English Church*, Batsford, 1981.

RODWELL, WARWICK and BENTLEY, JAMES, *Our Christian Heritage*, George Philip, 1984.

ROWLEY, TREVOR, *The Norman Heritage, 1066–1200*, Routledge & Kegan Paul, 1983.

SOULSBY, IAN, *The Towns of Medieval Wales*, Phillimore, 1983.

TAYLOR, CHRISTOPHER, *Village and Farmstead*, George Philip, 1983.

THOMAS, CHARLES, *Christianity in Roman Britain to AD 500*, Batsford, 1981.

WILSON, DAVID, *The Anglo-Saxons*, Penguin, 1981.

WOOD, MARGARET, *The English Medieval House*, Ferndale, 1981.

Index